NICE TO MEET ME

One Man's Journey Through Therapy for Sexual
Abuse to Meet the Boy He Left Behind

CHRIS CARLTON

MUGWUMP PUBLISHING

Mugwump Publishing
www.mugwumppublishing.com

Cover Design by Studio Grafik
www.studiografik.com

Ordering Information:
Quantity sales. Special discounts are available on quantity purchases by corporations, associations, and others. For details, contact the publisher at the address above.
Orders by U.S. trade bookstores and wholesalers. Please contact Mugwump Publishing Wholesale: Tel: (804) 380-3475 or visit www.nicetomeetmebook.com.
Printed in the United States of America
Publisher's Cataloging-in-Publication data
Carlton, Chris.
Nice To Meet Me: One Man's Journey Through Therapy for Sexual Abuse to Meet the Boy He Left Behind / Chris Carlton.
p. cm.
ISBN 978-0-578-09840-1
1. Biography & Autobiography (Personal Memoirs) 2. Psychology (Mental Health)

For my beautiful wife, Ellen, who I know will always be there to accept and love me for who I am.

Acknowledgements

A special thanks to my wonderful parents who, instead of turning away, chose to go through this very difficult journey with me.

For my siblings, and in-laws, who spent hours upon hours helping me move forward, riding the roller coaster, always there to talk and listen.

For Eva, while her body has failed her, her mind is still as brilliant as ever.

For my editor, Christie, and my cover artist and loyal friend, Ryan, at Studio Grafik.

For Lainie, Paul and Robbie, Dorothy, Greg and Karen, Jayne and Tom, Lynn and Angel, Shannon McK, Laura H, Jim and Janan, Ceil and Jay, Tony and Sue, Mike and Rebecca, Paige and Dave, EJ and Stever, Jean and Bill, Terry and Mike, Ryan and Kristin, Mark D., TSK(C), Chris and Caroline, Andy and Laura, Mike K. and family, Justin and Christine, Nick and Christina, Hansi and Tim, Marcia, Justin and Amy, Shannon M, Seth and Vicki, Brent and Megan, Patricia W., Steve S., Rob S., Rebecca G., Alex B., Andre L., Caroline H.G., Stef, Karina F.B., Jay C., Katie D.T., The best boss I've ever had-Bryan and wife Maggie, Christi M., Amanda D., Christina S., Adie S., Dave and Jenny, Don W., Ethel T., Frances and Andy, Kate McK., Barbara E., Heidi D., Jane T., Jenny H., Jenny V.S., Jill R.K., The Donoghue's, The Wylie's, The Cahman Family, Nancy D., Kelly and Shawn, KMR, Angela and Mike, Katie M., Laurie and Mark, Stuff and Megan, Miriam S., Mary C., Randy R., Robynn N.D., Tasha S.R., My online friends-JP, Felicia, Prozacblogger, Sue Ann J.L., Sharon, Patricia, SwordDanceWarrior, Cathe, Wendy Y., butterfly, Ercan, Gaby, Michael, c, Kathryn M., Daisy, Shawn, Jason, whatjulieslearned, Clara, life is terminal, Lori, traillius,

Mountainous Buck and my other brothers at MaleSurvivor, Annie, L, and anyone else I have inadvertently missed. For my friends at 1in6.org who I continue to be proud to be associated with.

To all of you, your continued support and encouragement at such a difficult time made the difference. All I can say is thank you.

Before We Meet Me

Ever have one of those dreams where you're being chased? You are determined to outrun a predator that is gaining ground on you, but your legs feel like cinderblocks? No matter how hard you try, you can't seem to generate enough speed. The predator is going to catch you. Suddenly, you wake up, frightened, confused, then delighted once you realize that your legs couldn't propel you forward because you are laying safely in bed, dreaming. A deep sigh of relief. It's over now.

For one in four girls and one in six boys, unwanted sexual contact is real. For many of them, this isn't a nightmare that they can awake from; it is a daily struggle to outrun a sexually abusive past. No matter how many hours they work, miles they run, beers they drink, pills they swallow, their traumatic past gains ground, year by year. But there is hope. With the right help and a steadfast dedication to recovery, these people can separate from the relentless predator of their past.

This book is about what it took me to stop being chased. I'm a survivor of sexual abuse. Seven years of incest, to be exact. It took me twenty years after the abuse ended to realize I needed help. Before calling a therapist, I looked long and hard for a book that would explain to me what therapy for sexual abuse would be like. Zero luck. So, I decided to live my life in a fishbowl by turning my recovery into an open book for others. I may not be trained to write about the psychology of sexual abuse, but I am qualified to write about what it's like to recover from sexual abuse. I'll forever be a student of recovery, constantly working to gain ground on my past, but after the last several years of hard work, I feel more like an honor student.

This is an honest, often flawed walk with me, from when my trembling hand first opened the door to a therapist's office, to when I finally noticed myself enjoying life again—and all of the fear, the pain, the confusion, the laughter, and the tears in between. It's a seat on the couch next to me, where you can safely witness me step back in time and re-connect with the boy I left behind.

Compared to other books about sexual abuse, my approach is less clinical, and more personal. Rather than explain the six phases of guilt someone goes through in recovery, I'm going to take you through what it feels like to pick up the phone and call a therapist for the first time. I'll talk about my physical reactions to cognitive psychotherapy, or EMDR, and the black hole of loss that arrives when I first realize my childhood wasn't as perfect as I thought it was. I'll take you through my frustrations with an arrogant therapist, and how I found a therapist that was right for me. This book was written to relate to sexual abuse survivors and non-survivors alike. Regardless of our past, we can all benefit from hearing an unpolished reality, so I'm going to show you mine.

This book started as a journal. I started writing just after my first therapy session in March 2010. It was an attempt to keep my mind clear and share my deepest, darkest emotions as I navigated my recovery from childhood sexual abuse. It was also therapeutic for me, as I posted much of this to the Internet on a blog and received tens of thousands of visitors offering support and encouragement. Often, all it took for me to keep going was the support of a family member or friend, or just a comment from an anonymous fellow survivor that read, "Me too."

As you read, you'll notice that I tend to make light of some things. This isn't because I don't take recovery or sexual abuse seriously. In my opinion, embracing a healthy sense of humor is vital for a sexual abuse survivor. Without my sense of humor, and throwing up my hands and laughing when times were tough, I don't imagine I'd be functional right now.

Walking into a therapist's office for the first time is a terrifying experience for anyone, especially when it requires sharing such a private, dark secret to someone you have never met. After narrowly clearing this hurdle, I go on to journal my next twenty-seven sessions over an eighteen-month period, some in more detail than others. I describe the emotions: the loss, the guilt, the pain, the shame, and eventually, the hope, empathy and admiration for a young boy.

Between weekly sessions, I write about whatever was going on in my mind. Sometimes I didn't want to write, but the act of sitting down alone in front of a computer allowed me to share the feelings I couldn't share verbally. I write about a broad range of topics, usually trying to make it relatable, hoping that survivors will understand what I am saying and that non-survivors can gain a better understanding of what a sexual abuse survivor must deal with.

At one point in the book, I decide to do some creative writing about how I am feeling at the time, another way to connect with those less familiar with sexual abuse. I title

7

these short paragraphs "*I Am.*" I do this at four different stages over a one-year period. It's an abstract way to briefly describe my mindset using everyday situations and language.

In Appendix 2, I have included five entries in which I attempt to deal with my emotions towards my perpetrator, Jack. Finding peace with your perpetrator is a challenging part of recovery, especially when that person is no longer alive. With very few avenues to confront Jack directly, I decided to use creative writing as a way to connect to this anger. In each of these sections, marked by [brackets like this] I have placed Jack in hell, where he is forced to speak with different demons that teach him about what destruction he caused in his time on earth. It is in the form of a fictitious dialogue between Jack and the specific demon that was chosen to teach Jack a painful lesson. For some, these entries won't make much sense, but it made sense to me at the time, so I have included them.

As you read this book, you'll notice that my anger begins to transform and redirect as the months and therapy sessions pass. Slowly but surely, I gain my footing and I process my pain. It's not always pretty, but if nothing else, it shows that progress can be made.

Overall, I hope the format makes sense. I haven't changed any of my writing, because some of the most imperfect moments, I believe, tell an important part of the story. My rigidity at times, discomfort, confusion, my cavalier style—it all means something and I hope it translates to a better understanding of a difficult but important journey.

A Note For Survivors

The biggest concern I have in writing this book is that I may, in some way, trigger another survivor and create a bigger set of problems for someone who is in a delicate stage of their recovery. Unfortunately, reading stories about other people's abuse can cause your pain to creep up on you unexpectedly, so I want to stress that if there is ever a time while reading this book that you start to feel unstable, or angry, or sad—please take a break for as long as it takes to feel comfortable again. If this happens, and you don't feel like you have a place to go to deal with your emotions, I have included a list of resources in Appendix 1 that have proven helpful for me along my journey. I can't stress this enough for survivors. Please be kind to yourself and respect what your body is saying.

Another hesitation I have is that a survivor might compare their recovery timeline to mine. I decided to keep the dates of my sessions because I think it tells part of the story, but please don't compare your progress, if you are in therapy, to my specific recovery timeline. We all have different personalities, experiences, and circumstances, and we will all have our own unique recovery pace. In the book, you'll read about my first therapist who, in an attempt to provide me with hope, put a timeframe on when I should start feeling better. This was a terrible thing for her to do. When those dates came and I wasn't where she said I would be, it set me back even further. Please don't burden yourself with a time constraint or compare your recovery pace to anyone else's.

You will read about my decision to use Eye Movement Desensitization and Reprocessing (EMDR) as a treatment method. This method may not be right for everyone, so please discuss thoroughly with your therapist because it can be difficult to manage at times as memories surface and the reprocessing occurs.

If there's one important thing I've learned about going through therapy, it is that there are ups and downs, and that's alright. Recently, I had a few bad days that hit me out of nowhere. I focused on accepting this brief setback and didn't allow myself to dwell over it. Shortly after, I felt myself ease up and relax. It happens to everyone, and as long as you keep reminding yourself that this is normal and focus on getting back on track, that is all you can ask of yourself.

As you read the book, you may disagree with some of the conclusions I make. Looking back, I often reached for answers when I just needed to let the process play out, but in my opinion it is important to keep all of this in the book to show how confusing connecting to your past can be. I always do my best to keep my writing honest and focused, but there are times when I get angry and irrational. It happens.

I'm glad you joined me and I hope you can gain some sort of perspective on your journey from my process. We survivors have such an important voice. Our voice, as difficult as it is to summon at times, is what will bring the sexual abuse of children, and the damage it does to so many lives, into the spotlight it deserves.

Invictus
William Ernest Henley (1849-1903)

Out of the night that covers me,
Black as the pit from pole to pole,
I thank whatever gods may be
For my unconquerable soul.

In the fell clutch of circumstance
I have not winced nor cried aloud.
Under the bludgeonings of chance
My head is bloody, but unbowed.

Beyond this place of wrath and tears
Looms but the Horror of the shade,
And yet the menace of the years
Finds and shall find me unafraid.

It matters not how strait the gate,
How charged with punishments the scroll,
I am the master of my fate:
I am the captain of my soul.

My Story

Anyone who has ever sat in a ninth grade algebra class probably remembers how badly they wanted the teacher to stop talking. As a ninety-pound freshman at St. Mary's Ryken High School in southern Maryland, I was no different. Math was supposed to be about numbers, and now this lady was talking about letters? "You see class, x is a number, but x is a different number than y and z," she explained. Uh, no it isn't. It's a letter…they're all letters. Ask my English teacher. Unfortunately for me and my FOIL method-challenged classmates, it wasn't going to be that simple. I looked to my left and right and saw my classmates furiously scribbling notes. Everyone was working like mad to get this silly talk on paper. Not me. I just sat there and wished I could leave. Then, as if someone was listening to my thoughts, there was a knock at the classroom door. *Yes*. She stopped talking. My prayers were answered. She opened the door to two men in business suits. They whispered. The class began to whisper. At least we had a break in the math madness.

What happened next would bring my life as I knew it to a screeching halt. My teacher turned towards the class and locked eyes with me. "Why in the hell is she looking at me?" I thought to myself. Then, she spoke. "Chris, could you please join me in the hallway?" she uttered. I could feel my blood vessels tingle, like they did after skidding to a stop on the highway, narrowly avoiding an accident. My face flushed. I had no idea why I was being asked to leave the room, but I stood up and started my journey towards the door, an unknowing journey that would demand my attention for the rest of my life.

The men introduced themselves as government agents. They needed to speak with me privately. My head spun as I considered all of the possible reasons. Did something happen to one of my parents? Was I being considered for a top-secret government program? Did they have the wrong person? Had I removed a mattress tag prematurely? For whatever reason, I didn't ask a single question—I was afraid to hear the answer. I followed them downstairs to a waiting golf cart where the school's principal sat in the driver's seat with a solemn look on his face. I said hello and sat down in the cart and we drove to the administrative school building. Why was I being handled so carefully?

The four of us entered the principal's office. The principal sat behind his desk. I was told to sit in one of the chairs that faced his desk, so I sat down. I was a good kid, never in trouble, so I trembled as I adapted to my first time in his office. The two agents stood behind me, which I thought was odd. After a few awkward pleasantries, one of the men spoke.

He said that one of my family members had filed a complaint with the police department in another state. She alleged that she had been sexually abused by her stepfather, some twenty years prior. This was the first I had heard about it, and it came as a shock to me. What also came as a shock to me was why I was getting emotional. Within seconds, I was crying uncontrollably. The men didn't say a word. I just sat there in my chair trying to gather myself. Eventually, once I stopped sobbing, they said that this is what they were afraid of. They were there to investigate any other family members who had come in contact with Jack over the years.

My real grandfather died in a plane crash long before I was born, and my grandmother quickly remarried, so even though we were unrelated, I had always considered Jack my grandfather. We saw him regularly. In fact, my family lived with Jack and my grandmother for three months when I was in fourth grade. My emotional episode was all they needed to see that I had also been affected by Jack. It was obvious. Scared out of my mind, I did my best to claim that he never sexually molested me, and that he had only propositioned me a few times. I stuck to that story out of fear, shame, and the countless other reasons why children are terrified to tell about their abuse. The agents pushed me to talk, but I maintained that there was nothing more to tell. After twenty minutes or so, they accepted my story and told me to return to my classroom. It was a cold, lonely walk back. I was terrified to open the door to the classroom, but I did, and my classmates whispered as I returned to my desk, my face swollen and red. I never talked about that incident to anyone at school, not even my closest friends who watched this interrogation unfold.

The agents followed up with my parents that afternoon, reiterating what I had told them and how I reacted. When I returned home that evening our family discussed what had happened. They filled me in on my other family member's claim and the pending court case. I kept my story going—telling my parents that nothing happened. The thought of going to court and talking about any of this terrified me.

That night, Jack began calling the house. He knew there was an ongoing investigation and he was beginning to act erratically. He knew what I knew, and he wasn't going to let me talk. After he called the first time and argued with my parents, I figured the episode was over. The phone rang again moments later, and I answered. Eager to free my mind from the mess, I didn't think he would call again, and I hoped instead that one of my friends wanted to talk about whatever ninth graders talk about. But, it was Jack on the line. I froze. I didn't know what to say. I was standing in the laundry room in the basement, shaking as he reminded me that nothing had ever happened between us. Out of fear, I agreed that I didn't recall any inappropriate contact. There was an underlying threat to what he was saying, and I knew he was serious. He asked me if he needed to come to Maryland to talk about it more. I told him that he didn't, that everything was alright. When I hung up the phone, I was in a panic. I feared that he might make the two-hour drive to keep me quiet, for good.

That night was the first night I slept with a knife under my pillow. It was a hunting knife that he had given me the year before. As I lay in bed, I thought about how I would use it. I didn't sleep for days.

That same week, just as pressure was mounting to testify in court against Jack, our family received a phone call. Jack was dead. He had died of a heart attack stepping out of the shower, fittingly buck naked. When I got the news, I immediately acted relieved, but after this initial emotion, I went back to my bedroom and cried. I was unsure of why I was crying, and further ashamed that I even cared.

The funeral was held at Arlington National Cemetery. His children, now adults, traveled across the country to pay their last respects. After the funeral, we all went back to the my grandmother's house—the same house that I had lived in for three months while our family waited to move into our new house. We had a small gathering and ate lunch, exchanging pleasantries. As the afternoon wore on, my mom was able to speak with his children privately. All of his children were told about the allegations, and all of his children spoke about their own abuse for the first time. It was becoming clear to everyone that Jack was a serial molester.

As we drove back to our home in Maryland, our family discussed what we had learned. "Chris, we're just so glad he didn't molest you," my parents reiterated. I concurred, regrettably. That evening we decided, as a family, to never talk about Jack again. And from that day forward, my secret was buried. For a while.

Our family moved back to northern Virginia after my ninth grade year. I enrolled in a public school and tried as best I could to move forward, but my first six months were lonely. I couldn't find the energy to socialize and meet new friends. Slowly, I began to adapt, as any good military brat learned to do. I excelled in sports and became one of the more popular kids in school, using the transition as a way to mentally block out my previous seven years of shame.

When it was time for college, I was eager to get out on my own. I worked hard to be accepted into Virginia Tech's highly-touted Mechanical Engineering department. I joined the lacrosse team and found a girlfriend. I worked and played hard in college, with my sights set on eventually becoming a Navy pilot, just like my father.

Upon graduation, I was accepted to the Navy's aviation program and reported to Pensacola, Florida to begin my training. Five days later, after finding out that I suffered from a rare eye disease, I was dismissed and returned home, humbled, broken, and lost. Instead of grieving the loss of my dream as most people would, I bottled it up and refused to let it affect me, a craft I had honed since I was seven years old.

I found a job as a Mechanical Engineer, which was not my passion, but it paid the bills while I sorted through my professional next step. I broke up with my long-time girlfriend and decided to join the Navy anyway as an Intelligence Officer. Even though it wasn't my initial goal, I was excited for the adventure and eager to travel the world. Later, I would realize that this decision wasn't about running towards a goal, it was about running away from reality.

I served six years in the Navy. I was a hard worker, a quick study, but I had an underlying anger and lack of respect for authority. While I was a decorated officer, the rigid chain of command structure was wearing me down, and my attitude would often wear down my supervisors. I turned in my paperwork for resignation in August 2001, and spent the next few weeks preparing for my transition to civilian life. On September 11, 2001, I was sitting in a classroom at Bethesda Naval Medical Center, receiving training on how to assimilate to civilian life, a requirement for any departing officer. That day affected everyone differently. For me, it meant that I would volunteer to retract my resignation and serve a tour in the Middle East supporting strikes into Afghanistan, an easy decision for me at the time, and one that I believe started my road to recovery.

I immediately deployed to Manama, Bahrain where I was the acting targeteer for U.S. Navy strikes, managing Battle Damage Assessment and intelligence gathering. It was hard work, but I was proud to be part of the effort; I was able to do something about the terrorist bombings, so I felt energized by the opportunity.

One late night in Bahrain, after months of twenty-hour days and as many beers, I found myself in a long conversation about life with a fellow officer. We were talking about our pasts, and then, suddenly, against my better judgment, I let my story out for the first time. I had never cried that hard and for that long in my life, and being a military man in my late-twenties, I was totally embarrassed. My repressed memories and disregarded pain had gained control.

I woke up the next morning, after about an hour of sleep, and promised myself that I was never going to talk about it again. I naively thought that it was all behind me now—I had finally spoken, so I was free. That amazing sense of relief was unfortunately temporary.

Over the next several years, after I left the Navy, the memories crept back more frequently. My anger became confusing and I found myself withdrawing from my family and close friends. I spent years keeping people at arm's length. If someone liked me, I held that against them. Social activity was becoming more and more difficult, and I felt I only deserved unhappiness, which I ensured.

It wasn't until I met my wife, Ellen, that I started to be more honest with myself. It came slowly at first, sharing with her the few details that I knew. Feeling like I could be myself for the first time, I realized she was the one for me and we were married two years later. I finally felt like I was normal. But, as the story so often goes, the anger and resentment re-surfaced, and it became clear to both of us that I needed to deal with this responsibly. My issues were bigger than both of us. It was clear that I needed to see a professional if we were to have the positive, healthy family we both wanted.

It took me about three months from the point of realizing I needed to see a professional, to when I actually picked up a phone and called for help. Being a self-sufficient male—an athlete, ex-military officer, from a military family—it was terribly difficult to admit to myself that I couldn't fix it alone. Poring through dozens of books on the subject and surfing countless websites was helpful, though just helpful enough to give me the strength to call a therapist.

This was the biggest decision of my life. It was awful, painful, and humbling, while at the same time empowering and life-changing. My story of recovery, however non-linear and imperfect, begins with my first therapy session.

Therapy Session 1: March 10, 2010

I sat there in my Toyota contemplating the inevitable. It was 3:25 p.m. I was having more chest pains; the kind that require you to inhale deeply in order to release the tension, if only for a few seconds. The pains weren't what worried me; I had been experiencing pains like this since I began facing the abuse several months prior. It was the other feeling that had my attention. Four more minutes. What was that? Was it nerves about meeting with a therapist for the first time? Was I nervous? No, I've been nervous plenty of times. This wasn't nervous. I finally pinpointed it—the feeling was fear. I hadn't felt genuine fear since I was a kid—the kind you feel when you might be harmed. Thirty six years old and I was scared shitless, hiding in my car, afraid to talk to someone about me. What if she doesn't believe me? Better yet, what if she tells me it's not worth her time? Three minutes. I sat there, almost in shock over what I was feeling, then swiftly swung the door open and lurched out of the car in a deliberate motion, reminding myself that I was in need of help. What I went through was real and it was wrong. It was ok to get help. I deserved to feel right. My family deserved it. My future children deserved it.

I opened the door to the office in an almost mousey fashion. I slowly stuck my head in. A man sat in a chair to the left, his head slowly raised and he looked at me with a distant stare—not someone I would feel comfortable entering a conversation with. There was a receptionist desk and another door to the right. I moved on to the receptionist. Shit. She was on the phone. I had to force myself not to make eye contact with the man in the chair. I stood there for about a minute. The receptionist kept talking and didn't acknowledge me. What the hell? These people don't even give a damn. I felt the urge to leave. I remember wondering if this was my Fight or Flight response kicking in. I calmed myself down and sat on the opposite side of the room from Angry Man. What was he here for? What does he think I'm here for? A few minutes later, the receptionist apologized and called me up to the counter. I gave her some paperwork and she said the doctor would call me when she was ready.

What felt like nine hours later, the doctor opened the door to the right of the receptionist's desk. An older woman than I had expected, she quietly walked over and asked, "Are you Chris?" I acknowledged I was and she reached out her hand. I stood up and we shook hands. She had a genuine smile on her face. In almost a whisper, she asked me to follow her. I started to calm down a bit as I walked, happy to leave the waiting room.

We walked down a hall, turned right and entered her office. It wasn't what I had expected. I really didn't know what I expected, but it wasn't this. There was a small white love seat against the wall on the left, with a matching chair flanking the far end of a coffee table that sat in the middle. Another chair was positioned on the right, opposite the love seat. On the right side of the room was a desk, obviously hers. A bookshelf lined the far wall filled with psychology books. I quickly noticed a few I had already read. The lighting was soft, but brighter than I had seen in the movies. It was comfortable, but not too comfortable. She told me to sit where I wanted, so I took the safer seat, the single chair at the end of the coffee table. Sharing the love seat would have been awkward.

She sat down, smiled and started off with "Remind me, what brings you here?" From there I basically shot-gunned a bunch of information, trying to keep things linear and brief but providing enough detail so that she could understand some of the sources of my pain. I doubt I needed to spell it out, but I did anyway,– probably just to make sure it was off my chest. When I went into any unsolicited details about the actual abuse, she quickly validated it with an empathetic gesture or comment. She was disgusted with what Jack did to me. It made me feel good that she reacted with disgust. OK, at least she isn't laughing at me.

This went on for about a half an hour. At the conclusion of my story, she validated it all. I felt a little emotion creeping up, but jammed it back down. Then, she pulled out the paperwork that her office had mailed me when I called and set the appointment. The paperwork was filled with random questions about how I was feeling, a sort of scorecard. She added up some of the numbers, and straightforwardly said, "Well, based on how you answered these questions, you are clinically depressed." That wasn't an easy thing for me to hear. I had always prided myself on my self-reliance, and my ability to overcome adversity. Depression felt like I had failed. Whatever, she quickly moved on. The next thing she did was pull out another few pieces of paper. For the next ten minutes we went through another set of questions about physical reactions I was having, sleep patterns, anger, etc. At the end of that, she added up those numbers and replied "You also have Post Traumatic Stress Disorder, or PTSD." In fact, on a scale of one to fifty, thirty-two being the lower scale of confirmed PTSD and fifty obviously being the worst, I was a forty-five. Hmm. That didn't sound good.

This was a lot of information all at one time. It wasn't easy for me to digest. I teared up a few times when she started talking about how it was perfectly understandable for me to be clinically depressed and suffering from PTSD given what I had gone through. She said she was amazed that I had kept it together for so long. I got more emotional then. I just sat there staring blankly at the wall. My emotion didn't really faze her, which actually made me more comfortable. My heart was racing. The chest pains were strong.

We spent the next twenty minutes talking about what we could do to get me in a better place. This was the good part of the conversation. She said EMDR (Eye Movement Desensitization and Reprocessing) was going to be the right treatment for me. In caveman speak, EMDR is a way of reducing the stressful impact that those experiences had on me by using exterior stimuli to retrain my brain. She was a national facilitator for EMDR, so I felt like I was in good hands. I had read plenty about EMDR, and from what I read and heard from others, it was the most effective treatment for male victims of sexual abuse.

She said that by July, I would be feeling significantly better. By September, I would feel like a different person. I immediately felt like my dog whenever I pull out a Milk-Bone. Now she's talking my language. I felt myself smile, but I tried to contain it for some reason. She kept talking but I sort of zoned out for a little bit as I thought about September and the promise of a normal life—free from the pain, the guilt, and the anger. I started thinking about great things like success, happiness.

She wrapped up the conversation quickly as we closed in on the end of the hour. We actually went a little bit over the hour, which I could tell wasn't her normal routine, but I couldn't blame her for wanting to keep us on schedule since therapy is a business and time is money. I think I was still buzzing from my Milk-Bone. We shook hands. She said to call her receptionist and make weekly appointments for the next eight weeks, starting in two weeks. She was taking a vacation the following week so we couldn't meet until the next week. Buzz kill. One hour earlier I was in a near panic attack in my Toyota, and now I was all but humping her leg for another appointment. I guess I did need some therapy.

Overall, it was a success. While I waited for my next appointment, I had some relaxation techniques to practice—basically some daily meditation training for me to focus on. She also gave me a book to read called "I Never Told Anyone." She said it would be another set of stories to continue to validate what I was feeling. These stories are like a sweet, soothing elixir for me, so I gladly took the book and went on my way.

As I walked out to the car, everything seemed quiet. I felt a brief sense of peace. I looked forward to my next session.

Jenga: March 18, 2010

I've spent some time trying to explain to people what it feels like going through life after being sexually abused as a kid. It's really hard for me to answer. I'm in a different place than I was when I was just getting through life as best I could. I'm in a more reflective position.

I'll continue to think about how to describe what it was like while I was going through it, but I can describe what it feels like right now looking back and analyzing what I experienced.

For a sexual abuse victim, life really proceeds like a game of Jenga. I have never liked board games because my smart older sister always won when we played, but for some reason this game seems like the right analogy.

If you don't know Jenga, it's a game that starts with about fifty small identical rectangular blocks of wood, stacked carefully into one larger rectangular shape. It looks like a square post, about a foot high with many pieces. There are two teams. One team begins by removing a piece of wood. The next team does the same. This continues until the structure eventually falls. Whichever team pulls the fatal block, loses.

Life for a sexual abuse victim starts with a fairly solid structure, although I imagine some abuse victims begin with a structure missing pieces. I was lucky and had a solid Jenga shape, with all blocks accounted for. Once the abuse begins, the abuser takes a piece. You respond and remove another. Sometimes you lose a seemingly inconsequential

23

block.   Other times, you lose one that feels invaluable. This goes on until the abuse ends, but somehow the game continues even though you thought you stopped playing. While the abuser stops taking blocks, you are still asked to remove a block from time to time.   Some years you don't touch the structure, but as you age, the requests come more rapidly.   The structure becomes more and more unstable. For me, I was very good at selecting which block to remove when asked.   I kept the structure standing when it should have been in shambles.   Eventually, no matter how well you play the game, the structure cannot sustain itself, and it comes crashing down all over whatever life you were living at the time.   That's the best way I can describe what it's like.

I guess the good news is that the game goes on in this version of Jenga.   You get the chance to put the blocks back one by one.   What I'm hoping is that therapy will give me what I need to place them back in the right order, in the smartest, most stable fashion to keep my structure strong. It might be the first board game I've ever won.

The Raw Nerve: March 19, 2010

The last six months have been weird.   For the past twenty-five or thirty years, I have compartmentalized my thoughts about the abuse.   I have kept what I felt guarded—even from myself.   My decision to face what happened has flipped my self-management modus operandi upside down. In the long-term, it will be a great thing and I will be better for it.   Right now, I'm a walking raw nerve.   Today, my nerve was hit with a flying elbow.   My parents, as much as I love them, are not willing to accept that I am not ready to spend time with them right now.   A lot of my frustrations with my abuse are tied to them, so it is very difficult for me. They were there to protect me and didn't. They didn't pick up on the signs when they should have. They didn't pursue the truth hard enough and suggest treatment when I cried about Jack the night the government agents interrogated me. They asked me never to talk about him again, so they wouldn't have to deal with it. As two Type A first-borns, they always get what they want and refuse to hear me if it's not what they want to hear—even though I'm now an adult. Seeing them sends me backwards right now. They know that, but they are not willing to accept that I'm not acting the way they want me to. They want to see me. I am not ready to see them. I have told them that. So, they choose the passive route and plan a trip to come into town to see other family members, and then copy me on the email. I can see it now. I will be pressured to hang out with them when they come into town and they will no doubt be bothered when I react the way I will react. It's because I don't want to be controlled right now. I don't want my parents telling me that I have to see them. I've listened to them before and it took a long, painful toll on me, so I need a break from that. The nerve is raw. It's unfortunate because I love my parents very much and I have told them that recently, but there is much more going on than they are willing to admit. I now feel like I'm a shitty son. I feel like a self-centered asshole. It doesn't feel fair to carry that feeling right now.

Better vs. Right: March 22, 2010

Living in reality is an ugly thing right now. It's a juggling act of highs and lows. It reminds me of what it's like going through a tumultuous, on-again/off-again relationship.

You've been through so much together, but for whatever reason, you can't seem to find a balance. Then you break up. You feel lower than low, and the only thing that can fix it is that one person. You wish they'd call. You wait, and wait, and wait. Then, one day, the phone rings and you're back on top of things. You feel alive again. The feeling is hard to describe, but you have a euphoric sense of relief. Right now, I'm in a low, and I can't seem to get my hands on that sense of relief.

This is because of my weekend. I actually had a great weekend with my siblings, both in person and on the phone. I was reminded how lucky I am to be surrounded by great people who genuinely care about me and I'm not just saying that because they're my family. These are some of the best people I will ever know.

A good part of this weekend was spent facing reality—going through my anger, describing it, and having those people I care about and trust understand me better. I wouldn't change a thing. Unfortunately, after spending that much time in reality, there is the inevitable low that follows. I think this is normal for someone in my shoes, but I'm not sure. This pattern is consistent and I now know to prepare for it. But you can never prepare enough. Anyways, after waking up, I had to make a decision— would I focus on feeling better or feeling right? This is an important distinction for me, because feeling better is something I've done for years. And it doesn't involve reality.

The first time I talked about my abuse honestly was in late 2001. I was in the Middle East, serving a tour in support of Operation Enduring Freedom. I was a lieutenant, a Targeting Intelligence Officer managing Battle Damage Assessment (BDA) for U.S. Navy strikes into Afghanistan. It was around Christmastime and we had been working long hours, seven days a week, ever since I stepped foot in-country in late September. We had a day off to relax and enjoy the holidays, and I spent it relaxing at an apartment pool with some friends. The booze was flowing.

I ended up at a friend, Miriam's, apartment, and we continued with drinks and got into a long conversation about life. I was drunk. The booze, the stress, something triggered my memories of the abuse. The next thing I knew I had lost control, breaking down into a mess of tears and snot—the kind of radical crying that you did when you were a little kid that usually ended in a nap. Let's just say it wasn't the most officer-like moment for this lieutenant. When I woke up the next morning, my head pounding, my eyes red and puffy, I felt worse than just hung over. I felt a low that was unlike any low I had felt before.

Unfortunately for me, I was signed up for a half-marathon that started about two hours later. It was an annual race from the east coast of Bahrain, to the west coast of Bahrain, approximately twelve miles of oil pipes, camel shit and sand. With our long work hours, I wasn't in running shape but I had run marathons before, so I felt like I should run; it would be a good way to get my mind off of things. The race field included some of Bahrain's best runners, and a handful of us U.S. military types who also had the day off—about one hundred runners in all. After my night of painful reality, I was determined to re-set myself and feel better, so I got into the zone. I made a deal with myself that by the end of the race, my breakdown the night before would be out of sight, out of mind.

The race was pretty grueling—no water stations, high winds, heat—and lots of oil pipes to hurdle. But, somehow, I felt stronger and stronger as the race wore on, and I finished in the top ten. I wasn't in shape and was ridiculously hung over, but somehow I clocked my best ever half marathon time—by a long shot. That day, I locked up the memories of the abuse and focused on feeling better.

Over the next nine years, I would have several of the same experiences. I would randomly lose it when my past would surface. Then, I would quickly wrap it back up and focus on feeling better. It's not a simple thing to do, but I was a pro. Unfortunately, the frequency of these "lapses" was increasing slowly—until the summer of 2009, when I could no longer stand it. I could no longer wrap it up and work on feeling better; I needed to focus on feeling right. And that's still what I'm focusing on. Granted, I don't get my relief prize at the end of a long weekend, but what I get is knowing that my foundation is being mended slowly and correctly, and that is okay for me now. I'm betting on a bigger sense of relief down the road.

Drive. Deliver. Think. Repeat: March 23, 2010

After my breakdown last August, I started to realize that I wasn't ready to start a business as I had planned. I knew I had to address what was happening to me, and the entrepreneurial lifestyle wouldn't cut it. My wife and I decided that the best thing to do would be for me to get a low-stress, part-time job. It would pay some bills, and keep me on a schedule so I could contemplate how to handle this hurricane. Within a few weeks, I lucked into what seemed like a good fit. What I didn't realize then was that this job would change my life.

I became a delivery driver for a program that delivers meals to senior citizens. Slightly different from Meals on Wheels, which delivers meals directly to people's homes, this company delivers food to churches and community centers where seniors congregate for lunch. It's managed by a large public company so I am considered full-time and receive fantastic benefits. The hours are perfect: 7:30 a.m. to 2 p.m., weekdays. It allows me to get home by 2:30, work out, and manage my mess.

I am responsible for delivering meals to the western part of central Virginia, so I have lots of driving time to think as I go from Hanover, to Goochland, to Powhatan and back to Richmond daily. While I drive, I listen to morning radio. Elliot In The Morning is my favorite mindless morning show, a ridiculous several hours with some insightful interviews. The host, Elliot, is a huge Washington Capitals hockey fan, as I am, so I like what he covers.

Elliot had an interview with former NHL great, Theo Fleury that changed everything for me.

Theo was promoting a book, "Playing With Fire", about his traumatic experiences with sexual abuse by a youth hockey coach in Canada over twenty years prior. On that day, while listening to the interview as I drove my van, I started crying. I remember thinking how impressed I was. One year removed from being a senior advertising executive on the ESPN account at one of the best agencies in the country, now I was crying while listening to morning radio as I delivered meals to senior citizens at eight dollars an hour. Paying my grad school loan payment felt like I was writing a check for that purple unicorn the Lucky Charms leprechaun sold me.

I showed up at my Goochland site looking like shit. Could I really deliver meals looking like this? When the site manager asked what was wrong, all I could think to do was blame it on my allergies. Yeah, those uber-common early-winter allergies. Good one, Chris. She felt bad for me—I was sure she knew I had been crying. My mess continued to my next site, where I kept the white lie going, and it followed me all the way back to my headquarters where everyone in the kitchen asked the same question. Yes, my allergies are the worst in all of North America. Fuck you very much.

Over the last few months, I have started to get to know all of the seniors and site managers at my sites. They greet me with huge smiles and hugs when I arrive with their food. At one of my sites, a grizzled military vet holds the door for me and salutes as I enter the building. He always has a motivational sound bite for me. I feel lucky to have this job.

What has been amazing to me is the number of abuse-related stories I keep hearing on the radio. In addition to the Theo Fleury story, I have been listening to Colin Cowherd's story on ESPN radio's "The Herd." Colin is in the middle of a major breakdown for abuse he endured as a young kid. Somehow, he has kept his radio show going, talking honestly about his past, and weaving it in with the sports stories of the day. It's hard to believe he's still working, but I listen to him every day after Elliot, and it helps me feel less alone. I also recently heard an interview with Todd Bridges, (aka, Willis, from "Diff'rent Strokes") who promoted a book called "Killing Willis." It details his story of sexual abuse by his publicist that led to his public meltdown and eventual jail sentence. I have an entirely new respect for Todd and how he has managed his recovery.

I catch myself wondering whether these stories are always all around and I'm just finally paying attention to them. Did I find this job or did it find me? Who knows.

So, since I spend a lot of time thinking and driving, I often find myself snotting and crying. Which leads to the ever-so-truthful allergy conversation once I hit my next site. The other day, as I walked into my Goochland site,

Susie, the site manager, greeted me at the door. In her hand: a box of Sudafed she bought for me on the way into work. This might be the best job I've ever had.

On Deck: March 24, 2010

Got a call that a session opened up on my therapist's calendar today at noon. She was apparently booked all week and I was told that I couldn't see her, but I could if a spot opened up. I was bummed then that I would have to wait, but as soon as I heard I could slip in today, I quickly realized I don't want to go. Seemed like a good idea at the time, but now I wish I was sitting in the dugout. Back to taking deep breaths again.

Therapy Session 2: March 24, 2010

This day started no different from the last day I had a therapy session. I woke up with immediate chest pains, wondering why I had signed up for therapy in the first place. I ran through my reasons why I shouldn't go. I also had a nice, subtle case of nausea going on. The night before had ended with me spending three hours filling out a ten-page form that went through all of the feelings I have had—past and present—and writing a detailed description of the abuse. Nothing like a little walk down memory lane to put you to sleep. All things considered, I slept alright, and I was happy for that as I left for work.

I told my boss I had a doctor's appointment, which was the truth. I guess I don't need to go into what kind of doctor's appointment, but I felt guilty for some reason. My delivery route was done especially early, which was great, and I returned to the kitchen at around 11 a.m. At around 11:25, I made myself a chicken salad sandwich at the deli counter. I took it with me to my car for my noon appointment. Before I started the car, I figured I'd wolf it down quickly to avoid eating while driving. About three bites in, my stomach told me my chicken salad sandwich was about to find a new home on my car upholstery. A nice sweeping wave of nausea hit me—the kind of two minute warning before a major spew. I stopped eating, drank some diet soda, and got going. It's amazing what physical things your body can do when feeling stress.

As I arrived at the doctor's office, there were several entrances from the main road, and I got confused and turned too soon, which landed me in the parking lot of a funeral home. I laughed a little, thinking how much easier it would be to simply check myself into a casket and just make this pain stop. I took a deep breath as I pulled into the parking space in the correct parking lot, calmed my nerves, and got out of the car. It was a little easier than last time.

It was 11:58. As I slowly opened the door to the office, I was relieved to see there was nobody in the waiting room. Huge win. Huge. I rang my therapist's buzzer to let her know I was there. I was a total veteran. The buzzer signals a small light inside her office that lets her know someone is waiting. If she's in there with another patient, it doesn't disrupt their session, but it lets her know it's time to wrap up. I sat down, glanced at the end table at a "Golf Digest," picked it up, and began flipping pages. I suck at golf. I stared at a picture of Tiger Woods. I got annoyed for some reason thinking about him and his "transgressions," and his need for therapy for sex addiction. Give me a break. You got caught. Stop hiding behind psychologists. I know that's not fair to think, because there could be a lot more going on with Tiger that I was unaware of, but that's how I felt. Ten minutes went by. Now I was annoyed. A woman in her mid-forties exited the office door, paid her co-pay at the receptionist's desk, and quickly left. That must be her other patient. She was sniffling.

Finally, at 12:14, the doctor opened the door to the right of the receptionist's desk and invited me in. She apologized immediately for being late—and that it never normally happens. She said next time to call her cell phone and remind her she's late. I was still annoyed and thought that she should have responded to my buzzer. Isn't that what it's for? Ok, no big deal.

I entered the office and went straight for my safety chair, the single chair next to the love seat at the far side of the room. We started talking. "Remind me where we left off," she blurted. She sat down and we caught back up. In those few moments, she must have been able to see that I was having chest pains. She stopped and asked if I was alright. We took a detour. She gave me a method for calming my breathing down, something that I could work on throughout the day, in addition to the progressive relaxation tapes I was listening to daily (uh…almost daily). We practiced. One one-thousand, two one-thousand…breathe. After a few minutes I was catching on. We got back to work. I returned to my chair. She stopped and said that I should probably use a different chair. I looked down, and realized that my safety chair was designed for someone half my size. She laughed at me. I liked my chair. I looked like a bear on a tricycle. She pointed me towards a large, soft recliner. I don't remember even seeing that recliner before. I switched. Much better.

I could tell she was having a hard time remembering the details of my story. I kept having to correct her as she recounted our last session. That bothered me. Was she not paying attention before? What's the deal here? Now I had two things that were bothering me a little. Ok, moving on. We started going through the ten-page document that I had filled out the night before. It detailed the way I feel about myself, my family, their history, our history, our feelings, our interactions, etc. As we went through the info she noticed that I would get mad any time my parents were mentioned. She asked me how mad I get when I think about certain things relating to them and I couldn't really tell her; I was just mad.

What she decided to do was have me fill out another form. A new form. This was called the "Personal SUDS (Subjective Units of Disturbance Score) Scale." She had me think about the angriest I have ever been. I thought about a time about eight years ago when my dad completely disregarded my wishes and forced me to do something that I had told him I didn't want to do. She asked me what I was feeling. She wrote it down. That feeling was my personal ten out of ten on my SUDS scale. She then asked what my least disturbed moment was. I immediately went to my honeymoon. Sitting with my wife in a cabana, doing a crossword puzzle, listening to a waterfall, feeling the ocean breeze. That was my personal zero of ten. I would then fill out two through nine so that we had a complete scale. She said from here on out in our sessions, we would use this scale to have me describe my level of anger. I got where she was going; I liked the approach.

Unfortunately, this took up some time, so we didn't have much left. I could feel her wrapping things up. We talked for about fifteen more minutes about the abuse. We discussed how the government agents pulled me out of class, the phone calls from Jack, and his sudden death. The fact that we buried it all as a family. She commented on what a horrifying adolescence I had. That's funny; I was always told by my parents that I had a great adolescence. It was clear to her that I had anger towards my parents, but she didn't think that I should have this much. She thinks I should have more anger towards Jack. I told her I didn't really. She said that was normal. It was odd, but with him dead for so long, I just didn't really have anywhere near the kind of anger towards him that I did towards my parents. She said we would be fixing that. I guess that's good.

I took a moment to mention to her that I had a blog where I was journaling my therapy. She was glad that I was writing, and didn't seem to care that it was open for the world to see online. That made me happy. It was time to wrap up. She reminded me to work on my tension with concentrated breathing. She wanted to make sure I did my progressive relaxation tapes every single day as well, so she gave me a log to fill out so she'd know if I missed a day. I told her that I get tense again about five minutes after I do the relaxation tapes. She didn't care. She said that was normal for now. She also told me to tell my wife that she shouldn't let me be tense towards her, and if I did, that I needed to apologize and say that I'd work on getting better. Noted. Until next Thursday.

As I left the building I got back into my car and took a deep breath. It wasn't that bad. I wasn't feeling any major improvement, but I knew I shouldn't yet. I drove onto the main road, past the funeral home. It seemed like a stupid thought to want to crawl into a casket.

Strength In Numbers: March 26, 2010

Like most men of my generation, I like sports, shiny objects and the movie "Gladiator" (I didn't say I like gladiator movies, just the movie "Gladiator"). In the movie, the protagonist, Maximus, and a handful of other gladiators are thrown into an arena for the first time to fight an overwhelming number of warriors whose only purpose in life is to kill gladiators. The warriors have the most sophisticated weaponry, armor, and vehicles—an advantage to say the least. Maximus and his fellow slaves have nothing more than old helmets, shields, and swords. They are on foot. But, the gladiators are fighting for their freedom. Using his experience as a military commander, Maximus convinces the other gladiators that they are all better off if they fight together as a team. "Strength in Numbers," he shouts. This team concept is unheard of for gladiators; these guys are convicts who want nothing more than to save their own ass and get out of there. But it works. By moving together as a unit, and using their shields as a wall, they are able to fight like a much larger gladiator. One by one, they overcome the stronger, isolated warriors and earn the right to fight another day.

I have never been someone who ever asked for help. I don't know if this was how my brain was wired at birth, if it was drilled into me at a young age, or if I developed it along the way because of the abuse. Regardless, help made me feel weak, plain and simple. Unfortunately, this trait, combined with the abuse, caused me to feel more and more alone as I went. The further I sunk, the less likely I was to ask for some help. It's part of a vicious spiral that is very common among those who suffer from depression. The best thing about my complete and total-life meltdown to this point is that I am able to accept that I need help. I can admit it, and it is a liberating feeling.

Since I started this blog about a week ago, I have given the web address to a few people I'm close to. There are many people I want to send it to, but I'm taking this one step at a time. What has astonished me is the percentage of people who have fully supported me and have returned stories of their own struggles—not small struggles, major challenges. These are some of the people I am closest to, and I didn't even know what they were courageously dealing with. I'm shocked and I can't stop thinking about it. The most common thing I hear is that people are also battling (or have battled) depression.

A few days ago, I found out one of my best friends has been winning his fight with depression for about ten years (way to pick up on that, Chris). His low point was about nine years ago, and since then he has stayed on top of it with some tools he learned in therapy. He still keeps in touch with his therapist, which is no surprise to me since he is one of the most loyal people I know. Recently, his therapist, impressed with how far along my friend had come in the past several years, asked him to write a letter for future patients who are battling depression. Being the writer he is, my friend jumped at the chance to put pen to paper. Here are the top five suggestions he had for patients:

1. Tell your therapist everything. He/She can't help you unless you do, and you will feel an unbelievable sense of relief once you're able to share your burden with someone. You can't trick your brain by hiding from your problems. It just doesn't work. I spent months falling deeper into depression because I held back some of what was bothering me. Don't make the same mistake. You've spent a lot of time wrestling with and running away from your problems. Now it's time to run towards them.

2. Take your medication every day—even after you are feeling better. Would you stop taking antibiotics once your fever breaks? Depression is an illness just like any other disease. Treat it accordingly and listen to your doctor.

3. Write in a journal every night. Just write your thoughts and feelings. Whatever is on your mind. You will be amazed at how this helps.

4. Exercise. I know you will not want to, but force yourself to do it. There is overwhelming evidence that touts the benefits of exercise in relieving symptoms of depression. Make it a goal to exercise at least thirty minutes five days a week. Ask a friend to join you for a jog a couple of times a week once you feel a little better.

5. Don't Give Up. You have too many people that care about you and too many opportunities ahead. Take comfort in knowing that you will soon feel more like yourself, and that better days really are ahead.

Knowing that I am not alone really helps. In addition to benefiting from their stories, the support, humor, compassion, and unwavering loyalty of my friends and family has kept my head up. What bothers me is why I didn't know any of their problems sooner. I would have wanted to know what my lifelong friends were going through. Maybe I could have helped. I would have returned their call faster, called more often, taken a trip. As I think about that I keep coming back to why I have been so afraid to admit my abuse—I'm no different from anyone else. Why do we hide so much from one another? Are we saving it for the life after this one, when it doesn't matter? We are all human. Flawed. We need to put more faith in the Strength in Numbers.

Rewind: March 26, 2010

I have been cheating. My goal with this blog was to document my progress, good and bad. I realize that I have been avoiding the bad for fear that people would worry about me. That's not what I want to do. I have done that my entire life and this is supposed to be my step in the right direction. The truth is that yesterday was a really, really bad day for me. I couldn't get out of my dark place. I had terrible thoughts about myself, what I'm doing, what happened, and where I am going. I didn't write anything because I felt like it was a waste of time, and I was a terrible writer. Luckily, yesterday was the day before today. So, this is making up for that in order to keep things honest.

Harvey Wallbanger: March 27, 2010

When I was in college, my roommates and I liked to play a game called Cat in a Box with our other roommate, Harvey Wallbanger. Harvey was a fun, energetic cat, the kind of cat that people would say seemed like a dog trapped in a cat's body. Harvey's most impressive attributes were traced back to a prize bull in Spain. He had cajones. Due to his reproductive stockpiling, he was relentlessly energetic—darting around the house, jumping on our food, basically throwing his body against the wall in a fit of excitement when we didn't play with him enough. This cat wanted to party. The only thing we could do to calm him down was to give him what he wanted. What could be better for a two-year-old energetic cat than a college townhouse filled with lacrosse-playing meatheads? Time for "The 'Banger" to rock out. We put him in the middle of a blanket—each of us at a corner—and flung him in the air, admiring his aerials, which were pretty impressive for a house cat (and he knew it). He would run around the house afterwards, justifying his surname. He was really in the partying mood now, and definitely wouldn't leave us alone—basically begging for more. So, being good roommates, we gave him what he needed. We put him in a little cooler, leaving the lid open of course; we didn't want to be rude. We would spin the cooler around on our linoleum kitchen floor. His eyes would get bigger and bigger as he spun. We would only do it a few times because we didn't want to hurt him. Now it was time for our form of Russian Roulette. We would all stand there, in the middle of the kitchen, and wait for the Cat in a Box to spring. Sure enough, Harvey would launch, like Kid Rock at a Hooters. He would fly around the house nonstop for about ten minutes. Finally, after his adrenaline wore off, he would calm down and take a nap on one of our laps. Looking back, this was no way to treat a cat. While we knew Harvey enjoyed the attention, this isn't something a PETA member would high-five us for over lattes.

Karma is a bitch. My wife and I went to a restaurant for brunch this afternoon to celebrate her completion of a 10k race. We decided to eat at one of the more popular lunch places, and we sat in the recently-refurbished enclosed porch. Brick walls, tile floors, and a wood ceiling—it was a volume machine. I felt my stress level rise the second we walked in. We sat down, ordered some Bloody Marys, and tried to have a conversation. We couldn't. The place was mayhem, with people laughing, glasses clinking, kids crying. I felt like Harvey inside the cooler, just waiting to launch and cling to the neck of one of the servers before running up the wall and firing myself into a ceiling fan. I have never been like this before but I'm pretty sure it's related to my anxiety about therapy and the whirlwind of thoughts rushing through my head. Whatever it is, I'm sorry Harvey. Make the cooler stop spinning.

Fake Happy Hour: March 28, 2010

Nothing is worse than getting into an argument with your spouse or significant other just before stepping foot into a social situation. Your fangs are out, your blood pressure is up, and the next thing you know, Bob from accounting and his sweet hair plugs are coming your way for a conversation about bathroom tile. You have no choice but to grin your way through two hours of small talk, faking your way through every conversation, just waiting to get back into the car so you can be yourself and deal with the original argument.

When I try to explain to people what it's like living life holding your sexual abuse to yourself, this is the only analogy that I can come up with that makes people get it. Imagine that happy hour extending for decades. That's what it feels like. Eventually, you will snap. Either you talk to your spouse and head for a private conversation to clear the air, or you jack Bob against the wall and rip out his hair plugs with your teeth before driving to his house to sledgehammer his bathroom. I'm choosing to talk it out with my spouse. I think it's the right thing to do.

Repression Lapse: March 29, 2010

When I first met with my therapist, she described what was happening to me as a repression lapse. When someone keeps a traumatic past hidden for a long period of time, eventually they can no longer repress the memories and they surface. Apparently this is common.

While it took me until March 2010 to enter therapy, I'm pretty sure my lapse began in the summer of 2009. At the time, I was having a lot of raw feelings surface, mainly related to my parents. Every time we would visit or talk on the phone, I would be agitated. As time went on, I had a shorter and shorter fuse with them and also with my wife. Something wasn't right, but I had no idea what. My wife was frustrated. I was frustrated. I was hating myself.

One night in July, after returning from a trip to see my parents, I broke down in the kitchen while talking to my wife. I couldn't figure out why I was so unhappy and I couldn't contain my emotions. It was surreal. Sure enough, the next time we saw them, it happened again. After some conversations with my wife I started to realize that my emotions were somehow related to the abuse. Up until that point, my wife knew that I had been abused for years, but I always kept the details vague. Slowly, the details started to surface and I confided in her that there was much more to the story. After thinking for a few weeks, we both agreed that I needed to talk to my parents about the abuse. I had to do something that I had been trained not to do.

I drove to their house one weekday evening. I was in the middle of raising money to start a small beer brewing company, and my parents had decided to invest, so the visit wasn't a surprise to them. I went there to talk business, but in the back of my head I knew I needed to cover the abuse. After we ate dinner, I raised the subject. My heart was racing. My mom quickly acknowledged what I said, but changed the subject. I went back to it. This went on for a few minutes; they were clearly not comfortable discussing "him."

After a few attempts I started to increase my level of commitment to the subject and they had no choice to but to talk with me about it. By this time, my heart was in my throat, and I could feel myself getting emotional. For the next hour or so, I became unglued. I told them there was more to the abuse than a "close call." I went into a few details, but mainly spent my time explaining how much it was haunting me. From the size of the snot bubbles formed on my face, it wouldn't take much to realize that I had an issue. Overall, they were good to talk with and we hugged it out as I left around 10 p.m. for my two-hour drive back to Richmond.

On that drive, my mind raced. I starting recalling memories that I didn't know existed. This was the scary part. I remembered sexual things he would make me do. Things he said. Specific details that I had never, ever thought about. I started to get worried. I called my sister to get out of my own head for a while. I spent a lot of time talking with her; she knew a little more than my parents did at that point so I felt like I had an ally, besides my wife. When I got home, my wife was asleep. I crawled into bed and tried to fall asleep. No luck. I got about an hour sleep that night, my mind wandering in and out of memories. I felt like my body was being invaded, like my brain had turned on me.

The next day, Friday, I needed to work on my Jeep. It was having some ignition problems. I worked on it well into the mid afternoon. My mind was elsewhere. I was trying as hard as I could to wrap the memories and feelings back up like I always had done before. It was starting to work, actually. Suddenly, I had a major problem. Not thinking about what I was doing, I loosened a radiator hose to get better access to the engine block. Not something I would normally do, but it seemed ok at the time. The pressure in the hose was too great, and the hose separated, shooting scalding antifreeze up my left arm. I just barely moved my head out of the way in time, but my arm and hand were badly burned. I jumped back and shook the antifreeze off. When I looked down, the skin on my left arm and hand drooped. Then it started to slide. Oh shit.

An hour later my wife and I were in the emergency room. They doped me up on painkillers and sent me to the burn unit at another hospital. I had second- and third-degree burns on a good portion of my wrist and hand. Luckily, the director of the burn unit was on duty, and I was in good hands as they removed the excess skin and bandaged the burns. They were worried about Compartment Syndrome, so I was admitted for the night so they could watch the swelling. With an I.V. full of painkillers, I visited many faraway places that night—most had rainbows and ponies and little people with big smiles. The amazing thing was that I was very calm when I thought about the abuse. I thought about it coherently and rationally. Instead of burying the memories like I always had, I was thinking freely about everything, not worried about containing them. I was comfortable facing the memories for the first time in my life.

From that day forward, I have been moving in the right direction. What I thought was a terrible accident, actually gave me the time (and opiates) I needed to contemplate how to handle my recovery. The real tipping point for me wasn't until December of 2009, but looking back, that day in early August was critical. I have never been someone to look up and say thanks, because I've always thought that I was one hundred percent responsible for everything that happened in my life. I feel that changing.

Spiral Awareness: March 30, 2010

Today was the first time I've caught myself having increasingly negative thoughts. Normally, when I have a bad day, it continues down into a flat spin of self-destruction until I wake up the next day feeling slightly different. When I was driving today, I started thinking about my life in a way that I have done many times before. I thought about what I would have been like if the abuse had never happened. I thought about myself as a seven year old, before the abuse began. I was jealous of that guy. He had a better self-image. Emotional stability. Some confidence. I thought about how he would have handled so many situations in college, his twenties. I pictured myself entirely differently and I felt completely gypped. I felt as if I was gypped out of the guy I was supposed to be.

These thoughts are so dark and they get me nowhere, but I have them often. I must have kept this line of thinking going my entire drive from Goochland to Powhatan, about thirty-five minutes. Just before I got to my Powhatan site, I caught myself. Why was I allowing myself to think about this? I don't think I've caught myself before. Maybe it's because of the conversations I've had with people about depression and hearing the "spiral" analogy mentioned over and over. I hear people talk about self-maintenance.

Before I entered the Powhatan site I sat in the car and thought about how thinking this way wasn't good for me. I couldn't focus on being gypped; it's a dead end. When I got back in the van I felt a little better just knowing that I caught myself. I'm not sure how to control these thoughts before the spiral starts, but at least I caught myself after thirty-five minutes. A small victory and I'll take it.

Closer to the end of my route I was listening to "The Herd" on ESPN Radio. Colin Cowherd is the radio host who happened to start therapy right when I did to handle his issues with an abusive father. I've been glued to his show because he talks candidly about it on the air. Colin suddenly got on a rant about depression, and how so many Americans are clinically depressed, something like ten percent. Then he mentioned the number of American soldiers in Iraq who are labeled clinically depressed, around eight percent. His next statement was that, of those Americans with depression, eighty-five percent improve with placebo. His ever-so-scientific conclusion was that typical Americans don't have purpose in their lives and just become depressed, and that the soldiers, while in a war zone away from their families, were better off because their lives had purpose. What a dick thing to say about so many people who suffer from depression. Suddenly, I was back to being down on myself and hating Colin Cowherd.

After work, I returned to my house pissed off. I went to my laptop and found "The Herd's" website and drafted an email to Colin, spewing fire. I've never written to anyone in the media. I've never really cared, but somehow this pissed me off to no end. I slammed the laptop shut and headed for the gym. Dick.

An hour later I was exercised, showered and feeling ridiculous for sending him an email. Why did it matter to me? Colin Cowherd, who I'm sure is a nice guy, is a radio host who lives and breathes ratings. Ratings write his paycheck. His sports fan ratings most likely took a dip after his public meltdown about his abuse. Sports dorks don't like touchy-feely therapy talk. He's got to put himself back together and generate buzz. So, he's ranting and forcing himself to feel better about himself. I get it.

What I'm figuring out is that I need to stop letting myself be controlled by outside forces, whether it's my subconscious negative thoughts or some guy with a microphone I don't know. I need to put more faith in what things I do know about myself. I need to remind myself more about how fortunate I am. I need to tell myself about the incredible opportunities I've had. I need to think about the great family, friends, and the love that I feel from the people I care about. I need to think about my amazing wife more and how lucky I am. I need to wonder about what color eyes my kids will have. I need to do all of this but it's not easy.

One Sock Wednesday: March 31, 2010

When I was in high school, I used to get a really nervous stomach before lacrosse games. By pre-game warm-up, my stomach would be a mess. I would often find myself stretching with my team, thinking about strategy, learning the other team's players, when suddenly, my colon blow alert siren would sound. Two minutes and counting. Oh boy. Time to come up with a plan…fast. I would excuse myself and run into the school, find a restroom, and dehydrate myself significantly before the game started. Much better. It was sort of a pre-game ritual, and I was used to it.

One day, we were playing at another team's school, and I was on the field stretching as usual. The colon siren sounded. Ahoy. Time to target a bathroom. I excused myself from stretching, and raced towards the school. I tried several doors. Shit. Locked. Maybe I could hold it?

"ABSOLUTELY NOT," my body responded. Roger that. Finally, just before launch, I found an open door and raced into the school and found a bathroom. Rent the movie "Dumb and Dumber" and you'll get the picture. What I realized next wasn't inspiring. No paper—anywhere. We've all been there, but this was an extreme case. I quickly remembered a tip that I had learned from our goalie and one of my best friends, Lumpy. When in doubt, rock the sock.

As I trotted back on to the field, I could see the concern on my teammate's faces. I was supposed to face off to start the game, and nobody could find me. I was just happy to be alive. We huddled for our pre-game cheer. I prayed nobody would focus on me. Sure enough, that one ever-so-observant teammate chirped, "Hey man, why are you wearing one sock?" D'oh.

One thing I've started to learn about Therapy Thursdays, is that they are preceded by One Sock Wednesday's. Luckily, I've learned my lesson and I now scout out my surroundings and heed the siren's blare immediately as to avoid rocking the sock, but nevertheless, I still have the same stomach. I guess tomorrow's the big game. I feel like I'm sixteen again.

Therapy Session 3: April 1, 2010

This morning started off better than my other two Therapy Thursdays. I wasn't having chest pains. I went to work feeling pretty good—maybe a slight upset stomach but I'd take that over the chest pains. The weather was amazing. I left work around 1:30 p.m. and headed home to fill out the rest of my SUDS (Subjective Units of Disturbance) paperwork before my 3 p.m. appointment.

Filling out the paperwork, I could feel my anxiety increase. I was asked to describe incidents in my past that have caused me to be angry. My chest pains were back. I inhaled deeply, as trained, doing my two second squares in my head to count my breathing. It wasn't working.

I got in the car and headed for my appointment. Damn, why was it so hot? Wasn't it just snowing a few weeks ago? Where the hell did spring go? We always get gypped out of spring. I got on the interstate. Some guy was tailgating me. Ridiculous. Seriously, dude? How can I go any faster than the car in front of me? What an asshole. Not only that, but the car in front of me had its left turn signal on. We were in the left lane. Really, man? You planning on taking a left turn here into the median at 60 mph? Fine by me. Finally, I noticed how agitated I was. What is wrong with me?

As I approached the therapist's office, I took a wrong turn again. This time into an office parking lot. My subconscious obviously did not want to go to therapy. I stepped onto the elevator. Another woman had walked on before me. She looked down. She had already pressed level 2, so I didn't have to push a button. The door closed and it immediately felt awkward. Where's the lame music when you need it? We arrived at the second floor. I gestured for her to exit first, she took an immediate left. I went right, to the doctor's office and entered, this time a little more confidently. It was 2:57. I rang the buzzer for my doctor to trigger the light inside her office. Ten seconds later, the woman from the elevator quietly entered the office. I knew what she was going through—this had to be her first time. We both sat and read magazines quietly.

At 3:09, I was still sitting there. I refused to call my doctor like she requested. The buzzer should have told her I was here. I went to the receptionist and abruptly asked her to check with my doctor. The receptionist rolled her eyes and put down her magazine. She got up and walked back behind the door. Two minutes later, my doctor opened the door and gestured me in. She discreetly set down an issue of "New York Times Magazine" as I walked into the hallway. As we walked she said that I should have waited until 3:15 to call her out of the office; it was 3:10. She said she was on a call and ended it because I was so persistent. Now, I don't know much about this therapy thing, and maybe I've spent too much time in the military, but what's up with that? If we have a 3 o'clock session, I'll be here at 3, ready. Cancel your calls with the "New York Times Magazine." Alright, maybe I'm being too hard on her. I'm completely agitated now. Is this one of those psychology experiments I read about it college to see if I would just sit there quietly until 3:30? Maybe I'm just nervous, but I'm not sure.

We got right back to work, going through my behaviors and emotions based on the paperwork I had filled out for the last session. We were still evaluating my condition. She asked a lot of questions about how I feel about myself. How I think. She broke the line of questioning with a comment about how ridiculously hard on myself I am. We kept going, describing how my wife and I are doing, our sex life, etc. She found it odd that I can't sleep naked. I told her some stories about Jack and it quickly made sense. She went further into sexual questions. They were difficult to answer but she was in no way uncomfortable, so that made it easier for me.

She then started asking questions about my childhood, just concentrating on our immediate family and not on Jack. I went through good things and bad things. She asked me for some specifics and I told a few stories about how hard my dad was on me and my sister. A few of the stories required more detail, which she pulled out of me.

To summarize, she was worried that I had a traumatic childhood, completely separate from Jack. I don't like to think of it that way, because there were so many great things about my childhood. She explained to me what trauma was and what trauma can do to a child. She ended with how my childhood and relationship with my parents has caused a great deal of stress in my life, void of Jack.

She gave me some new relaxation techniques to work on; she could tell that my stress level was still high. She also wrote down some things we needed to work on: learning how to be happy, learning how to compliment myself, learning how to accept failure. She went so far as to say that I needed more mediocrity in my life to learn how to accept it. She was worried that I was putting way too many expectations on myself and pulling myself down if they weren't met, and then I wouldn't lift myself up if they were met.

Then she said something that I wasn't expecting. She said the good news was that my depression wasn't that severe. She thought that it was very manageable and that I was borderline not depressed. She followed that good news with some bad news by saying that my PTSD was worse than she thought, that it was raging. She said that she needs me to see a psychiatrist in order to get a handle on it. Normally, she would feel ok moving forward, but in this case, she wanted me to get evaluated by someone who does this from a medical perspective. Evidently, the two-pronged trauma that I endured as a kid enhanced my problems and has complicated the treatment. I immediately felt like Jack Nicholson's character in "One Flew Over the Cuckoo's Nest." Great. I need another doctor. She followed that wonderful bit of news with the fact that I need to see a physician to evaluate my chest pains. She was worried that they were still occurring. I needed to get a full physical. Super. Duper. Two more doctors.

By this time it was 4:06, and I felt better knowing that I was getting my full hour. Maybe I was being too hard on her for the time thing. She asked how I thought she was doing as a therapist. My earlier frustration depleted, I said I thought it was going well but I wasn't sure. I said I had never been to a therapist so it was hard for me to know. I said I didn't really know if what she was doing was the right thing, but I had no alternative but to keep going. She stopped me and explained a little bit about her theory on therapy. She explained that she had been trained in several different types of therapy, one that focuses on just behaviors, one that focuses mainly on feelings, and another that deals with just thoughts. She said that her approach for me is to combine all three—that they are all so inter-connected it was valuable to have an eclectic approach. Uh, sure. Why not. I then told her that I was frustrated that we weren't moving forward faster. She told me I sounded like my dad. I know when I'm being fucked with, so I got annoyed at that. I corrected her and said it was that I really wanted to feel better, so I was anxious. I needed to start treatment, not just the evaluation part. She said she understood.

What I told her was the truth. I have absolutely no idea if she's taking me in a good direction, but I don't have enough ammunition to stop what I'm doing and start over with another therapist. Theo Fleury and I traded emails this week and he reminded me not to give up before the miracle. That sounds like goofy talk, but I'll keep going with my eyes wide open.

Before any miracle occurs, I've got two more doctors to see. While I'm frustrated, I also understand that it takes time and that understanding the complete picture upfront will save time and energy on the back end. I get it. I just want to feel right so badly.

The drive home was uneventful. Nobody was tailgating me that I noticed. No senseless turn signals flashing that I could find. Hmm. Drivers must be much better this time of day.

Survivors: April 2, 2010

"The world breaks everyone, and afterward, some are strong at the broken places."
–Ernest Hemmingway

I think in life there are people who are naturally drawn to groups and people who aren't. Some people feel very comfortable joining a running club, taking guitar lessons, or being heavily involved in a neighborhood association. I've never been one of those people. I'm passionate about things, but for whatever reason I feel more comfortable going it alone.

Discussion boards fall into that category of places where people congregate in groups and learn from one another. Even with all of my interests, I don't think I've been to a single message board, until today. Today I took the step to register and tell my story on a website designed for male sexual abuse survivors. Malesurvivor.org is a rare message board that has my attention. It allows people to tell their story and anonymously seek help from other survivors. For those who are further along in their recovery, it allows them to give back to those who need more encouragement or guidance or even just a little validation. The site is managed by moderators to keep an eye on the subject matter and jump in when someone needs the right nudge.

When I signed up, I got really nervous. I was afraid that nobody would think I was worthy of being included on the site. I was afraid my story wouldn't be significant enough. So, I really didn't say much. I didn't discuss any of the abuse specifically and I feel a weird shame for that. I know that it's because I'm afraid to show that I need support or help. I feel like I hide behind this journal because it gives me some control. I am the one writing. I am not relying on others (so I tell myself).

The more I scroll through the entries on the forum, the more respect I have for these survivors. Each story is heart wrenching. Each person is strong, maybe not in the sense that we normally think, but just by the fact that they are alive, telling an incredibly personal story in the open— many with great detail that must take forever to type. Most ask for help. Beg for help. I wish I had that kind of courage to show that kind of vulnerability. I'd like to be able to go back to the site and tell what happened—the physical stuff—and to ask people for help.

I don't know what this says about me now. I guess I've finally admitted that I need a group to bounce things off of, share with, and learn from. It actually feels good. I think being part of this group, if only for a few weeks, is a way for me to feel stronger at my broken places.

Building Faith: April 4, 2010

Early last fall, I had a typical man-moment. Staring into my backyard one afternoon, I couldn't help but notice how bad the carport looked. The dilapidated structure leaned slightly to one side, barely covering an old, inoperable, blue ski boat. The wood that framed the gravel floor had become detached in several places and gravel spread onto the lawn. Vacant bird nests filled the rafters. It looked bad. I couldn't imagine what the neighbors thought. I told my wife we should just turn it into a guest room and build an attached shed for our lawn equipment. My wife looked at me like I was suggesting we build a Sasquatch trap. She laughed. But, I pressed on. My hand had just recovered from the antifreeze burn, and I was looking for something to keep me moving as I was sorting out my overwhelming pile of emotions. I knew it would be a great project for me. Soon enough, I had a plan and an approved budget. Giddy up.

I was a carpenter on a mission for the next several months. I started with the foundation. It was a mess. The pillars weren't parallel, the spacing was off, so I had to re-set everything and level the base. The work was tedious but I was focused. It rained a lot, so I was seldom comfortable. Within a few weeks, the foundation was solid and level—ready for me to build, so I started by framing the walls. I added a new shed with a roof attached to the main room where the carport used to be. I added windows, a French door and siding. I hired someone to dig a trench from the house to lay the necessary wiring for electricity. I was getting somewhere. Unfortunately, Mother Nature had other plans. Excessive rains and cold temperatures shut me down. Bummer.

The winter was brutal. We had more snow than anyone could remember and I was stir crazy. Luckily, I had started my job so I had a little structure to my day, but overall, these were some really difficult months as I contemplated what I should do about my past. My fuse was getting shorter and my anger was steadily growing. Every time I looked out at the carport I got pissed, but there was nothing I could do. It was one more thing about my life that sucked. I had so far to go.

Finally, spring sprung, and now it was Easter. I can't remember a single Easter weekend that wasn't sunny and warm. I'm sure I've seen several Easters in the rain, but I can't think of one right now. That Easter weekend was no exception. It was a gift. With a clear schedule and beautiful weather, I was able to get back outside and begin putting the finishing touches on the new room and shed. I worked steadily on Saturday and most of the day today, and something hit me late this afternoon. I had really come a lot further than I thought I had over the winter. There wasn't that much left for me to do. Hmm. Strange. Every time I looked outside this winter, all I saw was how far I was from finished. The gift for me was more than the weather, the gift was the realization that I had really come a long way and I was really proud of what I had accomplished. I felt good about the time I put into the foundation—the floor was flat and strong, even after the deep freeze. The walls were all straight and the roof hadn't given an inch under several feet of snow.

One thing I need to work on is reminding myself that I've done some things right, and even though things may not seem good directly in front of me, my foundation is solid. I may not have all of the answers, but my faith is leading me. My faith isn't my religion; it's my compass forward through my recovery. I can always tell if I've deviated, so I should have faith that where I'm heading is in the right direction. What may not look so good at the time may actually turn out to be in pretty good shape. It was a happy Easter.

Mollusks in Stasis: April 5, 2010

In evolutionary biology, there is a theory called punctuated equilibrium. Don't get me wrong, I know very little about biology, but I vaguely remembered the theory from school, so I'll channel Wikipedia and sound smart. Punctuated equilibrium is when a species reproduces decade after decade and very little or no evolution occurs. The state is referred to as stasis. Mollusks are commonly one of these species.

When I got back from work today, I was feeling pretty on top of things. I definitely wasn't thinking about biology. I looked forward to getting to the gym. I had a quick bite to eat and pulled up ESPN.com to check out how Tiger Woods' press conference went. Instead of learning more riveting details about his transgressions, my eyes were immediately drawn to a story of Theo Fleury's recent criminal complaint filed against his abuser, Graham James. The story has been in and out of the news lately. James was a hockey coach in Canada's Junior leagues for years, during which he abused several young hockey players as he prepared them for the NHL. In 1997, Sheldon Kennedy, a former NHL player brought the first set of charges against James. At that time, Theo Fleury had yet to go public with his story. James was found guilty and served three and a half years in prison. After his term, James vanished and nobody could figure out how he disappeared so easily.

When Theo filed his complaint a few months ago, everyone expected James to surface and justice to be served. Nothing happened. Recently, another complaint was filed against James by an unknown accuser, so the pressure to get some answers quickly intensified. Today, the Canadian National Parole Board announced that they had pardoned James in 2007, and kept it hidden from the government and from the press. This afforded James a clean record, and freedom to live and work in other countries without their knowing of his past. I know Canada is a country that takes care of its people and oozes compassion, but this was unbelievable. Complete and total stasis.

If there's one thing that a childhood sexual abuse survivor can hope for, is that this epidemic will come to an end one day. People will openly discuss the topic because they know that if they sweep it under the rug because it feels uncomfortable, then abuse will thrive. Parents will consistently talk with their children and connect with them about how to communicate abuse. Activists will generate enough awareness that policies will be put in place and perpetrators will never be allowed to abuse again. My abuser is dead and I dig for closure every day with no luck, but one thing I can do is feel better knowing that slowly but surely, we are evolving.

But sadly, I hear about priest after priest that was simply moved to a different church. Boy Scout leaders were stripped of their positions with no penalty. Rabbis were protected by Orthodox Jewish leadership while their victims carried the shame. When is something going to change and what will it take? Of the one hundred fifty million males in the US, almost twenty million were, or will be, sexually abused as children. That is sixteen percent. If those twenty million demanded change, it would happen. With the media finally reporting story after story of abuse, it seems like more people are talking about it, and little things are being done, but it will take time for us to really evolve. Until we all stand up and make changes, we are no better off than the mollusk, stuck in a stasis.

Making The Call: April 6, 2010

People have asked me when I finally made my decision to go to therapy. I don't really know, but it was probably a lot longer ago than I think. What I do know is when I finally decided to call a therapist. The distinction is important, because between the two is a lot of time spent staring in the mirror.

Back in December, I decided to drive to see my parents and talk with them some more. I wanted to let them know where my head was and what I was dealing with. I felt like it was important to do, since I knew they were linked to a lot of my problems, and they would likely be involved in my recovery process. I brought a book with me that I was reading at the time: "The Right to Innocence." It was sort of a self-help book for those who weren't ready for therapy and a really good book for me at the time. One thing the book suggested was to write a list of the top ten reasons why I wanted to recover from the trauma of my childhood sexual abuse. It was not an easy thing to write, but I went all Spinal Tap and came up with eleven:

1. To be a better husband
2. To be a better father for my future children
3. To learn to love myself
4. To render Jack powerless
5. To keep me from abusing anyone in any way
6. To feel proud of myself
7. To be a better son and brother
8. To be a better friend
9. To prevent me from hiding pain with addiction
10. To prove to him that I'm stronger than he was
11. To one day help others recover

That day I took my parents through this list so they could better understand where I was headed and why. It was a good conversation and I left feeling like I had real focus. During the next few months, I spent time going through that book and doing the things that it suggested. While some of it was effective, there was still a lot of confusion and anger between me and my parents. What I thought would really help, had actually brought to surface new frustrations. It was a heavy few months, but I still wasn't ready to admit that therapy was the correct course for me. I was still walking the fence.

In late February I had what alcoholics, and Jules from "Pulp Fiction," refer to as a moment of clarity. It was the day of the gold medal hockey game between the US and Canada and I had invited people over to watch the game. What I didn't realize was that my wife had planned on doing a bunch of errands during the day, so she was really rushed to get back and help me prepare some food and clean the house for our guests. After they left, we had a really heated argument—you know, the kind of heated argument when the man doesn't say a word.

Knowing what was good for me; I left the house and went to a movie. As it turns out, what happened that night was a result of my wife holding a great deal of stress inside as she dealt with my recovery for months and months without dealing with her own emotions. This is incredibly common. A spouse is exposed to an unbelievable amount of stress when someone goes through this process of recovery. Fearing that she would be complaining when I was the one dealing with the big issues, she was holding all of it in and refraining from letting it off of her chest (hence, Chernobyl II). By the time I got back from the movie, we had both calmed down, and I made a deal with myself that I would call a therapist in the morning. I didn't know what was going on, but whatever it was, I had been breaking Number One on my list, and that couldn't happen.

Since that day about a month ago, I think we have grown more than we had in our first ten months of marriage. What we have realized is that we are both going through this together, as much as it hurts me to admit. A spouse must be able to deal with all of this mess as effectively as the victim. It's one example that quickly makes you see the ripple effect that abuse can have on a family.

I keep the list in my bedside table and I look at it every now and then. It's a quick reminder for me and it immediately helps me gain strength to continue on my path. When I look over at my wife I realize that my decision to call a therapist was the right thing to do. Time will tell how effective therapy is for me, but I know that Number One on the list required me to make the call, and I'm glad I did.

Skidding Into Thursday: April 7, 2010

Today is one of those weird days where I feel like I'm really heading in the wrong direction. I don't know whether it's related to tomorrow's therapy session or if I'm just having an off day, but my funk-meter is pegged. I'm actually starting to recognize a weekly cycle. The week begins okay, and then I get skittish by Wednesday. I dehydrate. Then I get chest pains until my therapy session. Then I feel great, which leads into a pretty good weekend. Not sure how long this cycle will continue, but until it changes, I'll keep hanging out near toilets and defibrillators. Don't really feel like writing about anything more. 'Nuff said.

Therapy Session 4: April 8, 2010

I started today in the same kind of funk that rounded out yesterday. I don't really know how to describe it other than it being a sort of murky, quiet, alone way of going about things. Interactions with people are dull. Little things that shouldn't get to me are bothersome. I find myself avoiding people. I don't really have interests. The morning radio show I listened to as I drove to my first site was frustrating me. Really, what kind of radio show talks about feral cats for thirty minutes? I don't like cats much, nor do I like conversations about cats...unless they're laser cats...but I wasn't so lucky.

I had to re-deliver a meal to a site, which sort of put me out of my rhythm, and on Thursdays, I like to have everything simple and predictable. That bothered me. I did notice that my chest pains were there, but they weren't that bad, which was a good sign. Work ended around 1:30, which was great, so I was home by 2 p.m. to change and prepare for my session.

My general funk carried into my thoughts about therapy and my therapist. As I drove to my session I started to think about how I should start shopping for a new therapist. It didn't feel like it was working out. I planned to go on to my discussion board and ask the members for advice on whether I should look for a male therapist to replace my female therapist. I was starting to feel like she just didn't understand me and what I was going through. As I drove, I noticed that I wasn't as angry as I was last week; that seemed good. But then again, I was definitely in more of a funk than last week.

I pulled into the correct parking lot for once, and headed into the office building. Elevator up, and into the office. It was feeling more comfortable. I was in my own world. I

62

sat down before ringing the bell, realizing that it was only 2:53. I glanced down at a "People" magazine. Jake from "The Bachelor" and his new fiancee cheesed the cover. I picked it up and thumbed through the pages. A picture of a seventeen-year-old Miley Cyrus with her arms wrapped around Bret Michaels caught my eye. What? Isn't that statutory rape? Granted, the story was about them just being friends, but c'mon? I put down the magazine and made a mental note about how long before Miley was on one of Dr. Drew's celebrity therapy shows. It was 2:58, so I got up and rang her bell, then sat down. The lobby music had James Taylor's "Fire and Rain" playing. It immediately took me back to a sailing camp I went to when I was in eighth grade. I calmed down as I thought about the crush I had on one of the older girls in the camp and how we became good friends. I was nothing more than a pre-pubescent attention machine to her, but she was something more to me. The lyrics suddenly caught my ear: "Been walking my mind to an easy time, my back turned towards the sun. Lord knows when the cold wind blows it'll turn your head around." I really liked that line.

Before I knew it, the therapist's door opened and a woman walked out. She had been crying. I felt bad for her. She quickly apologized to me, assuming she had made me wait. I made a point to say to her that it wasn't her fault. It was ok. My therapist quickly followed and beckoned me in. She didn't extend her hand; I think she's a germaphobe. I walked back towards her office and sat down in my big boy chair. I glanced at the tiny chair on the far side of the office. It was something from a Keebler commercial. She said we had a lot of work to do so we got right to it. We started by analyzing what my current condition was. She checked off what I was feeling. Sad, check. Stressed, check. On and on.

We kept going and stopped as soon as we checked "marital frustrations." She had always been so happy that my wife and I have a great relationship and felt it was my most positive sign as a patient. I told her about an argument that my wife and I had a few days prior. We quickly pinpointed that as the reason I felt down the last few days. Duh, Chris. She started to dive into what happened, and without going into details, she realized that I wasn't saying to my wife what I really wanted. She asked me why I wasn't being more assertive when it came to the situation at hand. I said I didn't know, but I just didn't want to control her, and I wanted to let her make her own decisions about certain things. She corrected me and said, "Your wife is a strong woman. Just because you say what you want, doesn't mean you'll control her and get what you want." A light bulb went on for me, probably long after her bulb went on. She said that I was trying so hard to not be like my dad (controlling), that I was over-correcting and denying myself my assertive nature. This was a major moment for me, less because I learned something important about myself, and more because I realized that my therapist was valuable. She had really helped me. Nice. We wrapped that part up, and I felt good knowing that I shouldn't be down about my relationship with my wife. I should feel good knowing that my small problem with my wife wasn't a big problem, that it was related to my current condition.

After all of this, she pulled out a sheet and started to tell me what a SUDS score was. I immediately stopped her and said we'd already gone through this. I pulled out my full SUDS sheet and showed it to her. "Oh, good, we did that already." Uh, yeah. Wake up and pay attention to our sessions. I felt my confidence in her recede.

She quickly decided to relax me. She put on a relaxation tape. This is the first time we had listened to a tape in her office, so it was a little awkward for me. I leaned back in the chair. All I thought about what how fat my stomach must look in the shirt I was wearing. No idea why this was my biggest concern, but I couldn't shake the thought from my head. She continued to focus me and we went through fifteen minutes of relaxation. At the end, I was a bag of sand. I needed that. She told me how we would be doing this as we began our EMDR treatment. Every session from here on out, we would need me to get to very relaxed state before we could begin. I felt good knowing we were getting close to some real therapy, real progress.

She said it was time to wrap up. I glanced at my watch. 3:53. I didn't enter her office until 3:07. Noted. Not the full hour. Gypped. I tried not to let it bother me, but it wasn't easy. As we walked towards the door, she mentioned how glad she was that I wasn't a patient who was planning on "bolting on her." I laughed and said that I didn't know any better. She didn't laugh. Awkward. Oh, well, whatever, at least I wasn't hiding anything.

As I drove home I realized that I was feeling better about her. There were a few things that still bothered me, but I felt good that I had learned something. I started to think about how few things in life that make you better are easy. This might just be one of those things. No matter who my therapist was, I was probably going to struggle.

"Been walking my mind to an easy time, my back turned towards the sun. Lord knows when the cold wind blows it'll turn your head around." I really like that line.

Silent But Necessary: April 9, 2010

Today was a big allergy day. I don't exactly know why, but I was unable to control what I was thinking and how my body was reacting. As I drove to my sites, my mind raced. My nose snotted. I was thinking a lot about the people who support me, and how lucky I am. I thought about what my life would be like if a few things had been different. What if I was a foster child? What if I didn't quit my job a while ago? What if I didn't marry my wife? I arrived at the common conclusion. Things happen for a reason, and what I'm doing now, however simple and structured, is for a reason. I thought about this journal. What I thought was just a way for me to write some thoughts down and possibly help someone in need of a nudge, is actually helping me unload a lot of baggage. I get to show my baggage to other people, as embarrassing as it is. But, it's not mine to hide and carry on my shoulders alone anymore. That's liberating. If you're only as sick as your secrets, then I just started antibiotics.

When I was an Ensign in the Navy, my first duty station was with an F-14 Tomcat squadron, the VF-31 Tomcatters. The F-14 was the fighter jet in the movie "Top Gun." My role in the squadron was Aviation Intelligence Officer. Basically, I helped train the pilots and navigators to keep them away from things that wanted to shoot them down. One of my main reasons for selecting an F-14 squadron fresh out of Intelligence School, over a Seal Team, submarine squadron, or intelligence watch floor tour, was so that I could fly in the back seat of the famous fighter. The rumor was, if your Commanding Officer really liked you, he'd let you fly in the back seat from time to time. Once I was accepted into VF-31 as their Intel Officer, a fraternal rush sort of process, I was laser-focused on getting some flight time.

Before flying, one of the requirements was to pass a complete aviation physical that included a swimming test, written test, full physical, and successful run through the altitude chamber. The altitude chamber is designed to teach people how their body reacts to hypoxia. Hypoxia is a pathological condition that occurs when your brain is starved of oxygen. For instance, if, while flying in the back seat of the F-14, the seal on the cockpit leaks unknowingly, I would be able to tell that there was a leak by identifying my unique physical reactions. Everybody has a different reaction, so this is really valuable learning experience that could save lives.

My squadron was located at Oceana Naval Air Station in Virginia Beach, but the altitude chamber test was all the way over at Norfolk Naval Air Station, about a thirty-minute drive. I had gone out the night before with a few friends, a few of which were going through the altitude chamber with me that morning. We were all a little hung over. We arrived, checked in, and were told to take a seat in the waiting room while the chamber was prepped. There were about twenty of us guys in the waiting room, all junior officers, with one very quiet female ROTC student sitting by herself in the corner. Being a college student and not an officer yet, she was clearly out of her comfort zone being around us older guys, as we laughed about the activities the night before. I decided to introduce myself. She quietly raised her head and said hello. She said she was passing this test so she could get some flight time and move one step closer to achieving her dream of becoming a naval aviator after graduation. We all tried to loosen her up. She was nervous.

The administrators called us into the chamber, and it was time to start. The chamber was a large, cylindrical structure with seats on the outside. We shuffled in and took our seats on the perimeter, facing the inside of the tube. A civilian behind a glass window at the end of the cylinder introduced himself and took us through the program. I just wanted to get this over with. I was kind of excited to see how my body reacted when I finally took off my oxygen mask at thirty-five thousand feet. He gave us our instructions. Some of us were to play patty cake with one another once our masks were removed. Some of us were to do simple dexterity drills. I was given a sort of word problem with some simple math and some counting. Cool. Before we got started the civilian made one comment. He said that due to the severe decrease in pressure as we ascended, the air in our bodies would expand and we would feel the need to pass gas. Imagine a helium balloon as it rises above the earth. He said to make sure we released the gas; otherwise it could be dangerous to our organs. This was no problem with our group. We had been practicing at sea level and we were professionals.

Masks on, doors shut, we began to climb. Five thousand feet... I could feel my ears popping. Seventy-five hundred feet, the air was starting to feel a little drier. We giggled and made childish comments as we waited. Intestinal gas began to flow freely. Some were loud, which summoned more laughter through our intercom systems in our masks. Much better. I started to wonder if I really wanted to take my mask off and smell the air inside this fart tube once we hit our desired altitude. Suddenly, right when we hit about twenty thousand feet, the female ROTC student cried out "STOP." What? What's the deal? "We need to go down, please, it hurts", she said. She was obviously not following protocol and letting it rip. "Ma'am, you're going to need to release the gas," the civilian sternly said. "I can't. It hurts," the poor girl responded embarrassingly. This went on for a few minutes. We were all getting impatient. Out of nowhere, one of the Lieutenants screamed, "Fart. C'mon, fart!" We all laughed. A few others aided in convincing her to accept her fate. I started to feel bad for her. After about five minutes of asking this young girl to fart, we realized we couldn't win. We had to go back down to sea level, a waste of about thirty minutes. The civilian was clearly agitated. The girl was crying. She had to be so embarrassed. She was forced to leave the chamber once we hit sea level. We closed the door and finished our drill. It was pretty interesting. I really didn't have any symptoms, other than passing out suddenly. Great. Not much of a learning experience for me. And, I was right about the stank once we removed our masks. I don't think I ate lunch that day.

As I look back at that moment, I think about the poor ROTC student. She seemed so genuine with her goal to become a Navy pilot. Did she deviate from her lifelong dream because she couldn't fart in front of a bunch of guys she didn't know? That would be sad. When I think about this journal, I realize that what I'm doing isn't exactly comfortable, but it's necessary for me to get to where I need to go. It feels like one of those things that will make me a better person, so I'll deal with the uneasiness every time I finish an entry. It turns out that farting in front of a bunch of people I may not know gets easier every day, and I'm starting to feel relieved.

I Am (Survival): April 11, 2010

I am a dog fight. I am a kid on the end of a diving board for the first time. I am a clenched fist. I am lying in a jungle with my hands around a machine gun. I am anger. I am a deep breath after skidding to a stop on the highway. I am tapping on a wall in Morse code. I am turning away from the mirror in disgust and then looking back. I am a hike through the snow with no shoes. I am quivering hands dialing a doctor for help. I am deciding it's too dangerous to fly today. I am the warm sun on a man's face after spitting out the cold metal taste of a pistol. I am dissociation. I am putting on a smile so nobody gets upset. I am the words "watch out." I am hate for a memory. I am one, one thousand, two, one thousand, three, one thousand, breathe. I am the first thing in my head this morning and the last thing out tonight. I am survival.

Vitamin Z: April 12, 2010

Ever since I was a kid, I've cringed at the thought of a visit to the doctor. I know I'm not alone here. The smell of a hospital or doctor's office. The quiet waiting room. The gown, no doubt designed by someone under the influence. The ricochet of urine off the wrist, into the cup. The awkward introduction. The cold stethoscope. The colder hands. The quick goodbye. It's just not natural.

Today, at the request of my therapist, I had to take a day off from work to meet with a physician and address the chest pains and anxiety that I have been dealing with for months. I actually don't have a primary care physician, because I've always preferred the 7-Eleven of hospitals, Patient First, so I went with a referral from my wife. It was a small doctor's office in an office park on the west side of town. It had a pretty comfortable waiting room, actually. I filled out the pile of paperwork and was in an examination room by 9:30. The nurse took my blood pressure and other vitals. BP was good, which was a relief. I also found out that I was six feet tall, not five-eleven like I had thought. Mental note: always get height measured in the morning when the vertebrae are well spaced. The nurse also gave me an EKG, and then asked that I go urinate on my wrist in the bathroom so they could do some standard tests.

When that was done, I returned to the examination room to find a clown gown waiting for me. Within ten minutes, I had figured out that the gap goes in the back. Right. Much better. The doctor entered and we started by talking about why I was there. I mentioned that I had a history of abuse, and that my therapist recommended that I receive a physical due to the chest pains. I explained my PTSD prognosis. He quickly understood and began a standard physical. In the end, all things were in good shape. EKG was excellent. He found my sports hernia, but didn't recommend surgery at this time. Sweet. He didn't play Dr. Jellyfinger, which I think just made my week.

We wrapped up the physical by discussing anti-depressants. He explained that as long as I was comfortable with it, he'd like to prescribe an anti-depressant to assist in my recovery. I told him that I'd do whatever it took to recover quickly, but that I had some hesitation when it came to drugs, specifically anti-depressants. I felt that they carried a pretty big social stigma, and deep down I felt that sometimes they're over-prescribed. He started by explaining that they are no different than a medication for high blood pressure. Would I be comfortable taking that? I said I would. He said there is absolutely no difference. Okay. I hesitated. He stopped and realized that he needed to explain it more. What he said was that anti-depressants were not just designed for depressed people. They are designed to level out the chemicals in your brain, specifically serotonin. I knew the word. He said that when a traumatic event occurs in our life, our body responds in a way to level out the trauma; we naturally calm ourselves down. This requires serotonin, no different than if you're almost in a car accident and your body freezes up and responds with anxiety, serotonin kicks in and your body begins to regulate. With long-term sexual abuse at a young age, my body has responded for a long time. The emotions have been tough on my brain, and the chemicals have been working overtime, he explained. The abuse was winning at this point, so the anti-depressant will do nothing more than give my brain more serotonin to help deal with the anxiety. This will help me respond better to the EMDR in therapy and accelerate my recovery. Ding! You had me at "recovery," Doc. I'm in. Zoloft it was.

We continued talking. He said that I should only take half of the recommended dose for the first week, and then take the full dose. It was best to let the drug slowly enter the body rather than hit it all at once. He talked about how seventy percent of anti-depressants will work well for me, but the other thirty percent would not respond very well with my body, and that this is normal. He thought Zoloft would be a good starting point and hopefully it would work. He mentioned that I shouldn't feel anything different for about two or three weeks, but soon after I should start to feel myself leveling off, and feeling a little more "normal." Hah. Normal. I almost don't know what that means. We were going to keep me on the drug for about six months, well into therapy, and at some point we would wean me off. If I started to ease back into my anxiety, I would need to go back to the drug until the timing was just right.

Ideally, he said, I should be able to quit the drug at some point, but he said everybody is different, so he didn't want to set a time limit. Some people simply need to take the drug for the rest of their life, and that if that occurs, it's ok. There should be no negative effect on my body, regardless of how long I am on an anti-depressant.

I had some blood drawn for the typical blood work and that was about it. We shook hands and he asked that I come back in about a month to follow up. Overall, I felt good about the visit. No petroleum jelly, I don't need surgery on the long-term hernia, good blood pressure, and I grew an inch. I hit up CVS for the prescription. I felt weird knowing that the pharmacist knew I was receiving an anti-depressant. She didn't act strange; I guess it was common. So, I just got home and took my first Vitamin Z. Before taking the pill, I re-read my list of eleven reasons for recovery. One tiny blue pill a day is a no-brainer.

Dare To Dream: April 13, 2010

I've never been a big dreamer. When I was a young kid, I remember having exciting, adventurous dreams. I'd have nightmares from time to time, but mostly I had the kind of dreams that made me want to go back to sleep so I could will my way back into my dream after being so rudely awakened, which never worked. For some reason, as I got older, my dreams sort of vanished. I've heard that this happens to a lot of people as they age, so I figured it was normal, but I missed dreaming. About three or four years ago, my dreams reappeared. Although, instead of diving back into dreams about relationships, bravery, or world-domination, I was having dreams about snakes. Like, three or four per week. Snakes in my hair. Snakes in the lake.

Snakes in trees. Snakes in my Cheerios. You get the picture. This went on for years, so much so that my wife started researching what these dreams meant. There are plenty of theories, but I can't say I bought in to any of them.

These dreams continued into 2009 as I started to have all of the problems addressing my past. Then I had a dream that I will never forget. It was the only dream that I have ever had about my perpetrator, Jack. In my dream, I was with the same two government agents who interrogated me my freshman year of high school. I was helping them find Jack. Sure enough, I broke the case wide open and made a valiant arrest. I walked Jack into the police station in handcuffs. I was a hero. I felt such a sense of accomplishment that I had finally apprehended this man after he molested people close to him for over three decades. I felt vindicated.

When we entered the police station, I took a few moments to unleash a torrent of expletives. I told him everything I felt, freeing myself from his abuse. He never said a thing. He just stood there staring at me through his black-rimmed glasses, in his light blue v-neck sweater, with his typical smirk. I finally calmed down and the two agents told me that if I was done, they would take him into the other room and book him. I relented. It was ok, it was over. The three walked into the other room. I could see them through the glass as they sat him down. Jack turned back to his left, looked at me, and smiled a wide smile. Then, the two agents looked my way, looked back at him, and started laughing. All three of them were laughing like college buddies, as he told stories about me. I just stood there, defeated. My hollow feeling immediately returned. I was alone again.

When I awoke he was all around me. I could smell his shitty musk aftershave as though he were a foot away from me. I could feel his presence. I can easily say that this was the most disturbing feeling I have ever had. I immediately got up out of bed, went downstairs and checked around the house. I still wasn't fully convinced that this was just a dream. After a few minutes of panic, my mind slowly accepted that everything was alright, and I went back upstairs and laid down.

What I have learned since is that when I woke up from my dream, what occurred was called an olfactory flashback. It's basically a vivid smell or taste from your past that suddenly rushes into the present as if it were happening again. Anyway, that night started about a month and a half of sleepless nights. Each night I went to bed begging for the sun to rise. I was so afraid to fall asleep and start dreaming, that as soon as I fell asleep, I would shake myself out of it to continue blinking safely toward the ceiling. It was a conscious nightmare.

Slowly, as I talked more about the abuse and starting facing my past, I started getting back to a better sleep pattern. I haven't completely returned, but I'm sleeping better than I had been. I also haven't dreamed about snakes ever since I had that dream about Jack. Were the snake dreams a precursor to this one dream? Was my subconscious telling me that there was something I needed to face? Was he the snake? Was this biblical in nature?

Just as a mother suddenly gains super-strength to lift a car off of her child, our minds can control our senses and plop us right back into a terrifying moment. What that tells me is that our minds must also have the ability to confront and overcome a horrifying past. Nothing will erase the past, but, hard work, support, and maybe some medication can balance it. Right now, my focus is to do everything possible to deal with what happened to me and get myself into a place where I can dare to dream again.

Z-Day Plus 2: April 14, 2010

It's been two days since my body was first invaded by Zoloft. When I took my first pill on Monday, it didn't take long, maybe thirty minutes, before my body started to react. I could actually feel a strange sluggishness in my head, sort of like when Nyquil first introduces itself. The fog only lasted about ten minutes, and then I developed a dull stomachache and I could feel my heart rate start to pick up.

About two hours later I was starting to get worried. I was becoming increasingly agitated and my heart was racing. My wife got home and we read through the pamphlet that came with the prescription. It said that some dizziness, nausea, and drowsiness, and trouble sleeping can occur as a side effect, so we didn't call anyone, but I was still unsettled. I didn't sleep well that night.

On Tuesday night, I was feeling a little better so I figured I'd play mad scientist and see what a glass of wine did to my body. Why not, right? Good call, Chris, way to think it through. A glass and a half later, I was a college freshman at my first frat party. Noticing what was going on, I put down the sled that I was getting ready to ride down my stairs, and put the cork on the wine. Noted. Dial back the wine, Turbo.

My head this morning allowed me to slowly extrapolate that three glasses of wine without Zoloft equaled one glass of wine with Zoloft. A cheap date, but also a lesson learned.

Today, after my morning grogginess wore off, my afternoon straightened out and for now, all I have is the

Tasmanian Devil heartbeat and a slightly foggy head. Party-boy will need to take a backseat for a while. It'll probably be good for me. Anyone need a sled?

Therapy Session 5: April 15, 2010

Just when I thought I was getting the hang of this whole therapy thing, I had my first ever panic attack today. All morning I was deep in my own head, which is never a good thing. I think I was wondering what we would be talking about in therapy, so I subconsciously started thinking about the different situations when I was abused. Throughout my life, I've trained myself not to think about it for more than a few seconds, but today was different I guess. This time I drifted back into the body of that young kid. I found myself in the situations when I was abused, and for the first time, I felt what that young kid was feeling. I was deep in thought; I don't remember hearing a word of what was said on the radio.

It was around 10:30 a.m. and I was on my final leg of my delivery route. My heartbeat had been racing all morning, nothing had really changed there. I was thinking about a certain incident at Jack's house. All of the sudden, I felt my rate of breathing increase. I had to take deeper and deeper breaths, although with each successive breath, I was getting less air. I started to get worried. It got worse. Eventually, I was barely getting any air and I could feel myself getting lightheaded. I started to panic. I swerved my van to the shoulder and slowed down. Luckily, I was aware of what was going on. Even though I'd never had a panic attack, I knew that's what was happening and I knew that I risked passing out. I immediately went back to my breathing techniques that my therapist taught me. Four square breathing. Draw a square with your breaths, Chris. Inhale for two sides. Exhale for two sides, complete the square. Increase the size of the square and I took longer breaths. Ok. I've leveled off, it's getting better. Within thirty seconds or so, I was under control. My heart was flying, I was a little light-headed, but I had enough oxygen and I had controlled my breathing. Shaken, I pulled back onto the road and continued on with my route.

The only thing that I can compare the panic attack to was a time when a friend of mine trapped me in my sleeping bag when I was six years old. I dove in head-first in an attempt to do a flip turn at the bottom of a bag and return out the top, but he stood on the opening and just laughed. He thought it would be funny, but I completely lost control and panicked. His mom was less than impressed with the total meltdown that occurred at that point, but I'll never forget the feeling.

I was a few minutes early for my session, around 2:57. The only one in the waiting room, I sat down and flipped through the same stack of magazines. I saw my therapist through the receptionist's window and she waved. Good, there should be no problem starting on time. At 3:09, she opened the door and invited me in. I can't win. Starting on time has got to be impossible.

We entered her room and I found my chair. We started going through my checklist of symptoms for the week. Was I irritable? Check. Anxious? Check. Panicked? Uh...Check. I told her about the panic attack. She immediately said that since I had just started Zoloft, that I was more prone to panic attacks. That would have been nice to know. She also said that my elevated heartbeat was very normal and that it would slow down once my body regulated the serotonin. She asked about the dosage, and I mentioned I was only taking half-doses, 25 mg, for the first week. She said not to deviate from that. Don't worry, after the spaz out on the side of the road, I had no temptations to increase my dosage.

The next thing she did was share with me a list of goals that she put together for therapy. This took her four sessions of collecting and compiling data, so it was a good, thorough set of goals. She, also, went all Spinal Tap and listed eleven:

1. Learn to get my SUDS score down to zero.
2. Report that I am less irritable with my wife.
3. Give myself at least one compliment every day.
4. Desensitize the abuse memories.
5. Reprocess negative beliefs.
6. Work through the anger towards my parents.
7. Give myself permission to be fully happy.
8. Work on understanding assertive, non-assertive, and aggressive speech.
9. Report appreciation of physique, body image.
10. Correct my "irrational ideas"
11. Report a return to my sex life.

We talked about each of these goals and both agreed that the list was accurate and complete. The only thing that I asked about was in finding closure with my abuser. She said while some people believe that this is worth spending time on, she doesn't believe, nor is there any research to support, that confronting the abuser is necessary or even helpful. This was good news to hear, considering my abuser is nice and dead.

We spent the next twenty minutes working on finding another relaxation technique. My homework was focused on practicing relaxation every day and charting my SUDS progress—the most relaxed I can get is a two. She said that before we begin EMDR, she needs me to be able to relax to a zero. Shit. That's like asking a dog to stop wagging its tail. We listened to a new tape, and I think I improved. By the end, I was a SUDS score of one. I probably could have been a zero if my heart wasn't beating like a hummingbird.

We finished the session at around 3:53. Forty five minutes is apparently an hour this year. We said goodbye and I felt relaxed as I walked out to my car. Believe it or not, I was starting to feel much more comfortable around her. Even though she bothers me with her complete and total disregard for time, I respect her knowledge and her approach to my treatment, at least for now. I started thinking about how far I've come in such a short period of time. I think it's only been a month since I first started therapy. I really haven't changed much, but the foundation is there, and that's the most important thing. Now I just need to learn how to stay outside the sleeping bag.

A Second Skin: April 19, 2010

Like everyone else, when I was a kid I loved watching cartoons on Saturday mornings. While I'm sure there are great cartoons on television these days, there was something really special about the old cartoons. Foghorn Leghorn. Bugs Bunny. Tom & Jerry. Road Runner. They all stuck to a very basic formula. One guy (Chaser) was trying to catch another guy (Chasee), who was always faster and smarter. So often, the Chaser would get close to catching the Chasee, only to be out-witted at the last minute, usually ending in a violent thump or explosion. The great thing about these cartoons is that in the next frame, after being crushed by a lead weight or a boulder, everything was okay and the Chaser was fine. All welts and stitches were gone. Even after a bomb exploded in the Chaser's face and covered him in burns, he simply unzipped his skin, and stepped out of it, to continue the chase with a comfortable new skin. For some reason, the formula worked over and over. I was mesmerized repeatedly, which may say something about me, but that's not my point.

My point is that life is no cartoon. One thing that I have said consistently in my life is that I'm not very comfortable in my own skin. I've had this feeling for as long as I can remember, without knowing why. It's not like I can't enjoy myself, or socialize and be fun. I can. But, there has always been an underlying discomfort. A feeling of not wanting to be going through life as myself. It's disturbing. As I've started to go through this process of recovery, this feeling, believe it or not, has intensified.

In my fourth therapy session, my therapist asked me how I was feeling. She asked about suicidal thoughts. We've talked about suicide several times, and whether or not my mind goes there. I mentioned that I didn't have any, but that I did have a feeling that was disturbing me. I told her how I didn't want to be in my own skin. To my surprise, she quickly leaned forward in her chair, her eyes lit up, and she focused on that sentence. She said how common that statement was for those with PTSD. Social situations elevate the feelings, and they continue until the PTSD is treated. I felt a wave of relief. The years and years of thinking that I was this odd, uncomfortable person began to make more sense. Is it not me? Am I not a freak?

Since that therapy session, I have started to feel more hope. What if the discomfort can go away? What if I have the energy to truly enjoy social situations? I've started to think about how great it will be to feel whole, confident, and comfortable one day. My life will have many frames.

After having a bomb blow up in my face at a young age, I actually might be able to unzip my skin, and get back to the chase.

Crash: April 20, 2010

"It's the sense of touch.   In any real city, you walk, you know?   You brush past people, people bump into you.   In L.A., nobody touches you.   We're always behind this metal and glass.   I think we miss that touch so much, that we crash into each other, just so we can feel something."
-"Crash," Lions Gate Entertainment, 2004

This opening line to the movie "Crash" has always made a lot of sense to me. I remember the days when I felt more. I would feel genuine excitement, and likewise, I would feel down and upset if certain things didn't go my way. As I got older, I noticed that my feelings became muted. Highs weren't as high. Lows weren't as low. I was sort of in this middle ground, cruising through life, mostly unfazed. People around me would get really excited about things we would do, and I would go along with them, smiling, but not feeling the same joy. When disappointment hit, I wasn't that devastated. I was fine, while others were slammed. People always commented on my composure. I saw it as a strength of mine, to always feel in control and stable.

What I have learned since is that this is not normal. While everyone grows up and learns to control their emotions, they still *feel* them. What I conditioned myself to do was to not feel the emotions, which is far different. This coping mechanism is very common for sexual abuse survivors. When trauma occurs at a very young age, and it's not managed, you force yourself to forget about the trauma as you get older and your body compensates. You attempt to wipe it from your emotion bank so that you can get on with a productive life without these negative feelings disrupting your daily routine. Unfortunately, what happens is that you wipe away an ability to feel a very large range of emotions. While lows don't feel as low, highs don't feel as high. This is a much less interesting way to go through life. It's only a matter of time before the real emotions surface and you begin to crash into things just so you can feel something.

This was very much my way of dealing with this muted existence. Since mind-altering drugs weren't in my vocabulary, I opted to push myself to the limit physically. Bungee jumping, cliff diving, Ironman Triathlon, adventure racing, marathon, scuba diving, tree skiing, wakeboarding. Whatever I could do to feel exhilaration, that's what I did. At night, I'd party as hard as I could. I'd try to be the last one standing. I'd drink at a party until I puked and wake up in the morning and go for a twenty-mile run. I pushed myself to my limits as a way of trying to get my sine wave up high enough so that I could feel something. When it came to negative feelings, I would shut them out. It gave me control. If a relationship wasn't going well, I'd run from it and quarantine my feelings completely. I'd concentrate on removing myself from anything negative, and most of the time it worked.

It wasn't until recently that I started to change. The more that I explored my abusive past, the more that I started to feel the full range of genuine emotion. In the past year, my range of emotions has been extreme as my memories surfaced and I started to face my feelings. It has been terrifying since genuine feelings of exhilaration, joy, and loss are foreign to me. I'm still learning what my normal range is, but this year has shown me little glimpses into several strangely familiar feelings. Some are frightening, some are terrific, but I'll take them all. No more hiding behind metal and glass and forcing a crash when I need to feel something. I have to take what life gives me by brushing and bumping into it like everyone else.

Therapy Session 6: April 22, 2010

Today, I woke up on time and went to take a shower. Before shaving, I spent a few minutes looking in the mirror, thinking about how I felt. I started to have the realization that the Zoloft was working. While I don't know if I'm feeling more "normal," I can tell that I am leveling off. I'm no longer racing down a steep hill on a skateboard, wobbling, waiting for a crash. I feel more like I'm cruising on a mountain bike, a few bugs in my teeth, but under control. Overall, I can tell my fuse is longer and my raw anger has faded slightly, which is nice. I shut the mirror, almost admiring who I was looking at. Almost.

As I got into my van for my first delivery this morning, I thought about how great I will feel if my improvement continues on this trajectory. Trying to manage my excitement, I couldn't help but admire how my last several days had been a steady improvement.

I had a simple delivery route. A quick out-and-back. On my drive back my mind started doing its thing again; I must have been thinking about my session in the afternoon. Sure enough, I started thinking about Jack. I remembered that my Mom recently told me that when they confronted him after learning about our other family member who was abused by him, he admitted to the abuse. He gave the excuse that he had been abused by his grandfather, decades prior, and therefore didn't know any better. I started thinking about that and felt really bad for him. How difficult that must have been at a time when there was no therapy or self-help books. Suddenly, I caught myself. How could I think like that? This is the man that fucking molested me for seven years, taking my innocence away from me, making me doubt and hate myself for the last twenty years. What is wrong with me? Why am I not more angry at him? I felt immediate shame and embarrassment for not hating him more. Before continuing down this road of self-hate, I forced myself to think about something completely different. NFL Draft on talk radio. Perfect. My day rolled along without interruption.

I arrived at my therapist's office a few minutes after 3 p.m. I was determined not to arrive early only to sit there thinking for fifteen minutes, so I was a little late on purpose. I thumbed through "Golf Digest." More Tiger Woods talk. Great, he's everybody's hero again. At around 3:08, my therapist opened the door and asked me to fill out a few forms in the waiting room before I entered. She wanted to see what sorts of things I had been feeling the week before. I was self-reliant this time, filling out paperwork without her help—a big boy. Anxiety. Check. Aversion to social situations. Check. Overall, I was feeling better, and I noticed that I checked fewer things this time. Cool.

I entered her office and we immediately went through my paperwork and discussed my week. She was really glad to hear about my decrease in anger and irritability. She was also relieved to know that I felt as though the Zoloft was working. We talked about a few small things, and she gave me a new relaxation tape. This was one that I could use any time, which was more focused on getting in touch with my inner-child. Yeah, that kid flicked me off a long time ago, but I'll see how it goes.

Then she gave me a choice as to what we did next. We could either begin the actual EMDR treatment, which she knew I was eager to start, or we could spend the session working on my assertiveness (number eight on our goal sheet). I asked what she thought. She suggested we work on the assertiveness because our next session wouldn't be for two weeks, and she preferred to start the EMDR when we would have a session the following week. I told her I'd prefer to get the EMDR started, but that I trusted her opinion. How assertive of me.

We started by role-playing situations where assertiveness, non-assertiveness, and aggression are used. I needed to identify which situation was an example of each. To recap, assertiveness is saying what you want in a way that respects you and the person you're speaking with. Non-assertiveness is speaking in a way that disrespects what you want and only respects what the other person wants. Aggressiveness respects what you want, but not what the other person wants. She said that at work and with my family, I am non-assertive. She also said that she bets my entire family, except for my dad, is non-assertive. She said we are all marionettes and he's the puppet master, and that's often how it works in families with personalities like ours. Hmm. Not sure. I started not enjoying the conversation.

We continued role-playing and she stopped and said that mentally, I completely get the difference. The problem was that when placed in the actual situations, I still wasn't being assertive. She reassured me that it was okay, that this was very common for someone who has been through what I have been through. Uh. Okay. Thanks for pointing that out. I was very uncomfortable and a little annoyed.

Before I knew it, our session was up and she said that our next session would be the uncomfortable stuff. The stuff dealing with the abuse, the beginning of EMDR. Great, this session was no trip to Busch Gardens. Way to pump me up for the two-week layoff.

I walked into the waiting room and went straight to the receptionist's desk to pay my co-pay. My therapist had walked behind the receptionist's desk and was handling some paperwork while I paid. I asked for a receipt from the receptionist and immediately my therapist snapped her head up and said that they won't write receipts for checks. This was the first time I wasn't paying with cash. Uh…oh. Ok, I said. She tilted her head and gave me a look. Crap. I mean…uh…it's important for me to have a receipt, please. She smiled, but still seemed annoyed. Bitch.

So, I realize I have a lot to work on, and none of it is comfortable. I guess if it were comfortable, I wouldn't be improving and I know that. For the next two weeks I'll be focusing on my homework. Relaxation tapes. Assertiveness practice. Complimenting myself daily. I just wish this were less painful. I'm afraid the mirror I'm using is a little too clear right now. I was hoping after not using it for so long, there would be a nice layer of dust on it, preventing me from seeing every single pimple. I guess that's not how it works. My mirror shows a scared shitless teenager with a raging case of acne. Maybe I'm picking things back up as that freshman in high school.

Recovery Reprieve: April 24, 2010

I am the type of person to go full speed when I want to accomplish something. Therapy and recovery is no exception. In an effort to take a deep breath from the recovery process and celebrate a challenging but wonderful first year of marriage with my incredible wife, we have opted for five days of sun and sand. This time tomorrow we'll be in a cabana, admiring a Caribbean sunset—SUDS level zero. I am a lucky man.

Therapy Session 7: May 4, 2010

Yesterday was my seventh therapy session. Well, that is, it was the seventh time that I have been to see my therapist. What I'm realizing now is that yesterday was the beginning of my treatment and the previous six sessions were simply there to get me through yesterday in one piece. My recent vacation with my wife was a great way to recharge my batteries and find some more strength. Thinking back, how foolish I was to go on vacation thinking that I had successfully navigated six weeks of solid therapy. I hadn't. I had simply laid the groundwork for what would be my first significant encounter with my past.

In the back of my mind, I knew what Tuesday would bring, which is probably why I only slept an hour or two on both Sunday and Monday nights. Since my therapist was going on a business trip for our usual Thursday session, we moved this week's session to Tuesday. And, since it would mark the beginning of my Eye Movement Desensitization and Reprocessing (EMDR) treatment, my therapist wanted to schedule me for the last appointment of her day, a 5 p.m. ninety-minute power session.

Despite the lack of sleep, I felt pretty good yesterday during the day. I worked until about three, and then went to the gym and had a good workout before heading to her office for our predictably punctual 5:14 p.m. appointment. I entered her office, targeted my chair, and sat down. We chit-chatted about my vacation and then went through my current list of symptoms. My social aversion was still there. A little bit agitated, but not too bad. Some trouble sleeping. Self-esteem still in the tank. But, she noticed I seemed pretty relaxed as I sat there in my flip flops, pretending I was still sipping gin and sodas in Playa del Carmen. She was glad that my heart rate had calmed down and my body had accepted the Zoloft. Overall, she felt like we were ready to begin the EMDR. As soon as she mentioned EMDR, I felt myself straighten up in my chair, my pulse quickened.

The first thing to do was to get me completely relaxed, as close to SUDS level zero as possible. I leaned back in my chair. Instead of listening to a relaxation tape on her stereo, she decided to talk me through the relaxation. She asked if it was ok if she touched my head. Uh…ok. She said as soon as she touched my head I'd feel a wave of relaxation move from my head down towards my feet. After about five minutes, she relaxed me enough to about a SUDS one or two, which she felt was enough to begin.

As I laid there, she got up from her chair, and went into the closet at the far end of the room. She banged around and knocked over a few things before reappearing with a tripod, similar to one you would use for a video camera. Instead of a camera, she held a two-foot wide, by two-inch tall, black piece of electronic equipment. She set the tripod directly in front of me, and after adjusting the handle, she faced the wide, thin, rectangular shape directly toward me. On the face of the equipment were about twenty tiny light bulbs, equally spaced horizontally. She plugged the apparatus into the wall socket, and a few of the lights illuminated red. There was a remote control that she carried with her as she sat down next to me. She tested the remote, which illuminated the lights. The lights flashed one at a time, from right to left, and back again, so that it looked like a red ball that went back and forth along the two-foot apparatus. It took about one second for the ball to go from one side to the other and back again. She said that I would be following the red light with my eyes, keeping my head motionless.

Feeling a little uncomfortable with all of this technology in front of me with no understanding of the theory, I asked her for a tutorial, and she realized it was important to explain. For years, psychologists had been using relaxation as a way of calming a patient's anxiety of traumatic memories. Basically, recalling a bad memory over and over at a relaxed state would aid in desensitizing those memories, associating the memory with a more relaxed state of being. About twenty years ago, one psychologist found out that the body can do this much more effectively if there is an external stimulus involved. They found that while reprocessing memories at a relaxed state, if you alternately stimulate both hemispheres of your brain, your brain for some reason can reprocess and re-associate painful memories incredibly well. I would start by closing my eyes, visualizing a memory, then opening my eyes, and watching the red dot go from side to side for about ten seconds. Then, I would close my eyes and work on a memory. She couldn't explain all of the science but she convinced me that it worked, and that's all I really cared about.

Not only would we be using this device, but we would be itemizing and safely securing my painful memories with the help of some mind games. Using my imagination, I would be placing my memories, one by one, into an imaginary container. She said for me to imagine something ceramic, like a jug, with a corked top. She was going to mention one of my traumatic memories, and I was going to think about that memory. I would open my eyes, watch the red light, and then close my eyes again. Taking a deep breath, I would then mentally place the memory into the container, and secure the cork. At this point, not only was I confused, but I was seriously wondering what she had smoked at lunch. Reminding myself to be patient, I complied and focused on the jug. In order to keep the memories from disturbing me after our session, she said that her office would be the only place where we could uncork the container. After placing the memory in the container I would need to repeat the words: "This will only be removed in here, and only if it aids in my recovery." Okay, Cheech, whatever you say. I closed my eyes, took some deep breaths to make sure that I was as relaxed as possible, and our treatment began.

The next forty-five minutes were awful. We went from sickening memory to sickening memory. She must have made a list of all of the instances I mentioned when Jack abused me, because she covered a lot of what happened, one by one. My tension slowly increased as we continued. My chest tightened. My muscles contracted. I found that my eyes had welled up more and more each time I opened them to follow the little red lights. Eventually, we got to a point where she ran out of memories for us to manage. She asked if I had others, and I did. I kept going, with a few of the other times Jack molested me—ones that I either hadn't thought much about, or hadn't come to mind when we talked or when I filled out paperwork. We continued until I couldn't think of anything more.

She asked me to open my eyes. She asked me how I felt. I was catatonic. I had tears rolling down my cheeks. I was shaking uncontrollably. I was a mental wreck. She asked me again. I still couldn't talk. My body shuddered as I cried uncontrollably. A few minutes went by and she asked me what my tears would be saying if they could talk. It was bad enough crying like a child in front of my therapist, but now I was being asked to talk like a fruitcake. I hated those kinds of questions. But, I answered anyway. I said that my tears were feeling so much shame. Uncontrollable shame. This seemed like it surprised her. I don't think she was aware of how I felt about the abuse, and really, I guess I hadn't realized how much I was still shouldering the blame. She continued on this line of thinking and tried her best to get my mind thinking clearly. I was obviously beyond reach, and she knew that at this point. She did her best to lighten the mood and we talked less intensely about a few other tertiary topics to move forward. She said we'd need to really focus on this in the future. We'd need to focus on my forgiving myself, which I clearly haven't done. Not fully.

Six thirty rolled around and we wrapped up. I was stripped of everything as I walked toward the door to her office. While it was a lonely feeling, for the first time I really felt her compassion and her understanding. I think I saw an empathetic, less rigid and robotic side to her. I guess I showed her a different side as well; it works both ways.

Since I left her office, I have been wading through an incredible low. It's as low as I have felt in a few months and it reminds me of the feeling I used to have the day after accidentally talking about the abuse. I don't feel optimistic. I don't feel proud. I don't feel happy. In my mind I know that this will pass, but I'm not feeling it yet. This feeling prevented me from writing yesterday, and it took everything I had today to write this. My wife and I took the vacation to get away and it worked. I was able to find new strength. What I didn't realize was how quickly I'd use it.

The Hyper-Stressed Chicken Breast: May 6, 2010

As I cruised down the interstate from Goochland to Powhatan on my route today, I clenched my jaw as tightly as my hands squeezed the steering wheel. My level of stress had definitely elevated since Tuesday. I just wasn't myself and was deep in thought as I drove. Without warning, an eighteen-wheeler barreled past me on my right. The airflow from the rig pushed my van to the left. As I snapped out of my daze, I glared at the driver. Unfazed, he continued on, my eyes moving to his payload. He was hauling what must have been five thousand chickens, neatly arranged in hundreds of coops. A few feathers flared from the sides. I caught the bulging, bloodshot eye of one of the chickens. He didn't look happy to be moving eighty miles per hour faster than his average. Man, was he stressed out, which made me start to feel fortunate.

Then I started thinking about the NPR interview that I heard a few weeks ago about high-stressed chickens. Apparently, if chickens are transported at speeds greater than sixty miles per hour, it affects their proteins somehow and the meat is tainted; the chickens are considered "hyper-stressed." The stressed chickens are then relegated to breeding, not to be used for consumption, and apparently the government is going to start holding farmers to this standard due to the alarming increase in anxiety-related disorders being reported in North America. I haven't seen the new mandated "stress-free" chicken labels on breasts at the grocery store, but I guess it's coming soon.

Of course, I made all of that up, but I enjoyed the thought as I drove, and I wondered if we'll soon watch a Dateline about something this ridiculous. Thinking further, how easy would it be to start a rumor about something like that? I bet it would spread like wildfire (well, maybe if some of the details were fine-tuned). Our reaction as parents and family members is to immediately worry about our loved ones and protect them from harm—it's natural and it's justified, given all of the frightening additives and quality issues relating to what we consume. And our fear is substantiated it seems with the rising cases of autism, Alzheimer's, depression, attention disorders, just to name a few.

My point, however indirect, is related to sexual abuse. If I can start a witch hunt for lead-footed chicken drivers, why can't we get people to talk openly about sexual abuse? Why does it get swept into the corner over and over, decade after decade? The epidemic is as clear as day, with disastrous effects, but as a society, we would rather spend our time fighting for something that doesn't make us uncomfortable. The damn chicken drivers and their need for speed. How dare they stress out those chickens and then feed them to our children? But, if a parent gets an uneasy feeling about someone who has been in contact with their child, they are probably less likely to raise hell. How do we talk about it without causing a stir? What if I'm wrong? What might be said about me? I'll just remove my child from that Cub Scout troop. But, once the child is removed, what about the other fifteen children whose parents aren't as aware? What happens to them?

I wonder if the answer lies in something deeper than the obvious discomfort for the topic of sexual abuse. I think we are trained by our society to push away the issue, and I don't think it's a conscious choice. I think it's an irrational human behavior that we learn very early in life. Instead of stopping to talk to as many people as possible about the topic and our fear, potentially saving countless children from abuse, we are more often removing ourselves or our loved ones from the danger, and moving on quietly and comfortably.

It reminds me of a marketing phenomenon related to irrational consumer behavior and the price of gas. Back in 2008 when hurricane Ike was rolling towards Texas, there was a lot of talk about the vulnerability of the oil refineries. The media covered it extensively as 110 mph winds roared towards Galveston. As the hurricane made landfall, the Governor of Texas made an announcement that the refineries were in good shape, that we had all dodged a bullet. But, consumers were still excited. And even though they had heard that everything was okay, they still topped off their tanks. The emotional commodity flowed at record rates from Texas to the East. Gas prices skyrocketed. But why? There was no reason to fill the tanks. If we all acted rationally, we'd be saving seventeen cents per gallon.

I think the way our society handles sexual abuse is no different. We are irrational in how we put a lid on the subject. No rational person would argue that sexual abuse is not a problem, but our actions don't support our rational thoughts. Something needs to change. Somehow we need to get everyone thinking about sexual abuse like they would a chicken with an elevated pulse. We need labels on all of the packaging. We need dishonest farmers locked up for good. A slow and steady increase in the awareness of this issue is occurring, but we can't be comfortable with that, not with so many drivers repeatedly breaking the speed limit.

Therapy Session 8: May 10, 2010

I stood at the top of the slope, mittens correctly looped through the pole straps, boots tight, goggles down—

fearless. I had just completed my first ski class, and my teacher said I had been one of the best little skiers in the class. I had spent my morning dominating the smallest slope on the mountain, but that nugget of information didn't matter as I stared down the intermediate slope determined to show my parents that their son was a skiing prodigy. In fact, at five years old, maybe I was the best skier on the mountain. Not sure, but it felt about right. My dad mentioned some crap about turning using the snow plow technique that I had been taught. Nah. I was moving on with my career. I had just graduated from ski class 1-A, obviously the top class, so I was heading straight for the bottom, turns were for beginners.

The next two minutes were possibly the most frightening and embarrassing two minutes a five-year-old could experience on the slopes. It's amazing how many people a fifty-pound projectile can take down with him when he doesn't turn. What's more amazing, is how many people will gather and laugh as the fifty-pound projectile throws a temper tantrum blaming the ski gear yard sale on faulty equipment.

I don't know how much of my personality is a byproduct of the sexual abuse, but one thing I am certain of is that my stubborn, overly-self-sufficient side was with me at birth. Today, when my therapist asked me how well my relaxation training went between last week's session and now, all I could say was, "I don't like being told what to do sometimes." She looked at me like I was a five-year-old projectile. I didn't really have an excuse. I felt ridiculous. But, nevertheless, for six days, I had been so unhappy with myself, I decided to boycott therapy or any sort of progress. I didn't do a single thing. I needed a break. I think she understood, but she didn't make it easy for me as she told me to look at her in the eyes and listen like a big boy.

"Stop avoiding your treatment," she said. Because I hadn't worked on any more relaxation, we would not be able to do another session of EMDR. Okay. Roger that. I realized I dropped the ball.

The session started at this high point and continued to soar. She asked how I was feeling, as she looked over my status worksheet. Really, nothing had changed. All social avoidance, anxiety, frustration, stress, sleep trouble, were still where it had been two weeks earlier. She handled this realization like anyone would who felt like someone was wasting their time—she just looked at me and didn't say a word. I had wasted both of our time. She made a note that I should ask my physician this week about increasing the Zoloft dosage. She said someone my size is usually taking 100mg, versus the 50mg dose I had been taking for the last month.

In order to get something positive happening, she decided to focus on where we left off last session. She was worried about how much shame I had about the abuse. At the end of the last EMDR treatment (the first EMDR session), I explained my shame as I melted down in front of her. So, instead of working on more EMDR for this session, she wanted to talk about just one incident to get a feel for what that little boy was feeling while abuse was occurring. She wanted to talk about the first time I was abused. Even though I said I had very few memories about the first time, she still wanted to use that as an example.

She asked me to recall the situation. I explained that it was in his car. We were staying at his and my grandmother's house for my aunt's wedding weekend, and he convinced my family that I should go driving with him. Jack said he wanted to teach me to drive on their property, a five-acre lot with a long, tree-lined driveway. I remember being really excited. We got in the car and he sat me on his lap. This is where it gets fuzzy. I know some sexual things happened but I was so confused I didn't understand what was going on. When we returned to the house, all I know is that I was terrified and ashamed. This is what my therapist wanted to talk about. She wanted me to explain what that kid was thinking at the time. I said that the kid felt ashamed. He felt guilty of something. He felt trapped. As I told her, I could feel myself getting uncomfortable and emotional. I was sitting up straight in my chair; my eyes were filling with tears. She said for me to now tell her what I am feeling about what happened then. I said that I felt ashamed. I was responsible. Even though my head knows that I was not responsible and shouldn't feel ashamed, that's what I felt. She asked if I felt anger. I said no. I said that I did, however, feel gypped. That kid shouldn't have gone through that. That kid was innocent. She said that my feeling was that of resentment, and that was good. It was very close to anger, which is where she wants to get me. By now, I was like a cat just after having its tail stepped on. I was so spun up that I didn't realize that my tears were flowing, my hands were clenching the chair, and my head was almost receding into my neck in recoil. She looked at me and had the nerve to ask if I was upset. I looked at her like she had looked at me when we started the session. Uh, yeah, was the snot on my lap the tipoff?

Her method was clear to me. She wanted to see me go back to that instance and explain everything I was feeling from the perspective of the little boy. Then she wanted to see how I was feeling now, looking back, and compare the two. I clearly haven't forgiven myself, holding myself entirely responsible. We have lots of work to do. She asked what my SUDS level was, I said and eight or nine—very stressed out. She said that it was important for us to bring me down to zero before I leave. It's important to always get your body down to a relaxed state after holding your body in that elevated stressful place thinking about the abuse. Doing this was the "Reprocessing" part of Eye Movement Desensitization and Reprocessing treatment, even though we didn't officially use the black box with the lights, we were trying to associate a more relaxed state of being with the traumatic memories.

She put on a relaxation tape and within about ten minutes, I was Jell-O, amazed at how quickly I was able to relax myself to near zero SUDS. This was a good sign, but I knew I still needed to practice. She said we were out of time, and that next time, we would be going through another EMDR session as long as I had done my relaxation homework every day. Oh, sweet, you're going to reward my hard work with an EMDR session? What, no promise of a fork in the eyeball to keep me even more motivated?

What I realized today is that I'm still the five-year-old on the intermediate slope. While it's good to have a strong opinion and a determination to go things alone, it's also important to let go of some of the things you don't know much about; leaving those important decisions to someone who does. Once you let go, listen to that voice of reason. Follow their instructions. It doesn't mean you're less independent, it just means you're intelligent enough to pick your battles. So, I've made a deal with myself to do my relaxation tapes every day until my next session. I'll do what's right to prevent the ski gear yard sale at the bottom of the hill.

Feeling Pretty Awfome: May 13, 2010

I am a beautiful woman. No, I'm not having a sexual identity crisis, but seriously, I'm hot. Like most graduating seniors, the end of my high school existence was capped off with an all-night graduation party. An all-night graduation party is when the parents tricked graduating seniors into abstaining from drinking for one night just before allowing them to head to the beach for a week of saturated debauchery. Luckily for my graduating class, we had a great group of parents who organized a really fun night of events. The final, and most anticipated event, was the womanless beauty pageant. Half of the football team donned makeup, heels, and skirts to see who could win over the crowd and take home the crown (and a fifty dollar bill to be exchanged for booze at the beach). Long story short, yours truly earned the crown by dazzling the audience with sass, seductiveness, and a huge sequin-covered rack. For me, it all came down to playing the part. I was able to leave my body for a while and step into another role. Finally, some relief (apart from the uncomfortable shoes). Different from putting on a smiling face to fool those around me while being abused by a monster, this bit of acting I enjoyed.

It was well before the womanless beauty pageant when I first learned how to fool people, but more importantly, it was somewhere between ninth and tenth grade when I learned how to fool myself. I went from hiding the fact that I was unhappy about the abuse, to literally believing that everything was fine. I could be an absolute mess on the inside and when asked how I was doing, I would respond that everything was awesome. I would actually think that I was doing great—the perfect life—but really I was feeling awful about myself. This sort of acting isn't a simple thing to do, and it has taken me over twenty years to understand my craft.

Because of this ability to build a wall between my thoughts and feelings, my therapist has noticed that what I feel and how I think are completely out of sync. So, we're slowly connecting the dots. When she asks me how I feel about the abuse, my mind is completely rational and I can tell her that it was wrong and that it wasn't my fault. I can tell her that I know this. Then, thirty seconds later, I'm a slobbering mess telling her that I feel entirely responsible. It's as though my thoughts and my feelings are finally coming together on the stage, but neither is really sure who's playing the lead role.

For so many years my head was the lead. Don't worry about what you're feeling, Chris, just power through it and do the right thing, it'll be awesome. Well, all of that is changing. I'm listening to what I feel more and more every day, and I know it's going to get me to where I want to be—truly happy with myself. There are times, of course, when what my mind says about little things should not be ignored, like whether or not to listen to that friend who is asking me to join him in the derivatives market, but for the big things that have to do with me as a person, I'm putting more faith in how I really feel, and that is a good thing. My full-time acting career, while entertaining at times, will need to come to a close. Maybe I'll become more of a freelance actor, only when the time is right, and only when what I'm feeling is the lead. But not to worry; I most certainly will be wearing comfortable shoes.

I Am (Progression): May 16, 2010

I am a pounding heart inside the chest of a nervous presenter. I am waking up in a cell and getting dressed. I am working out when I don't want to. I am not biting on the tailing slider this time. I am an olive branch. I am the decision to cry uncontrollably. I am staying out here until I land this trick. I am walking into her office without hesitation and not wondering who sees me leave. I am telling them not to wait up. I am letting someone down to keep myself up. I am the steps after one step back. I am pushing harder even though nobody is around to notice. I am not pouring the third glass of wine. I am I Have A Dream. I am speaking when I cherish someone. I am conviction despite consequence. I am progression.

Therapy Session 9: May 20, 2010

This morning kicked off with frustration. Another night of intermittent sleep. It's not that I can't fall asleep, and it's not that I wake up and can't fall back to sleep, it's that I wake up for a brief minute, about once every hour—all night long. It's been going on for weeks. I dragged my way through an ordinary workday that ended a little bit early, so I summoned all of the energy I had and went to the gym before my session. The workout was a good way to wake up. I ran home, showered, and hit the road, feeling good about having done all of my relaxation homework as prescribed.

I entered the office, found the clipboard with my name on it, and filled out my patient status worksheet while I waited for my therapist to keep me waiting. I checked the same set of symptoms that I normally do, but this time I wrote "improving" next to anxiety and irritability. I can tell there is a difference there, which is a great feeling. As I waited, I stared down at the sheet of paper to avoid any eye contact with the middle-aged man across the room. It's almost like standing at a urinal. Keep the eyes down or forward, no side to side. Thanks. I started reading the list of symptoms on the sheet and a few caught my eye. Labile mood. Somnolence. Organcity. Tinnitus. Shit, was I supposed to know what those meant? All of the sudden I found myself searching for "Feelings of illiteracy."

Around 3:08, my therapist opened the door and gave me her smile. I said hello and walked back to her office. We went through the list of symptoms as usual and she was glad to know that some were improving. She asked if my sleep pattern had changed and I took her through my hourly wake-up problem. She sat for a while and then said that she thinks it's related to my REM cycle. Her thought was that subconsciously, I don't want to let myself dream, so my body is awakening as I hit that stage of the hourly cycle. Wow. That's deep, Doc. Really? She sensed the hesitation, and she followed with some explanation. At the end of it, she said she wanted me to start taking a sleep aid. I told her I didn't like to pop pills, but she asked me to try it. She called my doctor, and within five minutes, I had a prescription sent to my pharmacy. I told her I'd try it, but now I'm having second thoughts. The last thing I want is more drugs in my body so I may instead opt for the psychological scolding next session. Not sure.

At this point it was 3:30, so she asked if I'd like to do some EMDR with our remaining time. I basically cut her off with my affirmative. For some reason I feel like EMDR is what will make me feel right the fastest. It's the real meat in this psycho-sandwich. I was motivated. Let's dig in.

We focused on my first memory. Back inside the car with Jack, on their wide open property with the two-story house. I was seven. Having already set up the horizontal black box with the lights for the desensitization portion, she started by getting my SUDS score to about two. I imagined the ceramic jar with the pile of memories. I took out the first memory. She asked me to think about what happened. I slowly found myself sitting on his lap in the car. His hands on my legs. His musk. His polyester pants. Inappropriate touching. I looked at the lights for about a minute. My SUDS score started to rise, I could feel it. She asked me how I felt. I said confused and awkward, and she pressed on. She asked me to keep thinking about it. I continued to dive deeper into my own memory. Deeper than I had before. I suddenly found myself walking up the steps into the house and feeling confused. I was talking myself out of what happened. I had to have imagined that. That didn't actually happen, did it? I went upstairs closed a door and sat on the floor by myself. I was very confused. She asked me to open my eyes and I watched the lights again. After a minute, I closed my eyes and returned to my memory. I found myself at the dinner table. I felt so uncomfortable. I was so small compared to everyone else. Jack was smiling and carrying on. Was this normal? Why was I feeling so alone? I couldn't tell my parents or my sister. I was too uncomfortable with what happened, and Jack seemed like everything was fine, so I just kept eating quietly. She asked me to open my eyes and look at the lights. I did and then closed them. She asked me what I felt. I said I felt alone. I went back to the lights and then closed my eyes again. She said to take a deep breath. We were done with the memory for now.

She then focused me on my relaxation. It took a few minutes but I was able to return to SUDS level one or two.

I had tears in the corners of my eyes but overall I was much more composed than our first EMDR session. When I finally relaxed, she asked me to look at the lights one more time. I did. Then she asked me to tell her if there was anything that I learned. I said that I learned that I was so young. That I was so innocent and unfairly taken advantage of. For the first time, I was actually thinking about myself correctly. I was seeing how wrong it was for me to be subjected to that kind of behavior. I was feeling my own innocence. It was a great feeling.

We wrapped up the session. I composed myself and we bantered about a few less heavy things before I left. I think this was the first session where I felt some real progress. I was pretty composed as I walked to my car. I was confident, optimistic, and energized. Now, if I can only bottle that.

Eva's Wonderful Life: May 21, 2010

The world works in wonderful ways. Just when the pressure of life feels too much to carry, you find that your existence, however awkward and inconsequential, may be helping someone else. This thought was the furthest thing from my mind when my alarm rattled me out of bed this morning. Instead, I thought about how, for another night, my body had failed me, jolting me awake every hour on the hour with clocklike precision. Stripped of all energy, the only thing that lifted me out of bed and put me in front of the bathroom sink, was Eva.

Every Friday morning for the past several months, I have been asked to pick up Eva, a ninety-one-year-old blind woman, from her home at 9:30 and deliver her to the senior center in Chesterfield along with the food. Since she was the only person who needed a ride to the center, she could easily sit up front in my cargo van and save my company from having to send a passenger van for this one passenger. Luckily for me, I really like Eva. A proud, kind woman from Kansas, Eva has been living with her daughter and son-in-law ever since she lost her eyesight ten years before. Her late husband is often a topic of conversation. It is clear that Eva is lonely as she wonders aloud why she isn't with him in heaven. "I'm ready to go," she routinely says.

I always look forward to my conversations with Eva. She is the type of person who doesn't seem her age. No matter what we talk about, she always has a smart, succinct comment to provide, one that leaves you thinking about it later in the day. The other seniors at the center saw this in her as well, and when I walked her into the center, they always circled around and helped her with her things. She has that certain je ne sais quoi. I guess that's why it's so sad for me to hear her talk about wanting to end her time here on earth. I usually re-direct the conversation to something positive, and avoid going further into the topic that she seems so comfortable discussing.

Today, as I drove her to the center, she politely asked me about the new puppy that I bought for my wife on her birthday. She always asked about my wife, and loved to press me on when we were having kids. Today she wanted to know how we chose the name Bailey for the puppy. I told her that one of the traditions that my wife and I have is to watch the movie "It's a Wonderful Life" every year around Christmastime. The movie was such a good reminder to both of us at that busy time of year, and the lessons of George Bailey, the lead character, provided inspiration year round. She said that she had never seen the movie. Surprised, I told her that it was a story about a man who contemplates jumping off a bridge because he feels as though his life has no importance, that he had not accomplished anything he set out to accomplish. After an angel is sent down from heaven to show him what the lives of all of his family and friends would be like if he had never been born, it becomes clear what an enormous positive impact he had on his family, friends, and the entire town. This gives him a new perspective on his life, and he returns home a happy man.

I expected Eva to delight in the positive story. To my surprise, Eva, with her head down, said, "I think about committing suicide every morning." Delivered without emotion, her comment caught me off guard. Immediately, I responded as anyone would. I started to tell her how great she was and how much she was loved by the people at the senior center and her family. I could tell that she had heard this kind of response before and she politely thanked me. Then, I did something a little out of character for me. I took a step further than I normally would. I started telling her about what I was going through. I told her about Jack and the therapy. I kept going with my story as she sat in silence. Arriving at my point, I told her that, if nothing else, she is here to keep me up. I told her how much I looked forward to her company at a time in my life when I needed something to look forward to. I told her that I needed her. We had just pulled up to the senior center and I put the van in park. Without hesitation, she placed her hand on my forearm, looked directly into my eyes as though she had regained her sight, and said, "What you just told me was so important for me to hear." She smiled and we sat there for a quiet second before I got out and helped her out of the van and into the center. We walked quietly, hand in hand, and then I said goodbye. She just kept walking towards her group of friends. I wondered if she had tears in her eyes and a lump in her throat like I did.

Like George Bailey, Eva had been reminded that her life was more important than she thought it was. We had connected as well as two people can connect in conversation and I'm certain we both walked away with the same sense of wholeness. It was a powerful feeling that I will always remember. As I drove the van back to work, I thought about how many meaningful conversations I had missed in life because I didn't take that one extra step to share my personal story that was so relevant to someone else's pain. But, I didn't dwell on it. I was still feeling good about my part in Eva's Wonderful Life.

An Unpredictable Riot: May 23, 2010

Nothing is more uncomfortable than feeling unhappy and not knowing why. Knowing the general reason isn't enough. I want to know why this weekend is so much harder than last weekend. What did I do wrong? How do these feelings start, and what can I do to not let it happen again. Everything else in my life, I control with hard work, or planning, or natural ability. This is different. There is an unpredictable riot going on inside my body, and I can't calm it down.

Thinking back, it actually started on Thursday or Friday. I felt pretty good after my therapy session on Thursday, but there was an internal discomfort I noticed that carried into Friday. And even though I had a good day, and a thought-provoking conversation with Eva, I knew there was something clawing at my core. That night, I had promised my wife that we would go out for a nice meal, but I had to break my promise when I realized that I couldn't sit in my own skin, much less have a meal in public.

Saturday, I was scheduled to participate in a local event. I didn't feel up for it, but I had agreed to participate weeks before, so I did. The Forest Hill Yacht Club (one of those fictitious yacht clubs) was having its inaugural event to celebrate the opening of a newly dredged public lake near our house. Each of the surrounding neighborhoods entered a six-person canoe team to race for the inaugural Forest Hill Yacht Club Cup. Our team was six men—all of us 180 pounds or more. Our canoe was a three person canoe, with a maximum weight limit about four hundred pounds less than what we stuffed into the boat. No paddles were allowed in this race. Just hands. Dismissing all laws of buoyancy, our boat won, if the race was to the bottom of the lake. Unfortunately, it wasn't. There was a great turnout, so everyone had a good laugh as our team doggy paddled back to shore, the canoe filled with water.

It was good for me to get out of the house and do something social. But immediately after the event, I felt the need to get home as quickly as possible. I've always been a fairly social person, so this is very out of character for me. Nonetheless, I was home thirty minutes later, on my couch with a gin and soda in my hand trying to calm down. I was so uncomfortable, I couldn't stand it. I had another gin and soda, since the first one accomplished its mission. By nine o'clock I was drunk. I was embarrassed that I was drunk and ashamed I caved to my desire to medicate this way. My wife quietly watched, never mentioning my clearly self-destructive behavior. Realizing how little control I had, I started to talk with her about what was going on. I told her that my desire to drink had really increased lately. I've always been able to control how much I drank, so it was a strange feeling to not have the control. I told her that I was reading on a website about Zoloft, and several people reported that their desire for alcohol rose suddenly after starting Zoloft. This had to be what was happening. I was definitely losing control. I sat there with my head in my hands. My wife rubbing my back. The riot was winning.

Luckily, today is a new day. I have a new perspective and increased resolve to gain control of myself and my recovery—without the use of anything but what a doctor prescribes. Losing control is a scary feeling. It's not something that I am familiar with. I'm already feeling different than the last four days. I'm more interested in things. I'm more energized. I'm optimistic about my recovery. I just wish I knew why.

The Effort: May 24, 2010

During my first six-month deployment to the Middle East, one of my F-14 squadron-mates, Ike, used to have a workout program. He called it "The Effort." He announced "The Effort" to a few of us late one night as we all sat around a table in the officer's mess, enjoying midnight rations or "mid rats" after a long day of flight operations. Our aircraft carrier had been turning circles in the Persian Gulf for about ninety days at that point and a lot of us were finding solace in greasy food, especially Ike. In fact, just by hanging out with Ike, I found myself eating more junk food and packing on a few pounds. But, Ike had a borderline serious look on his face. "Fellas, just watch and learn." For the next month we watched Ike never miss a meal. He never met a corndog or plate of fries he didn't like. Salad was not in his vocabulary. One night, as a few of us were playing cards to kill time, someone asked him

110

how "The Effort" was going. Ike said everything was going as planned. We all looked at each other. Uh…okay. By the time our ship returned to San Diego, Ike had literally gained ten pounds. Not letting him off the hook, I asked him where "The Effort" was now that cruise was over. He said he was almost to the end of Phase I. Catching me off guard that there were actual phases to this fitness atrocity, I asked him to explain. He said that Phase I was the most intense part. It was when he "bulked up, so he could chisel down later." After that I realized that everybody has their own weight loss strategy—and it doesn't have to make sense.

We've all been there. Everyone at one time or another has decided to focus on dropping a few pounds, and for most of us, it's not easy. It takes setting a goal, picking a path to achieve that goal, and following that path as closely as possible. When you first start, you get really sore. Your body constantly aches and you see zero change in your physique. You may even gain a pound or two at first. At that point, you make a choice. This is too hard, so I'll adjust my goal, or, I'm going to accomplish this, however painful. If you press on, you start to realize that your body starts to get less sore. You slowly start to feel better after workouts. Your energy may increase. But you really still can't see much of a change in your body yet. It's frustrating. After a good, focused effort, you start to notice something. Maybe a muscle that you didn't realize you had or maybe just a comment from someone about how healthy you look. Either way, it's some sort of positive reinforcement. You start to feel good. Then you go to a wedding one weekend and inhale some cake and do keg stands until 4 a.m. D'oh. Again, decision time. Do I get back to my workout schedule, or am I now so off-track, that I'm going to just fade away and tweak my goal. If you decide to get back on track, you feel good again pretty quickly. You stick to it and you start to see more and more changes. You get more comments. You see more definition. Now you're rolling. Then there's that one day. The one day when you look in the mirror and realize, dayom, I'm looking good. That's a great day. You have so much motivation, and you feel so good about yourself for sticking to it. From there, you coast to the finish line and prove to yourself that you can accomplish anything you set your mind to.

In an effort to help me get through these memories of abuse, the PTSD, whatever level of depression, anger, I've started to think about it like training for a big race. That's something I have done before and it's something I know I can do. I've started to compare my recent down days with those days when my muscles were sore at the start of training. When I had those days, I wasn't really seeing any changes to my physique. I was tired of dragging myself to the gym. And, it wasn't like I was training for a 5k race; I was training for an Ironman triathlon. This would take dedication. I wouldn't train for the swim by spending a day on the first step of the pool. No, I've done that for years. I've talked about the abuse with just my toe in the water, and then covered it up for two years. That doesn't produce results. I'm diving into the frigid water and I'm swimming as fast as I can until I can't go anymore. And then, I'll deal with the soreness.

That's what my painful past four days have been. Just soreness. Now it's time to start training again. I have to believe that this is what's happening, because that's all that I have to go with. I'm in the middle of my own version of "The Effort."

Therapy Session 10: May 27, 2010

Ten is my magic number. I can now say that I am feeling different. Others may have seen me improving, but today is the first day that I have felt as though I'm really recovering. I slept well last night. Only woke up once, which, compared to last week, made me feel like a bear after a long winter. I rolled through work, ran home to take care of the new puppy, and then hopped in the car for my appointment. Weather was hot, an August-like day. I cranked the music and weaved around traffic without incident. I felt very level.

I filled out my paperwork in the reception area. Nobody else was in the waiting room, but it didn't matter to me anymore. I noticed that I had checked a few less boxes this time. Anger and anxiety were definitely muted. I forgot to look up what organcity and the other Scrabble words meant, so I left those blank again. Ignorance is truly bliss in this case.

To my amusement, my therapist opened the door and greeted me at 3:05. What? Was my watch wrong? When's daylight savings? What's happening? I quickly forgot about it and started to think about what was ahead after exchanging pleasantries with the doc. I sat down. We reviewed my sheet and she was really glad to hear that my anger and anxiety were decreasing. I told her that this week was the first week of feeling marked improvement. She asked if I had done anything different. I paused…and then told her that I hadn't been drinking any alcohol since Saturday. She scowled. She thought I had stopped drinking any alcohol a long time ago. Do'h. Yeah…uh…sorry. Didn't tell you that. My improvement stole the show, though, and we quickly moved past my defiance and concentrated on the positive.

She asked if I had been having any dreams. I told her about a dream I had last night. I was looking through a scrapbook of pictures of my family, pictures that included Jack. In the pictures, it was clear that he was fondling me. His hands were always touching me. This dream is actually a reality…months ago at home I spent a few minutes with my parents flipping through old pictures…we all realized the abuse was clear as day. Every picture showed him with his hands on me in some form or another. My smile usually a half-smile.

She didn't worry too much about the dream. She was glad that it wasn't a realistic dream about him actually doing things. Then I told her again about my snake dreams. She had forgotten. I mentioned that, for years, I have had dreams about snakes. Like every few nights until about two months ago. She almost jumped out of her chair. She told me she did her dissertation on Freud's understanding of snake dreams. Wow. Aren't I lucky. She mentioned that sexual abuse by a male perpetrator often causes the victims to dream about snakes later in life. The phallic and evil nature of the snake is an obvious symbol for the subconscious. I felt good knowing why I had so many of these dreams. A nice "ah hah" moment always helps.

Then she asked about any other reactions I've had. I told her that my wife recently bought some Vaseline Intensive Care lotion for my hands (yes, I'm a guy, and I use lotion for my hands sometimes). The smell of the lotion made my skin crawl. I got chills. I couldn't use it. My therapist completely understood. She really didn't need to ask, which relaxed me. She said it was completely normal to have olfactory memories. Our brains hold on to traumatic smells forever. Again…I'm normal. Two for two.

Time for EMDR—time to open the ceramic jar for some more memory desensitization. I told her I was ready. She set up the machine. I relaxed to 1 or 2 SUDS and she asked me to envision the jar with the cork on and slowly uncork the opening. We removed only one memory, the same memory as last week, the first time I was abused. For some reason, she really wanted to concentrate on this first memory, however hazy. She asked me to go back to his lap in the car. Reluctantly, I did. We went through how I felt.

She was glad to know that I still felt like I was an innocent kid. Good. Last week worked. I looked at the lights for a few minutes, and then closed my eyes. She asked me just to let myself wander in my memories. Immediately I was in the house. He was playing with my ears, goofing around with me in front of my family. I was so uncomfortable but tried to hide it. We started playing a game in the other room—socializing—he had me on his lap. He was acting normal. I was so uncomfortable. I opened my eyes. Looked at the lights. Closed them again. I wandered back to the kitchen, where we were all standing. Jack was standing there talking with my parents. I looked down at his hand. He was nervously scratching at his thumbnail with the index finger of the same hand. He always did that. A nervous tick. My SUDS level rose. Lights on. Eyes closed again. I found myself with my sister outside playing in the leaves. I was somewhat happy, but I still was hiding the abuse. Lights on. Eyes closed again. Then I was at the wedding. The reason we were at Jack's house in the first place was because my aunt was getting married. I was the ring bearer. I was so uncomfortable at the reception. I wanted to tell. I couldn't. I smiled for pictures and felt alone. Lights on. Eyes closed. I was back at Jack's house. We were all saying goodbye. He pulled me in the other room and reminded me that what happened in the car was our secret. I listened and obeyed my elder as I was taught. Lights on. Eyes filled with tears. Eyes closed. It was time to wrap up. She asked me how I was feeling about that kid. I went through a range of feelings. Embarrassed. Alone. Innocent. She stuck up for the little kid every time I said something that marginally blamed him. She asked me to summarize what I felt. I told her that the little kid didn't deal with that terrible situation in the wrong way; he dealt with a terrible situation that was wrong. She lit up. Apparently that's a good thing for me to say. It wasn't that I didn't do something right. It's that I was forced into something that was wrong. That's a huge step for me. I actually felt it. That kid felt it now. Relief. Amazing.

We wrapped up by placing the memory back in the jar. We brought my SUDS down to 1. She put away the lights. Big deep breath. Progress. We talked about little things. It was the first time I talked with her and felt more normal, more connected. I have started liking my therapist. I not only have respect for her, but she has helped me respect her profession. I looked at my watch, 4:17. Whoa. Time really flies when you're having fun. We walked together towards the reception area. There was a woman there. We said goodbye and she immediately beckoned the young woman towards her, apologizing for her tardiness. I had to laugh a little. My issues surrounding her cavalier sense of urgency faded. It's incredible how far away ten weeks ago feels.

The Character Beneath: May 31, 2010

"A good character is the best tombstone."
                                    - Charles H. Spurgeon

Even though we all know what really matters in life, we often forget that what people show us on the outside is less important than what lies beneath. We all get caught up in the game. Instead of working on being better people, we focus on how we look, what we drive, who we know, what we read, where we live. The media grovels over celebrities and millions of Americans spend their days reading tabloids, trying to look and act more like last week's cover. Image is everything.

I've been thinking a lot about what people are seeing on the outside this weekend. But, I'm not talking about myself. I'm talking about what people are looking at, two hundred miles away in a graveyard in Arlington.

Few American customs measure up to the time-honored Memorial Day tradition of "Flags In" at Arlington National Cemetery. Today at Arlington, every single gravesite is decorated with a miniature American flag, placed one foot from every tombstone, centered. The ritual, orchestrated by the U.S. Army's 3rd Infantry and occurring annually since 1948, is a subtle reminder for all of us to be thankful for the many brave men and women who have given their lives for our country.

Unfortunately, Jack's tombstone was decorated by a 3rd Infantry serviceman this weekend. Visitors read his name, etched in marble, and felt warmth. Nobody knew any better. He is being celebrated as an American hero. The man who tortured innocent children. Who ripped the innocence from their backs. Who smiled in every picture and manipulated his way.

What has kept me level this weekend, after the thoughts of his decorated gravesite continually flash into my head, is knowing what lies beneath his gravesite is a tortured soul, forever suffering for what his body did on the outside. Image isn't everything. Nobody is honoring Jack today. We are honoring the sacrifices that many good men and women have made. We're honoring the character beneath. Even though Jack's physical tombstone is in a fortunate location, looking like a perfect tabloid picture, his lack of character beneath makes his gravesite an auspicious anomaly among so many American heroes.

These Two Things: June 2, 2010

While I paddled like a hamster on the elliptical machine today, I read a good article about the history of marriage therapy in the March twenty-ninth issue of "The New Yorker." Normally, I'd flip past an article on such a riveting topic, but these days I'm more in tune with my psychological side, so I read on. The article started by presenting that marriage therapy was on the rise, which, the author surprisingly noted, was inconsistent with the trend for divorce. For a second, it made me think that the quality of marriage therapy must be improving, that more people are having problems, but less are divorcing so marriage therapy must really be effective. Negatory. In fact, Consumer Reports rated marriage counselors the worst of all mental health professionals (Consumer Reports actually rates mental health professionals just like they would toasters).

Instead, to explain it all, the article cited a recent hypothesis that concluded that these diverging statistics coincided with a larger shift in American culture. It went on to say that too many people are heading into marriage with "heightened expectations for marriage as a means of self-expression and personal fulfillment." Apparently, couples are going to therapy for years and years, trying to "improve" their marriage, while never getting to the point where they are content, but never getting to the point of filing for divorce. Basically, millions of people are searching for a nuptial dream world—a world with ridiculous expectations in which they are trying to have the perfect marriage. What's worse, many are going to therapy thinking that the act of going to therapy is enough to get them to The Promised Land, but they don't work on the real problems, the honest issues. They don't actually want to change. But, for the record, they are "working on it."

I'm going to tread lightly here, because I have about as much experience with marriage as I do with therapy, but I have a little experience with both so I'll keep going.

Reading the article, I couldn't help but relate it to the therapy that I'm going through. I've been spending a lot of time reading online message boards for sexual abuse survivors lately. It's really good to validate a lot of the things I'm going through by learning about what other sexual abuse survivors have dealt with and how they're coping with their wide range of emotions. Many are in therapy or have been through therapy. I've learned so much from these people and I am consistently humbled by the intelligence and courage of so many survivors.

But then there are others that I can say remind me of the not-so-happily married couple that is "working on it." They aren't exactly dealing with the problem. Rather they're sort of holding on to the pain and guilt as a kind of coping mechanism and it keeps them safe. They list a wide range of excuses about why therapy isn't for them or how bad therapists are and how they're not getting anywhere.

I'm sure some of it is true—there are some bad therapists out there. But there's also a little bullshit in there somewhere. It's discouraging to see, but I understand what they're going through.

I don't want to get caught in that sort of pattern. Since I've always jumped into things with both feet, I think I approached therapy in the same way—all or nothing. Before I began, I needed to make sure I was ready. I didn't want to screw it up and drag it out. I wanted it to be as quick and effective as possible so I could get on with my life. It took me a while to realize that it's not that simple and clean. You can't just "fix it" like you can other things, but you can improve significantly with hard work.

I have committed to two important things that I hope will keep me moving in the right direction. First, I have dropped the BS. I finally leveled with myself. I admitted that there was a significant problem and I was completely honest with my wife and other family members about what had happened. That was hard. Second, I got to a point where I genuinely committed to recover. That was harder. I finally concluded that I was ready to do anything it took to feel right. What I've noticed is that keeping these two things going takes continual work. Every day involves making sure they are in place. Some days are better than others.

These two things, along with a great support system and a qualified therapist, are letting me progress. These two things have given me permission to improve. They're allowing me to be honest with myself and my therapist and to keep pushing when all I want to do is fire her and go back to my old life. Just as marriage isn't about waking up after twelve hours of spooning while wearing "Purrrrrfect Couple" cat t-shirts and then chest-bumping before watching the Stanley Cup finals with a cooler of Bud Light, therapy isn't about finding a best friend in your therapist and feeling immediate waves of relief after the first few sessions. Both are hard work, and both aren't pretty at times, but if you're honest with yourself and you want it to work, you'll get there. Well, that's what I think.

Who's The Blockhead?: June 3, 2010

Just when all things were moving along nicely, Lucy pulled the football away from me at the last second, and I found myself blinking at the ceiling from my back in the middle of the waiting room floor while everyone laughed. Today I showed up on my usual appointment day at my usual appointment time. My therapist came out and shook another man's hand at 3:04; he stood up and followed her towards her office. She caught a glimpse of me and gasped. "What are you doing here?" she blurted. Uh...hi...I'm your patient, Chris. I see you every Thursday at 3:00 p.m.(as well as 3:09, 3:14, and 3:19). "You're not scheduled," she responded. I sat there like a dying fish while the other four people in the waiting room pretended not to stare. She grabbed her appointment book and showed me that my name was nowhere to be found. Not this week. Not next week. Never again was I scheduled for therapy. "Did you talk to my assistant and extend your therapy?" she asked. Uh...no. Nobody said I had to do that. "We don't offer standing appointments," she chirped. Once again, news to me. "Well, we'll have to get you back on the books to continue your sessions, but I'm all booked up this week. Maybe next week I can fit you in." Ok. Lucy had not only removed the football at the last second, but she was now dragging me around the football field on my back, the crowd growing more excited. I felt like an idiot.

Tomorrow, I'll call her assistant and figure out what happened, but this sort of thing shouldn't occur. I know this is a job for these people. They come to work, they watch twelve people cry and help them with their problems, they go home. I'm sure it gets mundane. But, when you're the person on the other end, desperately getting your life back on track and depending on a therapist to help, and that therapist pulls the football, it feels worse than you would expect.

No big deal. I've dealt with far worse. I'll just continue my relaxation and focus on the positive. I wish there was some sort of guide for going through therapy. Chapter 1: How to not look like an a-hole in the waiting room.

Phil's Frankenstein: June 7, 2010

She may have created a monster. By slowly supplying the tools necessary to develop normal levels of self-respect, assertiveness, and confidence, my therapist just might have turned me against her. What a brilliant tragedy.

Today I called the office in order to get back on the books after last Thursday's miscommunication. I had every intention of scheduling another few months. When I called, the receptionist made it clear that it was my fault for not calling to ensure my sessions would continue. A little agitated, I didn't point any fingers and instead I moved the conversation to getting back on the books. I figured I'd settle the matter with my therapist once I saw her. The receptionist curtly said that the next available session was in mid-July. What? Are you kidding me? She mentioned that my therapist was going to take another three-week vacation—this only six weeks after her last vacation.

I found myself starting to morph into my therapist's worst nightmare: patient Frankenstein. I was taking what she had given me, and I was thinking for myself. I was going rogue. I now had enough self-respect to realize I deserved something better. I now had enough confidence to demand that I be managed appropriately. I was a monster. Only, I wasn't the evil Frankenstein from Mary Shelley's book that killed people. I was more of the late Phil Hartman's Frankenstein from "Saturday Night Live." This more introspective and friendly Frankenstein didn't say much. He just made indistinguishable monster noises and enjoyed singing Christmas Carols with Tonto and Tarzan, but we all knew what he was capable of. I always liked Phil's Frankenstein, it was one of the only times Phil ever broke character on "SNL." Moving on, I quickly made about five appointments in July and August, just to put something on the books, but when I hung up I knew that I had only one option. It was time to find another therapist.

I don't know if this is a common problem in the therapy world, but this sort of professionalism is generally unacceptable. I don't care what business world we're talking about. A good therapist wouldn't let this sort of thing happen. A good therapist would start sessions on time and if not, provide a good explanation of why a session starts late. A good therapist would ensure that the receptionist is pleasant, empathetic, and on top of the schedule. All of this just means so much to patients, as we are entirely vulnerable. While it might be a tedious profession for them at times, the good ones should know how to treat their patients, always. And, even though my therapist might have the most experience in EMDR, this is all starting to affect my recovery, and I can't have that. My life is on hold while I work on dealing with all of this. I am completely committed to my recovery and I should have a therapist who is as dedicated as I am. So, maybe I'll find someone better. Or, maybe I won't find someone and I'll end up right back where I started, but at least I'll know the landscape and I won't start losing respect for myself.

When Phil Hartman's Frankenstein is threatened, he makes strange noises and runs through walls. He takes action. It's time to take a little action.

Surviving Shaving Cream: June 9, 2010

Last night, Stephen Strasburg, the Washington National's highly anticipated rookie phenom, pitched his first major league baseball game. Strasburg threw a gem. He struck out fourteen batters—a franchise record for any pitcher, and the first time since 1971 that a pitcher in baseball registered that many strikeouts in his professional debut. Instead of airing the game regionally, Major League Baseball televised it nationally, which right there says what the league thinks of the twenty-one-year-old. Being a diehard Orioles fan, I didn't want to watch as the team across the beltway became that much more popular, but I watched it anyway. I enjoyed it. The guy can hurl. But what I enjoyed most didn't happen until after the game.

After the Nationals won, the network asked for an interview with Strasburg, which is normal for a television network to conduct with the player of the game. He stood there answering questions, giving his "aw shucks" statement that his agent probably coached him through months ago. He got about halfway through his second sentence when…WHAM!...one of his teammates slammed a towel-full of shaving cream into his face. Everyone had a good laugh since this is a well-known baseball tradition. Anytime a player wins a big game for his team, he usually ends up with shaving cream on his face/neck/back at some point in the postgame interview. He was handed a towel, big smile on his face. He wiped the shaving cream off, shot some residual cream out of his nose, and continued on. Halfway through his next sentence…WHAM!…another, larger towel with about twice the shaving cream filled his mouth, nose, and whatever else was left open above his neck. This was unheard of in baseball shaving cream circles. They literally weren't giving the kid a break, but it was well deserved given all the hype he received in the media this past year before even pitching a major league inning. It was a good TV moment and he took it well.

When I decided to switch therapists, I knew it wouldn't be easy. I guess that's why I dragged my feet for so long even though I was frustrated with my therapist. Now, not only do I have the frustration of knowing that I have to dig around looking for and qualifying a new therapist, but now I have to anticipate going through my entire story in detail again with someone new. My anxiety about that is back. That's a second towel of shaving cream that I wasn't expecting. I was finally at a point where I was comfortable talking with my therapist. She had finally stopped asking "Jack was your uncle, right?" My frustrations and trepidation with the entire profession had become somewhat muted. But, now I'm back at square one. I have the same fear that a new therapist will minimize what I'm going through. It might be a little less anxiety than the first time, but it's there. It's troubling to feel this in the middle of so much progress.

As if to test my resolve, I was handed a chance to turn back around today. I thought long and hard about it when I received a voicemail from my therapist's office saying that a last minute cancellation occurred. They could fit me in for one session tomorrow at noon—before she leaves for her sail around the world, or her climbing of The Seven Summits, or whatever she's doing on her mega-vacation. I sat there in my van, driving from site to site, talking myself into sticking with her. It's so inviting. The anxiety and frustration could all go away. I could get right back on the horse tomorrow and I'd be back in the saddle for good in three weeks when the globetrotter returns.

Suddenly, something hit me. I realized what was keeping me from taking that appointment. I couldn't disrespect myself enough to go back. It's not that she wasn't a skilled therapist. She might be the best in the city. But, she makes me feel as though I'm less than she is. I'm an afterthought to her and her staff. I always felt like I was in the way or I was causing them to work too hard. Little comments here and there were enough for me. It's like I was draped in a cloak of smugness when I walked in the door, from the receptionist all the way back to my therapist's office. I don't need that. I've spent the past twenty years feeling as though I'm not worthy of happiness or self-respect. What I don't need is a condescending group of people looking down at me. I know enough about people that I can weed through my options in the coming days or weeks. I'll find the right person for me.

So, that's where I am. I'm deciding to stick to my guns and find someone who not only makes me feel right about my past, but who also makes me feel right about myself in the present. I'm going to need to wipe away the second towel-full of shaving cream with a smile on my face, and then I'm going to need to fire it out of my nose onto the shirt of the cameraman. My gut is telling me this is the right thing to do.

Won't Get Fooled Again: June 9, 2010

The Who is ringing in my ears.

I haven't written twice in one day before, but for fear of forgetting this conclusion, I need to put this to paper immediately. For five days, I've been unsuccessfully trying to unwind, wondering why I'm so uncomfortable with my therapist and myself, and now I think I've finally identified the underlying reason.

As someone who has been molested by a family member—by someone whom I trusted and was told was on my side—I am incredibly sensitive to being misguided by someone that I've entrusted with my recovery. This is clear as day right now, and it's not something my therapist was going to help me figure out.

I may be over-sensitive to her administrative faults, or maybe I correctly pinpointed a major red flag, but either way, I know that it triggers a really strong reaction in me, and I need to listen to that. I'm the only person who knows what's right for me. I need to find a new therapist.

My "won't get fooled again" meter is pegged. Okay. 'Nuff said. Thanks, Pete Townsend.

The Blink Test: June 14, 2010

My favorite course in college was Psychology. I studied Mechanical Engineering. Way to follow your interests, Chris. I guess my interest in psychology is why I have always enjoyed reading anything written by "The New Yorker" staff writer and bestselling author, Malcolm Gladwell. While some may challenge his methods and assumptions from a professional perspective, I like how he takes very complicated issues relating to the human condition and packages them in a way that everyone can relate to. His books and articles rattle around in my head for years.

My favorite of his books is "Blink." He delves into neuroscience and psychology in a way that is easy to read. It addresses how our brains work, specifically, how we make decisions. It discusses the millions of little decisions each of us make every day and it offers some conclusions about how we go about making them. What's amazing to me is how many decisions we make in a split second by processing subtle clues. Little hints or gestures or inflections or data points is all we need to make a decision, and half the time we don't even realize we just decided on something. For example, a therapist can watch ten different married couples in conversation on videotape for five minutes each. At the end, he can pinpoint exactly which of the ten couples' marriage will fail. And he's right every time. Five minutes? How? In another example, a tennis coach can watch his student serve one hundred serves. Each serve, before the ball is struck by the student, the coach can accurately predict if it will result in a fault. What makes him know this? What are the clues? Often, the answer is, he doesn't know—he just knows.

My last few days have been incredibly frustrating as I've floundered around trying to figure out which therapist is right for me. Since I know that EMDR is working for me, I've narrowed it down to the therapists in this city who are certified to administer EMDR. There are four, one of them my current therapist. I made the decision to find another therapist. Sweet! My options are limited. Fuck.

As I drove my van last Thursday, I went to the top of my three-deep list and made some calls. First call was to a very qualified PhD. Plenty of EMDR work and a sexual abuse background, but after talking with her assistant, I found she wasn't taking new patients. No problem, her assistant referred me to someone that the PhD believed was a good alternate for EMDR work. That person was the number two on my list. Two birds, one stone. I called number two, this one a Licensed Clinical Social Worker, or LCSW (Basically, a post-graduate level counselor who can be a certified therapist. Some are better than others, but not a PhD or PsyD.).

I called and left a message. About an hour went by. She called back but I was away from my phone. Her message was strange. She was giving me "permission" to call her cell phone on Friday—a "one time only phone call to her cell phone, never to be used again without authorization" so that we could connect. She sounded condescending and rigid and generally annoying. Great start. I called her on Friday and we talked for about thirty minutes. I don't know exactly what felt wrong, but I didn't feel comfortable. She wanted me to fire my old therapist and have them transfer my records to her, before setting an appointment with her. What? That felt drastic and a leap of faith I wasn't ready to take. I wanted to meet with her first before making a decision. She wouldn't allow it. There were a few other comments that I didn't like. I couldn't pinpoint why exactly, but I knew she was double-faulting before she hit the ball. Abort.

The final therapist on the list, number three, was another LCSW. Her website seemed warmer and more inviting, more grounded. I couldn't tell if she had dealt with sexual abuse patients before, but her EMDR work looked solid and she practiced the "multi-dimensional" approach to therapy that I was familiar with. I left a message but it was late in the day so I didn't hear from her.

This unfinished business filled my weekend with frustration. I felt up and down. I was busy trying to keep myself focused and not let this momentary hiccup bother me. I drank some alcohol on Friday and Saturday nights to soothe the frustration. It may have worked a little, and it felt good to break my own self-imposed rule, but I ended the weekend realizing that I had abandoned my pledge to remove alcohol. I re-decided that drinking wasn't going to help, just complicate my ups and downs. It's such an easy temporary solution, but I know it's a dead end.

Today I was back to work, feeling more motivated. I found myself thinking about the book "Blink." I usually think about the book when I start to catch myself over-think something. I've been hearing people tell me to trust my gut lately. Hearing that always reminds me of the book.

I finally got a call back from number three late in the day. When I told her what was going on, she was hesitant to say much about my therapist. She said she needed to reserve judgment until she better understood my situation. And even though I wanted her to validate what I was saying, I liked her professional approach. I sensed her integrity, and there was something very human about her. I found out that she has done extensive EMDR work, as well as successful therapy with male patients for sexual abuse. Jackpot. She was talking my language.

The catch was that she wasn't sure if she felt comfortable working with me while my other therapist was on vacation. I found her almost convincing me to wait for my therapist to return, and then talk with my therapist about my issues with her and her staff to see if we could improve the relationship. She said her biggest concern was that it sounded like I had been making progress with the other therapist so she was sensitive to upsetting that progress by making a change. I told her that I felt very uncomfortable waiting until mid-July for my next treatment. I told her that I was ready to try someone new.

She asked if she could think about it overnight and call me tomorrow. No problem. Overall, I liked her thorough approach. She linked me up with her assistant to make sure my insurance would cover it, since all of this was a waste if I wasn't covered. I'll know tomorrow if it checks out, but her assistant seemed to think I was fine.

The decision I had unknowingly made was that I really liked this therapist. I made that decision about three sentences into our conversation. I don't know why, but I could tell she was a good fit for me. She's passing my "Blink" test and I'm forcing myself to trust my gut. Now I just need her to agree.

Z-Day Plus 65: June 16, 2010

I had another appointment with my physician today in order to evaluate how I'm doing physically. Since therapist number three on my list (the one I really liked on the phone) had agreed to meet with me on Thursday, I would be able to update her on my current medical situation. And, I've been riding the Vitamin Z train for over two months now, so I was looking forward to talking with my physician about the affect it was having on me.

BP and pulse were good. Lost some weight, always nice. I was hoping to be another inch taller, but no luck there.

Finally, we got to talking about the Zoloft. It's an interesting conversation for someone who has been hiding abuse for so long to have with a physician. When he asked me if I'm feeling more "normal," I just stared at him and blinked a few times. I didn't have an answer. I don't really know what normal is for me. Was I angry? No. Did I have a short fuse? Not really. Was I whistling zippity-doo-dah as I washed the dishes? Absolutely not. What I told him that since I've been living in my own little world for so many years, I thought my "normal gauge" was all out of whack. Some re-calibration was needed. The other thing was that I've been doing so many other things related to my recovery, that it was hard for me to pinpoint how much of an impact the drug was having, versus how much of an impact the cognitive and behavioral treatment was having. He understood, but he reassured me that everything was going well since I felt more level and I didn't have any significant side effects. We had found the right drug for me and we had found the right dosage (My magic dosage was 100mg. I started with 50mg, but that just wasn't enough for someone over 200 lbs, so about a month ago we doubled up. It took a day before it really made a difference.).

Before we wrapped up, I wanted to apologize to him for how rude my therapist was a few weeks ago when she called him, demanded that he come to the phone, and rudely told him to prescribe me a sleep aid. I said that I knew she was a little aggressive and condescending. He said it was alright, that sort of thing happens, and he would never have been bullied into writing a prescription anyway, but he was glad that I was actively looking to make sure I had the right therapist for me.

Besides the fact that he kept staring at the planet-sized zit on my chin, almost hypnotized by it, the visit was very productive and reassuring. We set another appointment for September to re-evaluate the Zoloft and see if we should start on a plan to slowly wean me off the drug. I liked the plan.

More importantly, I like the fact that I have an appointment with therapist number three tomorrow. When we talked she said she was comfortable meeting but she

132

wasn't comfortable performing EMDR on me until I made a decision about who should be my therapist. She didn't want to interfere on the EMDR side if I was going to end up doing EMDR with my old therapist again. It's sort of a professional code. Made sense to me. By this time tomorrow, I should be able to make a decision, so that part was irrelevant. Things are finally rolling forward, which is good—for me and my chin.

Therapy Session 11: June 18, 2010

If the shoe fits, you wear it, right? But what if it sort of fits and you desperately need a pair ASAP? What do you do then? We've all been there. You find a pair you think you like even though there is something in the back of your head telling you to keep looking and even though they sort of rub in some areas, you talk yourself into buying them because you're tired of shopping (well, at least that's how I shop).

So, you take the shoes home. You wear them a few times, but every time you wear them you notice how uncomfortable they are. Then, suddenly, they start to look stupid. You start to notice other people's shoes and wish you had bought a different pair. I bet they're comfortable. They're definitely cooler. And even after all that, engaging in a personal game of psychological warfare, you force yourself to wear them even more simply to justify your purchase. You're a walking martyr in goofy shoes.

Yesterday, I met with therapist number three. It was my first meeting with her, and even though I felt great about our conversation on the phone, I found myself with intense chest pains as I drove to her office. Wow, I was literally back to square one.

I entered the waiting room. It felt more relaxed. I liked the magazines I saw. Everything felt a little more real, less clinical and definitely less stuffy. The receptionist was very friendly with not a hint of smug. Already, I found myself more at home. At exactly 4:00 p.m., the therapist's office door opened. Another woman walked out and my therapist greeted me with a genuine smile and a germ-tolerant handshake. Everything was feeling right. And, strangely, on time.

We entered her office. It was polar opposite to the office I was used to. This was what I always thought that a therapist's office would look like. It was relaxed with modern furniture and soft lighting—darker, younger, and more soothing than the other office. There were several chairs and a big, comfortable-looking couch. She started by telling me which chair was hers, and then said to pick whichever chair I felt comfortable in. I picked a safe chair on the opposite side of the room. It was big enough for grownups.

The next hour was spent going through why I was looking for a new therapist. She never said anything negative about my other therapist; instead she focused on understanding what was bothering me about the other relationship. We went through the list, and by the end, she fully understood what it was that bothered me before. Her conversational style was much different and I felt respected and comfortable. I could tell that her priority was my well-being. I don't know how, but I could tell.

At one point she asked me how I felt about the visit. I told her that my chest pains were back, but besides that I was very comfortable. I told her I really liked her. She asked why I thought my chest pains were back, why I was feeling anxiety. I told her I thought that it was because I had this sinking feeling that she wouldn't believe me. I told her I had it before with my other therapist. She then asked if I had a lot of experience with not being believed. I told her no, that my entire life, people usually believed me. When I told my parents about the couple of "close calls," they never questioned whether I was telling the truth. They made me feel believed. She found that odd, that I would be worried about nobody trusting me at this point even though I had always been trusted. We talked a bit further, and before I knew it, we had uncovered that it wasn't that I was afraid she wouldn't believe me, I was afraid that I wouldn't believe myself. I've read about this—that an abuse victim often doubts whether it ever happened. But I didn't realize I was carrying the same doubts. I guess I still am.

The point is I really liked the way she led me with open-ended questions until I got to an answer. My other therapist didn't do that; she usually hand-fed me her explanation. Right or wrong, that was the answer that I would have to accept. This new therapist made me feel less like a patient and more like a partner in my own recovery. This is a significant difference and one that makes me feel better about myself. It makes me feel like I'm partly responsible for my own improvement, not solely reliant on a therapist's professional skills to lead me to my recovery.

At the end, we talked about what to do next. I told her that I wanted her to be my therapist and that I'd like to close out with my original therapist. She agreed to work with me, but she wanted to make sure that if I switched to her, she wouldn't be put in a position to look like she had stolen me from my other therapist because that's not what happened. She was worried about how that could look in a small town, in a close-knit industry. I completely understood and I told her that I would talk directly to my therapist when she returned from bungee jumping in the Himalayas, and I would tell her why I was deciding to make the change. I never intended on revealing either therapist's name to the other and being direct with my old therapist when she returned was my plan all along.

We set my next appointment. She was fine with standing appointments and she gave me her personal cell phone in case I ever needed to talk with her directly. She said not to hesitate to call anytime. That's the way I thought it should work. I felt relief. Finally, I had a therapist I was completely confident in and comfortable with.

What I have realized was that my old therapist, while technically skilled, was like that pair of shoes that don't fit exactly right. I tried to wear them in. I tried to convince myself that they looked good. But, at the end of the day, they were rubbing me the wrong way and I needed a new pair. So, I trusted what my gut was telling me, I leveled with myself, I shopped a little more and I found the pair for me.

Therapy Session 12: June 22, 2010

"Whenever you take a step forward, you are bound to disturb something."

- Indira Gandhi

Yesterday was my second therapy session with my new therapist and, while productive in many ways, this step forward in my recovery required that I duplicate a step backwards into my past. That's the hard part about switching therapists. You have to re-tell your story—the entire story—not just one memory. You have to lay it all out there for someone new, like you would a stack of pictures when you get back from a long trip. When you lay all the pictures out there, you start to reminisce a bit. You look at the journey in a new light. You realize how much you did on your trip. In my case, not only did I see my entire story with a new set of eyes, but I was reminded, even after the progress I have made, how far I am from normal.

We began on time. A friendly hello from the receptionist and a prompt start and warm smile from my therapist felt like gifts. I was very comfortable. My anxiety was better compared to my first session with her. I had done my homework the night before—a ten-page client questionnaire, an agonizing description of myself, my family, my symptoms, and my past. This was the same ten-page client questionnaire that I filled out for my first therapist, the same one that I was denied a copy of when I called my previous therapy office a few days before. Apparently I have to wait until my former therapist returns from vacation before I can get a copy of my file. No big deal, but still a little annoying to have to spend a few hours duplicating paperwork.

She began by asking how I was doing, how I was feeling about being there. I told her that I felt good. She immediately brought up something I had written in the therapy summaries I had given her. Basically, during my last visit, I gave her a copy of my first ten therapy session journal entries. She said it would be helpful. I didn't give her the URL to my blog. I'm still not sure if it's a good idea to tell her about it; I'm still thinking about that. What she brought up was the session where I wrote about my eleven goals for my recovery. She said one of my goals jumped out at her. Goal number eight:

8. Understand assertive, non-assertive, and aggressive speech and report consistent assertion.

She quickly tied this goal to what I was doing in changing therapists. She asked me if I felt as though I was being assertive by putting my foot down and switching therapists. I hadn't really thought about it much, but she was right. My decision to change therapists was an act of assertion. She said it was good for me to realize that. I'm not the type of person to ever pat myself on the back, but, if you don't force yourself to acknowledge that you've done something positive, you'll never feel like you did. She was forcing me to acknowledge it. I liked what she was doing.

Then she mentioned that she made a decision not to do any EMDR until I have a conversation with my old therapist, ending that relationship. Even though I was telling her that she was hired as my new therapist, she wanted me to close that door before beginning EMDR. I get it. I told her I understood. I would be able to talk with my old therapist on July fifth. In the meantime, I knew I still had to catch her up on my past, so EMDR was a few weeks away, regardless. We moved on.

Then she asked a simple question about my past based on what she had read, and without realizing how much I was ready to talk, I just started yapping uncontrollably. She would stop to ask a question here and there, but then I would go right back to yap on. This was much different from my old therapist. I didn't like to talk much with her. This new therapist for some reason makes me feel comfortable droning on about everything. I take that as a positive sign, even if I didn't stop talking for more than three seconds for the remainder of the hour.

She ended by saying that what I had gone through—all of it combined—was very, very difficult. She said that it takes resilience to get through life with so many obstacles. I didn't pay much attention to the compliment, but instead I merely enjoyed the wave of relief because I knew she believed me, she acknowledged that what I told her was real. Her simple validation was like a drug.

When I started this process of facing my past, I disturbed a lot of things. I disturbed my career. I disturbed my marriage. I disturbed my relationship with my family. Now, I'm forcing myself to understand that this step backwards is really a step forward. I've disturbed my own progress a bit, but it's okay. Just like my career and my marriage and my family, it's necessary for me to disturb some things in order to continue taking forward steps.

Unlikely Hero At Center Court: June 28, 2010

In November of 2004, the NBA experienced its worst nightmare. In a heated game between the Indiana Pacers and the Detroit Pistons, in an arena just outside of Detroit, a player did the unthinkable. He jumped into the stands and attacked a heckling fan, and then, returned to the court and punched out another fan who had funneled down to the court amidst the mayhem. What followed was the longest non-drug or betting-related suspension in the game's history, and a league scrambling to salvage its image.

That player was Ron Artest. A Queens, New York native, Ron had established himself as a defensive power in the NBA. An aggressive player, Ron was actually known for many things, including his immaturity and his knack for losing his cool. Things went from bad to worse for Ron on that night in 2004. Slammed with a seventy-three-game suspension, he was at rock bottom, alone to deal with the anger issues he had been harboring since his days on the streets of Queens.

Fast forward to one week ago. Now, an NBA veteran in a supporting role on the Los Angeles Lakers, with a reputation still tied to his mistake six years earlier, Ron held the NBA Championship trophy in his hands for the first time. For eleven years in the league with five different teams, the coveted trophy had eluded him, as did the respect from a large number of NBA fans.

But Ron played like a champion throughout these playoffs, which explained why he was rushed by almost everyone with a media badge once the clock ticked down. His determination and grit was a major factor in the Lakers' victory. When interviewed on primetime television at center court, trophy in his hands, everyone expected him to talk about his role in the dramatic game seven win. Instead, Ron thanked his psychiatrist. His psychiatrist.

There was a pregnant pause by the reporter, clearly floored by Ron's candor and honesty. But Ron was unfazed. He knew what he said and he was proud to tell everyone that he couldn't have done it without the mental and emotional guidance of his therapist.

I have noticed something that continues to happen to me as I work through this recovery process. Ever since I started telling people about what happened to me, removing this weight from my shoulders after twenty years of lugging it around, I have found relief in that honesty, that candor. It's no longer a secret. No longer do I have to put on a fake smile and make everyone feel comfortable. I can take a deep breath and be myself. But, when I see someone for the first time, someone who I know is aware of my journey, if they don't directly mention anything about my recovery or pretend like things are fine for whatever reason, I start to feel like I used to feel. The elephant in the room is staring at me. I'm faking it again until they say something. Just say something. Anything. I desperately want people to ask how it's going, or make a comment to some effect that acknowledges what they know. Just any little comment to remove the elephant before it smothers me.

What I've realized is that I'm not being fair. I'm not being fair to others or myself. I can't expect other people to venture into this uncomfortable territory if I'm not willing to. I need to get the conversation started sometimes, however awkward, because it's only right.

What I've realized is that what Ron did was something inspirational. He started the conversation. He cleared the air. He made it more comfortable for the millions of people watching. He gave us a glimpse into the man behind the uniform and taught us all a lesson. He made people in therapy feel less weird. He made people in need of therapy take a step closer to picking up the phone and calling for some help.

As survivors of abuse or trauma, we are dealing with a wide range of emotions and challenges. But that shouldn't mean we need to wait for others to make us comfortable. However powerless we feel, we are in the lead. We have the power to force ourselves to clear the air because, you never know, maybe that's what everyone is waiting for.

Go Away White Knuckles: June 30, 2010

On Monday, my new therapist called my cell phone. I saw her number and I felt my pulse quicken. My mind raced. Had she decided not to work with me? Was she questioning what I had told her? Did she talk with my old therapist? Did she find my blog and was she mad that I had written about her? All of these questions flooded my mind in the second it took me to answer the phone.

I quickly learned that her call was simply to ask me a few more questions so that we could have a more productive session on Thursday. She wanted to know if I had ever seen the psychiatrist that my old therapist talked about and that I had written about in one of my session recaps. I explained that since I had found a physician, there was no need for the psychiatrist to write my prescription for Zoloft. She also wanted to learn a few more things about the techniques that my old therapist had been using so that she could better understand what was working and not working for me.

I took a deep breath. First, I was floored that she cared. I couldn't believe she was worrying about this—a major departure from my previous doctor-patient relationship. Second, I was impressed that she was willing to learn. She was comfortable hearing a few specifics about what my other therapist had done. She was pushing her own professional ego aside for my recovery. That meant everything to me.

We talked for about half an hour. I could tell she was taking notes. She finished by asking again how I was doing. I said I was doing okay. I said the word "okay" in a way that made it clear that I wasn't perfect. She paused…and then said that it was alright for me to say anything to her that I wanted to say. I was a little confused about what she meant. I asked if she meant I could say something specific about her or that I could say something about myself. She said it didn't matter, that I could say anything I was thinking and that it was alright. I realized that she could sense something. I thought for a second. Then I said that I was really anxious. I told her that ever since I stopped the EMDR, ever since I had started the new therapist search, I had begun to feel very uneasy. For months I felt like I was improving and then all of the sudden, I was dead in the water. I told her I really liked her so far, but that anything in my voice that seemed hesitant was only my need to get back to work on my recovery. She understood. We were on the same page.

I then told her that I didn't want to be in therapy, but that I wanted to, as quickly as possible, resume my life, my career and this hiccup was slowing that down. She laughed out loud when I told her I didn't want to be in therapy—I could tell she was not used to that kind of candor—but it was necessary for her to know my plan. I wanted to be on top of this as quickly as possible. She got it. Now we were even more on the same page. She said, almost reluctantly, that she was thinking that maybe we should speed up my start to EMDR, that she was feeling more confident that I had moved on from my old therapist. Sweet. We ended the call and again I felt like I had the right therapist for me. All pistons were firing.

Since that call I've thought more about why I said the word "okay" like I had. I didn't explain it to her in enough detail. The truth is that I'm doing less than okay. I'm hanging by a thread. I'm barely keeping it together. I can tell that I've moved significantly backwards in my recovery in order to find the right therapist. Stopping EMDR, midway through my treatment, was taking its toll on me. I'm white knuckling like I was before. I'm doubting my progress, my optimism is slipping, and I'm feeling that spiral again. I'm not in control right now. My deep breaths aren't deep enough. I am relying on alcohol to relax me. I need to get back to where I once was.

I can write every day in this journal and force myself to think through things and stay focused, to keep my mind pointed in the right direction. The problem lies in how I feel. I can't control that with my mind. My mind can tell my white knuckles to go away, but they just sit there, staring at me, all white-knuckly, waiting for something more powerful to change them. I wish they listened. I need to get back to work on my recovery.

Therapy Session 13: July 1, 2010

Yesterday was America's two hundred and thirty-fourth birthday. Flags were flying, ribs were smoking, and laughter was echoing through backyards across the country. Yesterday I wished I hadn't been born. Instead of celebrating our country's independence, I was busy fighting for my own independence—the independence from myself.

A few days earlier, Thursday, July first, was my third therapy session with my new therapist. I was annoyed the second I woke up. I weaved through traffic on my way to work, pissed off at everything within a few car lengths. The little things were bothering me again. I was completely on edge. I had been that way for a while. I entered her office and took a seat. It was good to see her warm smile and hear her genuine interest and mutual respect. At least I had that going for me.

When she asked how I was doing, I told her that I had been struggling. I was hanging by a thread. Anxious, agitated, stressed. My chest pains were back again and my deep breaths were just shy of however deep they needed to be to keep me calm. She asked why I thought I was on edge. I told her that I felt like I needed to make some progress. I felt that, with every passing day, I was treading water less and less effectively. I needed to move forward. She understood which was good. I told her that I thought EMDR was helping and then all of a sudden I stopped improving when I stopped EMDR and had to change therapists.

We talked for a while longer about my theories. She nodded her head more. I kept talking, pretty much dominating the conversation. She kept listening. Finally, she said, "Okay, here's the deal." Then, in a direct but at the same time considerate way, she told me that what I was saying was wrong. It wasn't that I had stopped improving. It was that I was beating myself up for not improving faster. Hmm. Interesting. I quickly shut up and thought about what she said.

For the next few minutes she took me through her opinion, firing holes through my self-evaluation like any professional would. I couldn't disagree with her. She made me understand that I was trying to control my recovery and that never works. I needed to slow down, I needed to put less pressure on myself to recover quickly, and I needed to respect the process more. No more Type A approach to therapy; it just doesn't work.

Then she explained why she thought I was doing what I was doing. She thought it tied all the way back to my childhood, and she didn't think it was the sexual abuse that caused it. She said it was due to the way I've been conditioned. I've been conditioned to excel—always. I was conditioned to not accept any sort of mediocrity and to push myself harder and harder. In some ways, this mentality is good. It benefitted me in the military and in business school, but this self-judging, never-satisfied, Cro-Magnon approach to life and success can be self-destructive if not managed properly, especially when applied to therapy. She was right. I knew she was right. I was at war with myself and I was losing.

She thought that it was important for me to get in touch with my optimism. I needed to shed this layer of stress of micro-managing my recovery, and look at how far I have come in a few short months. I needed to tap into that optimism I felt a month or so ago. We set up the EMDR machine and worked for about thirty minutes on finding that optimism, remembering it, and holding on to it. We finished and I felt a slight improvement. I don't know if it was the EMDR or if it was her shaking me out of my funk by calling me out for being too hard on myself while linking it to my childhood and distancing it from who I really was. Whatever it was, it was helpful.

The past several days since that session have been up and down. My entire family was in Colorado this weekend, everyone enjoying a retirement home that my parents had just built—their dream home. I couldn't go. I'm just not ready for that yet and I was mad at myself for not being well enough to go. It took me until today to realize that I was being unnecessarily hard on myself for not being there.

It's time to claim my independence from myself, from that version of myself who is never satisfied. While I may not have been launching bottle rockets from my butt crack and shot-gunning Bud Light until the wee hours this weekend, I was somewhere on my road to recovery. The least I can do is take my foot off the pedal and celebrate how far I've come.

Therapy Session 14: July 6, 2010

On this Tuesday, I found myself less concerned with how my therapy session would go in the afternoon as I was with how my conversation would go with my old therapist. She had finally returned from her uber-vacation and I could finally talk with her about my decision to cut bait and find a new therapist. I was a little nervous, but convicted. I called her office early in the day, around 9:30, as I drove to one of my sites. I had about a thirty minute drive in front of me so it was perfect. Her receptionist said she was in the office and available, so she put me on hold so she could

146

transfer me. Twenty-four minutes later, still on hold, I hung up. At some point during the day, she called me back and left a message noting that I was not on the line when she came to the phone. Whatever. When we finally connected, it was about 3:45 p.m., and I was getting my head prepared for my 5 p.m. appointment with my new therapist. This conversation was so defective, it deserves to be repeated word for word:

Me: Hello?

Old Therapist: Hello, Chris. We finally connected. What's going on?

Me: Yes, we finally did. Welcome back. I'm not sure if your receptionist mentioned it to you, but I have decided to take my treatment in a different direction.

Old Therapist: Yes, she did, but she didn't say why?

Me: Well, for several reasons. One, you never called me and explained the mix-up that last session when I showed up but I was no longer on your schedule. Then, when I called, the receptionist implied that it was my fault. To top it off, she then told me that you were going on vacation for three weeks so my next appointment wasn't going to be for five weeks. I never heard from you throughout all of this. You never told me about your vacation. None of this felt right to me, so I decided to see what other options I have for treatment.

Old Therapist: Well. First of all, I thought I apologized to you in the waiting room that day. Second, it wasn't my receptionist that you talked to, it was the other receptionist. She's not good. She's actually a bitch. And third, you should have seen the sign posted in my office that said I would be on vacation for those dates. Did you not read the sign, Chris?

Me: Are you kidding me? You can't expect your clients to look around for important information like that without explaining to them that you'll be gone, that they'll be on their own, without treatment, for a long period of time.

Old Therapist: I was available by email. While I was on vacation, I emailed with all of my patients.

Me: What? You've never once given me your email. I had no idea I was allowed to email you. And if I did, I would have. Also, I'm not new to the professional world, even if the receptionist isn't yours, she's coming into contact with your patients, and that is a direct reflection of you as a doctor. I won't accept that answer.

Old Therapist: Well, I'm sorry you feel that way, Chris. Come on in for another session and we'll talk this through. This is obviously related to your recovery and your condition. We can uncover why you feel this way.

Me: I know why I feel this way. As for coming in, I'll consider it, but not until after I've met with other therapists. I've decided to move on for now. I'd also like to request a copy of my records.

Old Therapist: Ok, then. Let me just take a look at your chart really quickly. Well, look at that. You started with severe PTSD, a score of forty-five. That's really severe PTSD. And, based on the last assessment, we have lowered that significantly. So, you know how the saying goes, 'If it ain't broke, don't fix it.'

Me: Well, with all due respect, it is broken, and I'm fixing it. I'd like to get a copy of my records.

Old Therapist: I don't release records without doing a final recap, so you'll have to come in to talk through and close out your file. I don't mind not charging you for that last session.

Me: I'm sorry. That doesn't work for me. I'll just move forward and be in touch if I feel up for a final session. Thank you for everything you've done for me. I appreciate what you've done to help me.

Old Therapist: Okay, Chris. Good luck and stay in touch.

This dialogue may seem like it was embellished. It wasn't. The condescending approach, thick with old-school pretense and bullshit is what I have been dealing with for months. The painful conversation was a great way for me to feel complete closure on that relationship. I felt great after I hung up the phone. I got everything off my chest and I stood my ground when I had to. Patient Frankenstein has officially kicked through the wall and moved on.

I drove to my therapist's office feeling good about the phone call, but the heat was fucking killing me and I was annoyed at the terrible traffic. Does anyone have coolant in their radiators or are we all going to break down in the middle of the road?

I entered my new therapist's office right on time. Five o'clock on the nose. I sat down and we caught up with small talk. She asked how I was doing and I told her that I was up and down. Overall, I said that I thought our last session had really helped me. I told her how I had really focused on giving myself a break and that I realized that she was right. She said she just caught me smiling for the first time since she's known me.

She asked if I had been in touch with my old therapist. I took her through a quick recap and mentioned that I had severed that relationship. I think she was as relieved as I was that there were no more ties to Dr. Bitchface. I said that I was going to leave my records there, and she understood. She confirmed that we'd be fine without them.

She asked why I was down over the weekend and I took her through what I thought. I was hard on myself about not being well enough to be in Colorado. Suddenly, something jumped into my head that I hadn't even thought about. I remembered that, when I first met with my old therapist, she told me that I should be feeling considerably better by July Fourth. I completely forgot about that. I told her that maybe this was why I was struggling, because I felt like I hadn't achieved that goal. She confirmed what I was thinking and told me that setting any sort of date or timeline for my recovery was not something that a therapist should ever do. Everyone moves at their own pace. I took a deep breath. That felt right.

She asked how my wife was doing. I told her that we had a fight over the weekend but we had talked through it. My wife had decided to see a therapist as well, simply to have someone professional to talk with as we go through this process together. My therapist agreed that it was a great idea. She also noted that every time I talk about my wife, I play with my wedding band.

Then she said something that startled me. She said that she wasn't sure what to do next. Huh? Whatchu talkin' 'bout, Willis? She explained it further. She said that my case was very complicated. Obviously, I had the sexual abuse to work through, but I also had another layer of conditioning that she needed to work with. I was terribly hard on myself, which was hurting my recovery, so she had to work with that carefully. My way of managing myself was off. We talked for a while on what to do, and we both agreed that we should move forward with EMDR on the next sexual abuse memory, and then deviate to handle the conditioning part when it calls for it. She also said that we could fit me in for an EMDR session on Thursday—only two days away—as long as I was comfortable with meeting twice in one week. My affirmative cut her off.

I really respect the way that she showed me her indecision. She made it a joint decision (or at least she made me feel like it was a joint decision) on our course of action.

Before we wrapped up, she asked how I felt about myself as a boy, specifically, how I felt about that boy now? Did I feel compassion? Did I feel shame? I told her that it was difficult to say. I felt sad. But I felt differently about the seven-year-old boy than I did about the nine-year-old boy. I felt that the nine-year-old boy wasn't strong enough to tell anyone, and that the seven-year-old boy was taken advantage of by an adult. She found that interesting. What it did was provide us a starting point for our next EMDR session. There was a clear line between how I felt about myself after the first time I was abused, and how I felt about myself after subsequent incidents occurred.

I said goodbye and left feeling great. I felt a little proud of myself and optimistic about the future. I handled my former therapist well and I now had a good hold on where I was heading. The heat and humidity was ridiculous, but I barely noticed it. I caught myself smiling.

Boneless Chicken Ranch: July 8, 2010

The Far Side was my favorite comic growing up. I couldn't get enough of the overtly ridiculous humor. My favorite of Gary Larson's creations was the Boneless Chicken Ranch. A ranch, strewn with literally boneless, amoeba-like chickens, just hanging around. It was stupid, but for some reason it always got me.

Today I had a long and painful EMDR session with my new therapist. I started out strong. I ended up a snotting, exhausted, boneless chicken, which is where I am now.

Tomorrow, I'll recap my session. Today, I'll just hang around.

Therapy Session 15: July 8, 2010

I have been avoiding this post. Kind of like how I avoid a pile of dirty laundry, walking past, trying not to make eye contact, wishing it would go away. Both are necessary; good for me and those around me. Thursday's session was the first real EMDR session with my new therapist, and it covered the most terrifying part of my past, when I was nine, the four months or so that we lived with Jack. A big pile of laundry.

I didn't sleep well the night before. I was up for a few hours in the middle of the night. I'd been through this before. What was different this time was that I had an understanding of why I was awake and this allowed me to tell my wife in the morning what was going on and why I wasn't in the mood to talk. I was anxious about the memories I knew we would tackle that afternoon.

This was the first time I had two appointments in one week. My new therapist thought it was alright to have multiple sessions per week. She said that once you start working on a new memory, you can continue with that memory in the same week as long as you are stable. Luckily, my insurance accepted unlimited sessions.

We started the session on time. I sat down and she asked the standard "How are you?" question. I've realized that I need to answer this honestly with her, not the pre-meditated "good" response I give most people. I told her I was really anxious about what we were about to do. She knew what I meant. I also told her that my old therapist had sent me an email apologizing more completely for our misunderstanding. I guess she had thought about it more and felt the need to apologize. It felt good to get some sort of real apology, instead of a mind-game about what happened. I told my therapist that I wasn't sure if I wanted to respond. She said for me to give it some time before I made a decision.

We started EMDR pretty quickly. Her thought was that we should save as much time as possible for EMDR, that the twenty minute mini-sessions my other therapist had administered weren't long enough. She asked me to relax. I spent about two minutes settling down. I was better at relaxing myself than I used to be. Then, she handed me a laminated card that had a scale of anxiety. The left extreme, one, being relaxed, the right extreme, ten, being extremely stressed. It essentially was a graphic form of the SUDS scale that my other therapist used. On the back of the card were about fifty phrases for expressing feelings. "I feel out of control" and "I feel like I have nowhere to go." It was helpful for people who had a difficult time expressing what they were feeling. She said I could use the card if I wanted, but that I didn't need to if I could express myself without the card.

We jumped in. The black box with the lights was set up in front of me. Eyes closed, I drifted to 1983, stepping foot into the house I never allow myself to think about. I was in the basement. Our family slept in the basement. My parents on the fold-out-couch in the living room with the television and my sister and I in sleeping bags on cots in the laundry room. We would sometimes sleep in the back bedroom but not always. I was in my sleeping bag. Waiting. Anticipating Jack's ritual of coming downstairs to make sure I was sleeping naked. Somehow he knew to come down when my sister wasn't in bed yet. He sat on my cot. Said a few creepy things and asked me to show him that I was naked. I wasn't. I tried to fight it the first few times. He told me that I needed to listen to him. I was very uncomfortable.

My therapist told me to open my eyes and look at the lights. Sixty seconds later my eyes were closed. I was getting ready for school. Just before leaving with my sister and mom, I remembered that Jack told me I had to wake him up in the morning. I thought it was odd, but I did what I was told. I cracked the door to the bedroom, my grandma asleep on the far side. Jack awoke and opened the comforter and stood up. He was naked. I froze. He walked towards me and in a quiet voice he said "Good boy. See, this is how men should sleep." I couldn't move. His naked body within inches of my face. It looked like a snake. I was embarrassed and uncomfortable. Two minutes later, I told my mom that Grandpa was naked when I woke him up. This was the only time I reached out for help. I didn't say enough—it wasn't enough for my mom to know what I was saying. I tried but I was too embarrassed and ashamed.

My therapist asked me to open my eyes, look at the lights. Eyes closed again. I found myself in the kitchen, fixing dinner and setting the table with my mom and grandma. We were eating in the dining room, which was adjacent to the kitchen and Jack's office. Jack called my name from his office. I walked in. He was behind the desk, only visible from the chest up. He told me to shut the door. He told me to walk around the desk and sit on his lap. I did, reluctantly. He grabbed my hand and placed it between his legs. To my surprise he was exposed. He made me touch him for a while. I pulled away; I couldn't take it anymore. I smelled Vaseline lotion. My face turned red. I looked away and finally was able to free myself from his grasp. He muttered something about it being alright and our secret. I walked back into the kitchen, disgusted and confused. I tried to blend in. I walked into the pantry and up the pantry stairs towards the attic. I sat on a step in the dark. I didn't move. I was alone.

I opened my eyes again and watched the lights. My eyes were filled with tears. I closed them and found myself at dinner. I couldn't hide on the stairs anymore. I had to sit next to him and watch him eat dinner and converse as though nothing was wrong. He even asked me what was wrong. My dad gave me hard time for not eating. He elevated his voice, threatening that I wouldn't be able to leave the table until my plate was clear. My mom kept asking me to cheer up. I wasn't being social enough. Jack grinned at me. I was trapped.

The memories continued throughout the house. A blend of days and nights, specific actions and perverted conversations alone with Jack. I couldn't escape. I was so young and so defenseless. I hated how I felt. I had to pretend like I was okay to keep everyone happy. What was wrong with me?

I opened my eyes for the last time and she said to take a deep breath. Tears were flowing down my face. I hadn't thought about that house in detail since I left it. I could smell everything. I could see the carpet and feel the pain. She told me that I was so young and innocent, that this wasn't my fault. I agreed. She asked another question and suddenly I was hit by a wave of uncontrollable emotion. I fell apart. She sat quietly. I couldn't speak.

Once I composed myself, we talked more about what I was feeling then and we worked on some of the incorrect thoughts that I had. I couldn't tell if I felt any better. All I knew is that I was out of control, exhausted, and wishing I could escape.

My therapist then said something about my technique. She asked if I was visualizing anything while I watched the lights. I told her no. I said that my old therapist said it didn't matter if I visualized anything while I watched the lights. My new therapist disagreed completely. She said that I really needed to be visualizing and thinking about memories while I watched the lights, that I was doing it backwards and it probably wasn't as effective as it could be. Uh…really? Okay. Once again, my frustration with my old therapist surfaced. My new therapist told me that if I was having a hard time visualizing while I looked at the lights, we could use vibrating paddles to stimulate the left and right sides of my brain while my eyes were closed. I didn't have that option before, so I said that would be great. She pulled out two small paddles—one in my left hand, one in my right. They vibrated left, then right at about the same pace as the lights moved left and right. She said it would allow me to reprocess without using my eyes. My brain would be stimulated while I had my eyes closed.

We needed to wrap up the session. It was already five minutes after the hour. She said there were two people waiting. She told me that my next few days would be tough. She said that we still had work to do on this memory, so until then, I'd be filled with thoughts and memories of what happened. I'm glad she warned me. She offered that I could come back the next day if I really felt bad and we could talk through more. I said I'd let her know, but if not, I'd see her next week. I just wanted to get out of there. I was spent.

I said goodbye and opened the door. My eyes red and puffy. Immediately, I made eye contact with a man sitting in the waiting room. He looked away, confirming that I looked like shit. I wished I hadn't looked at him. I dragged myself to my car and headed home. I could barely think.

Since Thursday, I've been in a funk. I can't escape the thoughts of that house. But, I'm alive. I made it through that session and this journal entry. One load of laundry at a time.

Extra Medium: July 11, 2010

Given that this country invented the Super Big Gulp, I wonder why we haven't invented the extra Medium t-shirt yet. I bet, every now and then, someone could benefit from a shirt that's just a little more medium. Medium is a fantastic size with great heritage, but what about those times when you need to take things just a little more medium? What then? Large and Small both flaunt their improvement—XXL and XS to name a few. But, Medium doesn't take that extra step. It enjoys a simple solitude, content with its place in the world. Maybe there's an unwritten rule among t-shirt manufacturers to never mess with the sacred Medium, like in baseball, you don't talk to the pitcher in the middle of a no-hitter. Nobody would dare try and make the Medium t-shirt...more mediumer. Still, with all of its under-improvement, the Medium enjoys great success.

As I work through this long and unpredictable recovery process, I have begun to accept my under-improvement. I can't do anything to make myself more than what I am right now, or make myself feel better than how I feel. Respecting this process is really important for me right now. Doing this removes a layer of stress that I don't need. It took hearing it from a few people, not just my therapist, but from people who have taken a journey similar to mine and are now looking back with respect for the long recovery process. It isn't pretty. It's medium, and it isn't getting any mediumer.

My Truman Show: July 13, 2010

This week falls somewhere in between sneezing with your mouth full and eating rice with one chopstick. Not cool. It seems like the world is playing a prank on me. Okay, that's it. Everybody come out from behind the curtains. Joke's over. Seriously, who nibbled through eighty-nine percent of my shoelace? And, who made the lady in front of me keep swiping her driver's license through the credit card reader when I was late for work? I'm waiting for a stage light to fall out of the sky and for a director to turn on a microphone and start talking to me from behind the clouds. Am I starring in "The Truman Show?"

I sat there in traffic this morning. I was late to my first delivery. By that point, I had lost track of the day's nerve-provoking mementos. At least I was at the front of the line of traffic. I sat waiting for the construction worker in the orange vest to spin the little sign from the red "STOP" to the orange "SLOW." Just spin the damn sign, man. Finally. I was given the orange sign and accelerated, veering left into the single lane of traffic. I drove about ten feet before I noticed the sedan coming right at me at forty miles per hour. We both swerved, luckily in opposite directions. I narrowly avoided the cement barrier—the same cement barrier whose only purpose seemed to be to prevent me from skidding into the freshly planted grass and going home without a giant cement scrape down the side of my van. I swallowed whatever organs had become lodged in my throat, and slammed on my brakes to figure out why the man in the orange vest slept through sign spinning class. The incident didn't bother him much. The warm glass of bong water he enjoyed this morning no doubt kept his emotions in check.

The rest of the day followed suit and now I'm still trying to catch my breath, keeping myself busy enough not to think. I've watered the plants so many times I've altered the water table. I've taught my dog, Bailey, every trick I know—he is iPhone proficient. I've gone through my bookshelf looking for new things to read. Turns out I have seven "Dummies" books. I wonder how many "Dummies" books I have to buy before Barnes & Noble actually labels me a Dummy on my account. I'd rather not know. I really have no reason to write, other than to get some thoughts out of my head. That, and to prove that I'm smarter than Bailey.

These kinds of days come and go. They feel like a test or at least a reminder that I could be in worse shape. So, I'll keep knuckling my way through it and I'm looking forward to waking up tomorrow morning and feeling a little different. Well, assuming the director with the microphone likes that storyline.

Therapy Session 16: July 16, 2010

When I used to run a lot of triathlons, I would often overheat. My body, in an effort to keep me safe, would start shutting down if I didn't have enough salt or water or nourishment. I would start to feel weak, then light-headed, and then, if those warning signs weren't acknowledged, my body would start turning off important sections, like my brain—an essential section of the body for triathlon. I blacked out once in a race, collapsing to the ground and losing my sight. After that, I realized that my body was in control. No matter how badly I tried to keep pushing, I needed to listen to what it said.

Yesterday was the first session where my body failed me. I had to stop about half way through the session or risk my body shutting down important sections, like the ever-important "vomit control" section.

We started the session a few minutes late, but got right to work. I caught her up on my last week. I explained how bad last weekend was, and then took her through my gradual improvement as the week went on. She was glad to hear that I had been on an upward swing after the difficult EMDR session the Thursday before.

We started another EMDR session. We discussed how I needed to think through memories as I followed the lights with my eyes. Before, I was clearing my mind as I watched the lights, which apparently is the opposite of what I was supposed to do. Doing this properly would help me better re-process the memories, stimulating my brain from left to right hemisphere and back.

We went back to 1983. I was sitting on the basement couch with Jack. He had his arm around me, playing with my ear and whispering odd comments. We were watching "The McLaughlin Group." He always wanted me to watch with him but it bored the hell out of me. He had his hand on my upper leg. He tried to put my hand on his leg. I was incredibly uncomfortable. I could smell him, his cheap musk aftershave. Someone opened the upstairs door to the basement and walked down the basement stairs. He removed his hand from my leg.

My therapist turned on the lights. I watched for about two minutes as I thought about how uncomfortable I felt with Jack. I remembered quickly finding a reason to talk with whoever walked in the room, my own version of a cry for help. My therapist stopped the lights. I took a deep breath.

I went back to the house. We had just eaten dinner. It was dark outside. Jack had to go to the drug store to buy something and he asked if I wanted to come with him. I politely said no. Then, Jack went to my mom and asked her if it would be okay. She said that it would, but it was up to me. He kept pushing until I relented. I knew he just wanted me alone again.

We got into the car and went to the store. I had the feeling that he didn't really need anything; he was just trying to get me alone with him. We left the store, got back in the car, and started driving home. He asked if I wanted to drive. I declined. He kept pushing. I didn't know what to do. He pulled over to the side of the street. It was a darker than normal street, void of street lights. The ground was wet from rain earlier. Out of the corner of my eye I could see him fidgeting with his pants around the zipper. I wasn't sure what he had done. He told me to sit on his lap. I said I was fine not driving, that I didn't think I could handle the wet streets. He quickly side-stepped my argument. A few seconds later I was on his lap. He smelled different, like lotion. He put my right hand on the steering wheel. He took my other hand and put it in his lap. As we continued with EMDR, I started having memories that I never knew existed. I found myself fully engaged in touching him—very specific details of how much we did were surfacing—his hand directing my hand as we went. I was in hell. I was so uncomfortable. I wanted to scream. I felt like crying.

As I sat in her office, staring forward, tears rolling down my face, I started to feel very uneasy. Within another minute of thinking, I started to feel nauseous. It got worse. I could tell I was about ten seconds from vomiting. I told her I had to stop, that I wasn't feeling well. She ran to the corner and grabbed a trash can for me to vomit into. The room was turning white; I was sweating those cold sweats. I forced myself to think about something else for a few moments and slowly, I gained control. I wasn't going to be sick.

My therapist agreed that we should stop. We were only halfway through the session, so we needed to talk about something else. We decided to talk about my family and focused on how many people Jack had impacted in our family.

I explained the dramatic details of my real grandfather's death, and Jack's immediate marriage to my grandmother, and how he, just after they married, moved the family to Canada. My dad didn't go because he was in college at that point, but his thirteen-year-old brother and three-year-old sister were forced to go. They visited their own hell in Canada.

At the end of the session, my therapist told me that when my mind wanders back to that memory this week, to try and visualize the memory like I'm watching it on a moving train, that I'm not on the train and I'm seeing it outside of my body. I knew what she was saying; I told her I'd try.

At that point in the session, I had controlled my nausea. I wasn't feeling great, but I was stable. I was exhausted. We said goodbye and I walked out into the parking lot feeling like I was on another planet. How could my mind have hidden those details from me for so long? How could my body know that I needed to stop EMDR? I felt weird knowing that I had been so involved with touching him. I didn't know what to think about that.

Today, I feel better than last Saturday, which was surprising, considering how difficult the session was. I have been thinking about that triathlon when I blacked out and how my body knew what was right for me. It knew that I needed to stop running, so my body made it happen. In this therapy session, my body had come through for me. It somehow knew that digging further into that night in the car wasn't a good idea just yet. I needed to take it slower. So, the memory is sort of percolating right now and I'm okay.

Therapy Session 17: July 23, 2010

Last Thursday night, my wife and I drove up to Baltimore to meet some friends for an Oriole's baseball game. It was a long way to go to see baseball's most win-challenged team, but it was fun to get out of town for a night. The game went as expected. My Oriole's were trailing five to zero heading into the eighth inning. This made it easier for my wife and I to hit the road before the game ended for our three-hour drive back to Richmond. We said goodbye to our friends and walked up the aisle, past the empty seats.

Just as we reached the top of the steps, we heard the remaining crowd cheering. We turned around to see a teenager, most likely out-of-his-gourd drunk, running freely through left-center field, a big smile on his face as he soaked up the applause. He high-fived the second baseman. He jogged towards third. At this point, you could start to see reality setting in. The 'this seemed like a good idea a few minutes ago' look on his face was evident as a policeman met him at third. The kid touched the bag, and then made a break back towards second. Gutsy move. The crowd went nuts. For the next five minutes we laughed at the circus-like attempt to wrangle the half-baked teenager. Eventually, after embarrassing all nine cops with his drunken, yet surprisingly nimble moves, his endurance wavered. He stopped, and finally walked towards the cops. The crowd cringed as he accepted his fate, which ended up being a little more forceful than necessary. But, despite the pain, the kid kept smiling, clearly proud of his accomplishment. Those five minutes were the best five minutes of the game.

This week started rough, but it slowly improved, despite last week's painful therapy session. I started to relax and feel optimistic, like I was going somewhere. But in the back of my mind, I knew I was no different than that teenager, enjoying my five minutes of fame. I knew I had to accept my fate. I had to go back to my therapist's office and think about that time in the car with Jack.

I entered her office and sat down. The crowd cringed. I knew what I had to do. The cops had won. My fun was over.

She started by asking how I was feeling. I gave her the honest answer—that my week started off really rough. Last weekend was difficult, but by the time Wednesday hit, I was actually feeling good. She was glad to hear that but wanted to learn more about why I was feeling down over the weekend. I told her that I was feeling strange about learning that there were memories I was unaware of, that it was frustrating for me to know there could be more. That thinking about a night in the car with Jack made me uneasy and it carried over into my weekend.

She said she understood, but she kept pushing for some reason, trying to figure out if that was the only reason I was down. After about ten minutes of discussion, we arrived at the real answer. Unbeknownst to me, I was beating myself up for having to quit halfway through the last session. I felt like I had failed, that I wasn't strong enough to endure the entire EMDR session. I really didn't know I was doing this, but it was clear to her that this is what was happening. Hmm. Am I really being that hard on myself? I guess I am.

At this point, we were about twenty minutes into the session, and we had to decide whether or not to go back to the memories and start EMDR. I really didn't want to, but I told her that I would if she felt it was the right thing to do. She said that it was, so we set up the black box with the lights. Reality was setting in.

Just before we started, we engaged in a conversation about who I was. This led to a thirty-minute discussion about my true self. I was telling her that the abuse had made me question who I really was, that I thought maybe it changed me. I had read about this. These sorts of thoughts are normal for an abuse victim, questioning everything as you go through recovery. We went back and forth about this. I don't think we really got anywhere, but in the back of my mind, I was glad that I didn't have to dig into my memories of Jack for the time being. I guess subconsciously, I derailed the EMDR session because I wasn't ready. That was becoming clear to me as we continued. At the end of the session, she mentioned a type of treatment that she had used at times to help people who seemed lost about who they naturally were. I told her I would consider using this treatment, so she gave me a website so I could check it out.

Just as most things in life, my session had taken an unexpected turn. I didn't spend the session digging through the abuse memories, and instead, we took an introspective look at Chris, the person. Instead of accepting my fate and being slammed to the turf by nine police officers, I was allowed to step back and slow down. While I had prepared myself for the beat-down, and prepared myself to force a smile as it happened, I was glad we didn't force the EMDR session. I needed to take a deeper breath.

Mandatory Recall: July 28, 2010

Nothing beats finding out that the fruit you've been eating, the workout water bottle you've been drinking from, and the deodorant you've been using, have been increasing the chances of your body developing cancer, an auto-immune disease, and a number of genetic disorders that could one day affect the children you've barely thought about creating.

I was reading an article the other day that brought these fine facts to my attention, and within a few hours, it had me smelling like an un-deodorized armpit and sanitizing my hands every few minutes while designing a new backyard garden. I'm waiting to find out that this little portable machine I'm typing on is assisting in the growth of back hair…if I had back hair…which I don't of course. What?

The amazing thing about the article was that it talked about how difficult it is to enact a mandatory FDA or FTC recall on products that "point towards" consumer danger. Too often, by the time a recall or warning is issued, the damage is done: the kids have already chewed on the toys for months; the dangerous compounds have made their way into their bodies. All because nobody in charge of warning the public wanted to be a whistle-blower, or an over-reactor, or dead wrong and risk getting fired. It's a shame we don't err more on the side of caution and let companies work out the kinks with the government should an incorrect recall occur. I guess that's big business, and in an unstable economy, I guess a few big mistakes could have drastic economic consequences. But a mandatory recall is necessary sometimes. It can keep us safe. It's not very easy to do, but sometimes it's vital.

So yesterday, something horrible happened at work. One of my fellow drivers was backing his van toward the loading dock to unload his empty coolers after a long day of deliveries. He backed his van just shy of the loading dock door. He put the van in park, and then got out of the van in order to call the security guard via intercom to notify him to open the dock door. At some point, he jumped back into the van, and just as he did, the van lurched backwards with his one foot in the van, and the other still on the ground. As the van lurched, the open door knocked him over and he was thrown under the vehicle, which proceeded to run over the left side of his body before slamming into the loading dock door. Chaos ensued. He somehow pulled himself up and put the van back in park before falling to the ground in pain. I happened to return from my deliveries about thirty seconds later to find him laying on the ground, buckled over, the loading dock door crushed by the back of the van.

Long story short, the driver is going to be alright. He got incredibly lucky and should make a full recovery. The fact that he is alive is a miracle.

Even though I was a non-factor in the accident or his treatment, arriving at the scene not knowing if he was still alive was one of those adrenaline-filled, skin-tingling moments that will stay with me for a while. I've spent a lot of time today thinking about that, which has made me think about how lucky I am to be here. However painful it is at times, I have a lot going for me. I'm alive and I'm better than I was twelve months ago.

This month marks one year of my recovery process, so rather than just forget about my positive thoughts today, I'm going to go ahead and institute a mandatory recall of the crap I've been holding on to for the past year. Those negative beliefs have been toxic, and they're being replaced by much healthier, consumer-friendly thoughts. So I've created an abbreviated list of categories where I already see improvement:

> Category: Who I was as a child.
> Recalled Product: A participant in sexual behavior. Weak and not worthy.
> Revised Product: An innocent victim, now recovering and gaining strength.
>
> Category: How I think about relationships with other people.

Recalled Product: Nobody can get close to me. If they like me, they are flawed, easily mislead.
Revised Product: Honest with myself and with other people. If they like me, they like who I am.

Category: Who I see in the mirror.
Recalled Product: A fake. A liar who's overweight and ugly. Two hundred twenty-five pounds in July 2009.
Revised Product: A fighter. Not overweight, just sturdy. Two hundred eight pounds in July 2010.

Category: How I disagree with my wife.
Recalled Product: Short-fused, angry. My frustrations outweigh her voice.
Revised Product: Calm, balanced, fair. Respectful of her differing opinion.

Category: My thoughts on therapy and recovery.
Recalled Product: Therapy is for people who can't manage themselves.
Revised Product: I'm in need of help. By surrendering, it somehow puts me back in control.

I'm stopping there, but looking at these five categories, I am starting to see significant progress. Life-altering progress and it's only been a year. Somehow, seeing how close my co-worker came to disaster yesterday was enough to make me look back and appreciate what I have right now. I can't let this moment pass. I have a great wife, parents, siblings, in-laws and friends. It must be so much harder for abuse victims without support. I finally have an air conditioner in my car and in my house. Our furnace works. I still have absolutely zero back hair. The dining room has a table, and I've made a lot of progress in my recovery. We never know how long we're here, so my taking a look back and seeing how far I've come—how many toxic products I've recalled in twelve months—is exactly what I needed to do today.

Therapy Session 18: July 29, 2010

The majority of my life has been spent listening to everyone's gut but my own. And since I was lucky enough to be surrounded by very smart, passionate, and opinionated people, who all did very well by their guts, I had plenty of help formulating a strong opinion. Unfortunately, that opinion was never mine.

One challenge that incest survivors have is that that they often learn to ignore their gut at a very young age. Someone took their own voice from them, someone they trusted. Now they don't trust anyone or themselves. They conclude that their guts aren't up to par with others' for some reason. Others around them are confident and strong, while they are stupid and weak.

I felt that way. So, what did I do? I faked it. Shit, I didn't know any better. I didn't even know I was faking it. I became incredibly good at hearing other people's opinions, suggestions, warnings, hints, complaints and then smashing them together to make a decision "for myself." And since I was good at acting, I knew how to give everyone what they needed, with a smile on my face so it seemed like it came from me. For a little while it worked; even I was buying into my own "confidence." But deep down I knew it wasn't mine. I wasn't listening to my own gut. My gut was telling me to run, to go do something that I needed, to stop listening to everyone and acknowledge who I was: A survivor of incest, and a believer in a better way.

I woke up on Thursday anxious about my therapy session that afternoon. In our last session we had talked extensively about who I was, and at the end of the session, my therapist mentioned a type of therapy that helped some of her patients who were searching for answers. She said it was an alternative treatment called Human Design. She had taken some courses in Human Design and she found it helpful for some. I didn't think much of it when she told me, but when I got home that night, I started doing some online research.

Human Design was developed by a man who had a vision while he lived in a mud hut on a small island in the Mediterranean Sea. Originally from Canada, he worked in the business world before disappearing in 1983 to find himself. In 1987, after eight days and nights of listening to the "Voice," he developed Human Design and re-emerged to share his enlightenment with the world. A combination of astrology and spiritual science, it uses birth dates and birth times to generate a chart for every person. The complex diagram is used to help people better understand themselves and how they fit into the world.

It was way out there, to say the least, and my therapist warned me that it wasn't for everyone. After my research, it was clear that this was not something for me. I could tell that she believed that it worked for some people, and I trusted her, but I was conflicted because my gut was telling me not to go down that road.

I walked into her office, found my chair and sat down. My mind was more fixed on the Human Design conversation than it was any EMDR treatment. She asked how I was doing and I gave her the standard answer— nothing too much, just "I'm doing pretty well." She made light of the situation by saying "I'm just glad you came back." It was necessary levity at an anxious moment, and it allowed me to segue into the conversation about Human Design.

I started by telling her that I thought it was interesting. She could sense my hesitation, and she followed by saying she knew it was way, way out there. But she said that some of her patients really found it valuable, so it was something she offered as an option. She asked if I found out my time of birth, an integral part to developing a Rave Chart that would eventually unlock vital information about my "design." I told her that I did find my time of birth and that I developed my chart and learned about it. It was interesting and a very complicated process of figuring out how I was wired at birth, which was the necessary step before untangling that wiring and "de-conditioning" myself from thirty-plus years of programming. I'm an introspective person, and a science geek, so I found the idea fascinating.

The primary problem, I told her, was that aside from the radical and fruity nature of the material, I got a really bad vibe from the founder of Human Design. He went by the name Ra Uru Hu, a name he gave himself after hearing the "Voice." He has several videos posted on the website. In those videos, he tells his story: his deep and passionate experience, his reasons for making a bundle of money from his experience, and his need to keep spreading his word. What made it worse is that he seemed either sedated or hypnotized. This is where I recoiled. Everything seemed wrong to me. It felt like a money-making scheme or a cult. His ego was entirely too large, his delivery too slick. My gut was telling me to stay away. I told my therapist that I didn't want to insult her professionally, but that I needed to trust my gut and stick with just the EMDR and the other traditional methods of treatment.

I held my breath as I waited for her response. She simply said that we didn't need to incorporate Human Design into my treatment at all, that it was just one of many tools that have helped her patients. Her response helped me relax, and I quickly realized that it didn't matter to her if I chose not to integrate the treatment. She knew that many people find it to be just a bunch of hocus-pocus, and she completely appreciated my candor. We took a few moments to make sure we were both "cool." We were; it was a good meeting of the minds. We were all straight.

She asked if I was up for EMDR, and I said I was ready. My pulse quickened as I realized that I might uncover more sexual memories that I had hidden deep in the corners of my mind for the past twenty years. We hooked up the lights. I leaned back in my chair and took a few deep breaths.

We immediately went back to Jack and my grandma's house. We weren't in the car. I didn't want to think about the car for the time being. Jack was talking with me at the piano. His hand was on my leg, telling me how much he liked me and how good I was. I found a way to distract him enough to let me stand up and walk towards the kitchen to get the attention of my sister. She came to see what I wanted. I asked her if she wanted to go to the basement to play soccer in the laundry room. I was relieved when she agreed and we barreled down the stairs. I had escaped. We played for a while. My mom called down the stairs from the kitchen to tell us it was time for dinner. I opened my eyes and watched the lights, thinking about how I felt as I walked back up the stairs for our meal. I felt like I had escaped—temporarily.

My therapist stopped the lights and asked what I was thinking about. I was back in the basement in front of the television with Jack. Nobody was around. He was giggling and playing with my ear again. I hated it when he touched me. He told me to follow him to the tool room. I did, reluctantly. The tool room was in the farthest corner of the basement, the area of the house where I felt the most vulnerable. He walked in and turned on the fluorescent light. He wanted to show me how to work on something at his tool bench. He stood behind me, pressing himself against my back. I quickly came up with an excuse. I pretended like someone was calling my name. I played it off pretty well, enough for me to leave the tool room and start a conversation with my sister. She was wondering where I was. Another escape complete.

I opened my eyes and watched the lights. I felt my eyes get heavy. It was hard to keep them on the lights as they moved back and forth. I was deep in the basement, wandering, hiding. She stopped the lights. I found myself at school. Since we had just moved to Virginia from Texas, I had very few friends. The one friend I had was a kid named Randy. Randy had just moved from New Orleans and he was moving into the same subdivision we were moving into. His house was right around the corner from the school but a good thirty minutes from Jack and Grandma's. That made it difficult for us to play after school. All I wanted to do after school was go to Randy's apartment and play. I couldn't go back to Jack's house. But convincing our parents to drive all over town for a few hours with Randy was a tough sell, especially because my mom was pregnant with my younger brother.

I opened my eyes and watched the lights. Randy was at Jack's house with me. In a failed attempt to invite myself over to Randy's house, he ended up at Jack's with me. I couldn't let him be involved with this mess. He was my only friend. We had to work on a project for school. We were building a replica Jamestown Fort out of Popsicle sticks. I begged my mom to stay with us, to help us out so Jack would stay away. She did. I was relieved.

My therapist stopped the lights. I found myself thinking about my mom and dad going to the hospital in October when my brother was born. I was excited, but at the same time I was alone. I was fending off Jack without anyone but my sister around. I didn't want to go any further. I was exhausted and luckily, we were almost out of time. I felt a slight smile creep to the corner of my mouth. I had made it through the session. Nothing too bad.

My therapist paused and said she wanted to talk about how innocent I was and how resourceful I was to keep everything together for my family. I didn't want to disrupt our family happiness, so I was able to put on a smile, but I was resourceful enough to protect myself when Jack tried to get me alone. I was juggling well for a nine-year-old. It was good to hear her validate that what I was going through was difficult for someone at that age. I felt bad for that kid—and so did she.

While I felt a little sad, I felt great that I had made it through in one piece. I didn't blow chunks on her carpet or pass out in the chair. I didn't even cry this time. I think that's a good sign, but I'm not sure. The best part about it was that I trusted my gut. I didn't try to make my therapist happy, I did what I thought was right for once. It's been a good weekend.

Professional Gnat: August 3, 2010

Two degrees and three careers in ten years. Not many people can say they've achieved, or even attempted, such a feat. You could say that I've managed my career with an astonishing gnat-like focus. As soon as I smelled success, I would rev up my spaz-machine and re-invent myself professionally. This career-hopping is a common thread among sexual abuse survivors, and most of the time, the survivors have no idea why they can't keep a consistent, successful career. In my case, through all of this change and repeated self-sabotage, there has been one common denominator: I always found a way to be around professional sports.

It was the summer of 1999 and I was in Virginia Beach, sitting in the ready room of our F-14 hangar. We had just returned from our six-month deployment to the Middle East, so we weren't doing much more than stealing things from other squadrons and watching how far we could shoot milk from our noses at lunch. Our skipper, or commanding officer, walked in and asked if anyone liked baseball. Huh? Jackpot. I told him I loved playing baseball. He corrected me, and said that we weren't going to be playing baseball. Instead, our squadron was offered an opportunity to perform the fly-by at the Major League Baseball All-Star game at Fenway Park in Boston. This was bigger than a jackpot for me. I was a huge baseball fan. I knew that the All-Star game was celebrating the All-Century team since it was the final All-Star game of the century, and every Hall of Famer was invited to the game to be recognized. It was one of the biggest nights in baseball history. Within a week I found myself in Boston, on top of the right field seats, helping orchestrate the fly over. It was an amazing night. The sun was setting behind the diamond formation of F-

14's as they barreled over Fenway's Green Monster just as the national anthem ended. The jets were low and they were loud. Very loud. In fact, many of the players on the field fell to the ground out of fear. Several FAA violations later, myself and the eight crewmembers celebrated at the after-party with the likes of Cal Ripken, Jr., George Brett, Reggie Jackson, and Ted Williams (in one of his last public appearances). It was probably the single greatest professional day of my life. It was so great, you would think that I would make this job a career. Nope. The Gnat would soon be looking for something more exciting.

Fast forward four years. I was getting an MBA from Arizona State University, living the good life in the desert, going to school full-time and working full-time in a sleep-deprived marketing internship at the Arizona Diamondbacks. I had managed to work my way into a front-office position at the ballpark, managing community relations projects for the team. This meant that I often got to wear a uniform and play on the field with community groups when the baseball team was away. Dream job, right? I remember one day working with The Boomer Esiason Foundation, an organization founded by the former NFL quarterback to fight Cystic Fibrosis. I was standing there, in a Diamondbacks uniform, in the middle of Chase Field, the home of the Arizona Diamondbacks, hitting pop flies off a fungo bat to Boomer, Billy Crystal, Louis Gossett Jr., and other celebrities. It was a great afternoon. Who couldn't keep this kind of job forever? Uuh…The Gnat.

Fast forward two more years. I was working at an upstart Event Marketing Agency. We were courting new clients, so I was part of a pitch-team that was presenting event ideas to a prospective client, CARFAX, the vehicle history report company. They ended up liking my idea of

177

sponsoring a NASCAR race, the soon-to-be CARFAX 250 at Michigan Motor Speedway. Within a year, I was with my clients, at our inaugural CARFAX 250, standing next to the CARFAX CEO as he prepared to hand the CARFAX 250 trophy to Dale Earnhardt, Jr., the winner of the race. Just as the trophy was being handed to Junior, Carl Edwards pushed past me and got in the face of Junior because of some final lap contact that sent Carl crashing into the wall. I was literally standing there, within two feet of two NASCAR legends about to brawl. Unfortunately, cooler heads prevailed, and the celebration continued, but you can't ask for a better seat in sports. Unless you're The Gnat.

Fast forward another two years. Dissatisfied with that awful dream job, I had just started working for a top Advertising Agency. A position on the ESPN account had somehow landed in my lap and suddenly, I was an account executive managing several ESPN television and print campaigns. While I had very little advertising experience, my sports business experience was enough to get me in the door. The next few years included several week-long trips to Aspen, Colorado and Los Angeles to enjoy the X Games as a VIP, as well as trips all over the country to shoot commercials with professional athletes. You couldn't beat it and still, The Gnat wasn't happy.

The more that I have learned about the effects of childhood sexual abuse, the more I have eased up off myself for being The Gnat. I've started to realize that I was never happy because of what happened to me, and because I saw myself as not worthy, I didn't allow myself to be happy. This is a very common and very frustrating cycle.

The best book that I have read so far on the subject of male incest survivors, is a book called "Victims No Longer," by Mike Lew. In the book, he details many of the post-abuse life patterns of male incest survivors. To name a few:

1. Numbing with alcohol, drugs or other compulsions
2. Changing ways of life through religion, meditation, personal growth, etc.
3. Excessive work hours to avoid thinking about the past
4. Extreme athletic endeavors to feel something positive
5. Geographic escape, changing locations to start fresh
6. Constant changing of careers and friends
7. Pursuing academic degree after degree
8. Avoiding authority figures, older people, friends and lovers

There are several more, but these are a few of the most common. The book goes on to say that these patterns shouldn't be regarded as bad things. These are the patterns that keep survivors alive.

I've been beating myself up for doing many of these things throughout life, wondering why I was searching, and running, and achieving with no focus. Now it's finally making sense.

Knowing this will change the way I look at myself forever. I've been discovering the innocence of my childhood when I work through EMDR, and now I'm finding innocence in the ever-confused young adult the more I read. Relief. The Gnat, and my other pseudonyms, are finally catching a break.

Therapy Session 19: August 5, 2010

I walked into Thursday's session a little distracted. My head was spinning like a tornado from other things, so when my therapist asked me if I was ready to start some EMDR, it sort of took me by surprise. Uh…sounds good…I think. Unlike my first therapist, my new therapist put the ball in my court and asked me what memory I felt like discussing. I liked this method much better than being told what memory to address; it gave the control back to me. If I wasn't ready to think about something, I didn't have to. It was comforting. I felt like I had exhausted my memories of living in Jack's house. Well, except for one. The situation that was percolating in the back of my brain was the memory of being in the car with Jack on that rainy night, the one I couldn't continue with a few weeks earlier because I started to feel sick.

Since that session, I've been thinking about what bothered me so much. It scared me that I hid memories from myself. The specifics of the abuse that I started to reveal were so new, and so vivid, that it took over my body and all of my senses. I had to respect that my body wasn't ready for all of that at once. Now, with a few weeks of percolating under my belt, I was ready to return to the innocent boy on Jack's lap in the car.

As I drifted back to the memory in the car, I thought how strange it was that my mind could go back to the scene as soon as I gave it permission. Immediately, I found myself sitting there, with his hand dictating what my hand would touch. His whisper in my ear, as though this was all part of a normal childhood. I smelled the same smell, I felt the same awkwardness.

This continued as I opened my eyes and stared at the lights for about a minute. Then, my eyes were closed. My mind kept working. I remembered being startled by how it ended. He just sort of stopped and zipped himself up and asked if I was ready to drive. I was confused, but I wanted everything to be normal so I quickly concentrated on the new task at hand—driving. We had a good time. He showed me how to drive with one hand, then with one finger. The car swayed from left to right in the lane as I tried to control it with my nine-year-old index finger. We laughed. He let me pull the car into the carport as we returned to the house.

I opened my eyes again and watched the lights. Jack and I walked into the house, where I quickly found my family and told them about how well I drove the car. Jack followed and continued to praise my driving. I acted as though everything was great. If I said everything was okay, maybe it would be okay?

At this point, I started to feel nauseated, but I continued. I opened my eyes and watched the lights again. I started thinking about the way that I carried on about how much fun the drive was. I started to feel shame. The lights stopped and I closed my eyes again.

I found myself walking down the stairs into the basement. This time, my entire family was watching television together. Jack was on the couch. My grandma was to the left of Jack, and my sister to the right. My parents were against the far wall, sitting in a couple of chairs. The big wooden box of a television was in the near corner, to the right of the fireplace. My hair was wet and freshly combed. I was in my pajamas, as though I had just showered. I bounded down the stairs, assessed the seating arrangements, and immediately headed for Jack's lap. The nausea got much worse. I told my therapist I was feeling sick and she brought the trash can over. I told her I had to stop or I would vomit. We stopped what we were doing and I took a deep breath, focusing on getting ahead of the nausea.

Since we still had about twenty minutes before the end of the session, we talked for a while about what I was feeling. I told her that I was feeling terrible that I had provoked him. I couldn't believe that I was engaged in the abuse. No wonder he abused me—I basically forced him to.

My therapist stopped me there. She quickly corrected this flawed line of thinking. She explained that what I was doing was surviving. I was doing what any kid my age would have done to keep everything as normal as possible in order to prevent upsetting our entire family. She reminded me that I had sacrificed myself to keep everyone happy. I had a hard time fully understanding what she said as it was so much easier for me to apply what I knew as an adult to that innocent child. She was right, I had to remember how old I was when this all happened.

The session ended and my spinning head was now a tropical storm. I had too many things moving. Too many thoughts, too many new revelations about the ways in which I would seek Jack's attention. Why did I do that? It didn't make sense. Why would I continue to cover everything up and make it harder for people to help me? I was giving him the wrong signals. What was wrong with me?

Knowing that I didn't have the mental capacity to deal with this disaster of a day, I did the one thing that I didn't want to do. I decided to numb myself. I was drunk by 9 p.m. It was the only thing I could do to get through the night. I woke up on Friday ashamed of the role I played in my abuse, and disgusted with myself for drinking so much. This spiral was tight and fast.

I've spent three days thinking through the session. I've done some reading. I've listened to my tapes. I've spent a lot of time alone with my thoughts. It's taken me three days of thinking to chip away at the thick layer of disgust for myself. The worst part is that my mind knows that none of the abuse was my fault, but my body feels what it feels and time is the only thing that will fix it. I'm better than I was yesterday and Saturday was better than Friday. So I just need to hold on and trust what time will do.

Therapy Session 20: August 10, 2010

A week ago, my therapist and I decided to schedule two appointments each week since we noticed I was feeling anxious for another session by the time Tuesday came around. It was really my idea, my overly-ambitious personality kicking in again, but she's seemed okay with the idea for the time being. Tuesday and Thursday will be my sessions. I'm thinking that the Tuesday session will be focused on tying up all of the loose ends from the Thursday EMDR session the week before. And then by Thursday, I'll be ready for another intense EMDR session. This makes me feel like I'm getting more accomplished. Time will tell.

My first real Tuesday session was two days ago. I walked in still feeling odd about how much of a role I played in my own abuse. I hadn't quite forgiven that kid for sitting on Jack's lap and for projecting how much he liked Jack. We started there. The conversation went as I expected it to, and then we shifted to talking about grief. We talked about how I really don't connect with my negative emotions. I never let myself grieve, no matter how difficult the circumstances.

She wanted to focus on this. I didn't think much of it, but she thought it was important. We pulled out the EMDR lights and started going through my past, exclusive of my time with Jack. She wanted me to think about times when I experienced disappointed, let down, or failure. I found myself thinking about a time when I was twenty-one. I had just returned from Pensacola, Florida after failing to pass a physical exam required to start training as a Navy pilot. I had already taken my oath, so I had committed to the Navy, but now, since I had failed the eye test, I was honorably discharged.

Everything I had done for the four years prior had prepared me to become a Navy pilot—my dream since childhood. My engineering degree at a top engineering school didn't come easy for me. I stayed up all night studying, over and over, with my goal driving me.

I had sacrificed so much, but in a blink of an eye, I found myself on a flight back from Pensacola, by myself, with no direction in life. My dream was over. When I got off the plane, my parents greeted me at the airport, tears in my mom's eyes. I just smiled and pretended like I was fine. I never once let myself feel down. I charged forward and found a job. Why cry about it?

I opened my eyes and watched the lights for a minute, my mind drifted to my childhood. We moved every few years because my dad was active duty military. I drifted back to each time we moved. I thought about the friends I left behind, the sports I had to quit, the progress I had to abandon. But each time we moved, I put on a smile—not because I was happy, but because that's what you do when you're a military brat. You find ways to push through it with a smile.

I closed my eyes. My therapist mentioned how she noticed a very troubling pattern—a complete disconnectedness with my emotions. In an effort to keep myself up, I completely separated myself from pain, which is equally disruptive in a more subtle and longer-lasting way. I shrugged my shoulders. I really didn't know what to say other than I don't like feeling down, so I don't let myself feel down. Hmm, was all she said. I laughed. She noted that I laughed a lot as I talked through a lot of these difficult periods in my life. She found that interesting.

Then we ended up in a conversation about how I continually feel like the worst is always yet to come. Yes, I can be optimistic at times, but for some reason I'm always waiting for any happiness I feel to come to an abrupt, tragic halt. This troubled her also. We kept going into the conversation, my honesty obviously not making her feel any better about my personal Modus Operandi.

She linked it to several things. One, the sexual abuse. Two, the fact that my life was spent adjusting time after time, each time we moved, and being expected to put on a smile. That's a real strain on a child's psyche. I would start to feel happy at the end of two years in one town and then, wham, as I expected, I was the unhappy new kid again. To make matters worse, showing the pain wasn't an option.

After the previous week's session of finding out that I had pretended like I enjoyed Jack's attention in front of my family, finding out that I've been avoiding emotion my entire life was difficult to hear. It was starting to become clear that I was not the emotionally healthy person I thought I was. Nothing was what I thought it was.

It felt like I was in one of those old coffee commercials. I'm sitting there, enjoying my cup of premium blend Columbian coffee, when some waiter walks up and tells me with a smile that I'm actually drinking Folgers's Crystals. What? Folgers's fucking Crystals? You're telling me that I've been enjoying a cup of Folgers's fucking Crystals this whole time? I was under the impression that I was enjoying a delicious blend of imported coffee beans. I hate Folgers's fucking Crystals.

Let's just say it's not a good feeling.

I hope I start getting used to the new coffee. After all, it was delicious, before I knew what I was drinking. Okay, gotta run, I'm late for today's appointment.

Therapy Session 21: August 12, 2010

When I was in eighth grade, I took a pre-algebra class in order to prepare for high school algebra. At that time, I hated math, mainly because I wasn't very good at it. I remember sitting there with my mom and dad, night after night, trying to understand the nebulous concept of the imaginary number "x." For the life of me I could not grasp that "x" represented a number and to make matters worse, this letter was a number that we didn't even know. This concept was inconsistent with everything I had learned about letters, numbers, and certainty. Algebra was evil.

Then, one day, it clicked—like swimming with goggles for the first time. It all suddenly became clear. From that point forward, I enjoyed math, and eventually went on to ace my math classes in high school and college.

When I took my chair in my therapist's office on Thursday, I knew we would need to revisit why I enjoyed spending time with Jack. It was a concept I couldn't grasp and I was beating myself up every time I thought about it. It just didn't make sense.

My therapist asked me how I was doing. I told her that I was doing fine, no better, no worse than the last time I saw her. She asked if I was feeling up for some EMDR and I said I was ready. When she asked what I wanted to work on specifically, I answered quickly. There was no doubt that I needed to understand why I made it so easy for Jack.

She set up the lights and I sat back in the chair. I took a few deep breaths. We started talking about the little kid.

She asked me if I still felt like he was guilty and I told her that I did. I felt pretty strongly that he was an accomplice in the abuse. We started with that. I watched the lights. I closed my eyes after about a minute and thought about how I would seek Jack's attention, his affirmation. I would volunteer to work on things with him; I would spend time with him around the house. I felt nauseated.

We continued on this track for the next twenty or thirty minutes. I found myself in all sorts of situations where I was seeking his approval, or his attention. The more I thought about it, the more nauseated I felt, until finally, I had to stop. I was going to vomit.

She quickly stood up, fearing for the life of her office rug, she turned off the lights and put away the tripod. I took a few more deep breaths and my nausea leveled off. She told me to relax, reminding me that I was safe.

I couldn't believe I was so involved in spending time with Jack. My therapist took a seat in a different chair and started a conversation about the memories I was navigating. She asked me how that kid was feeling. I told her that he was ashamed. He was lonely.

She latched on to that word—lonely. We talked about what the kid was going through at the time. We had just moved from Texas to Virginia. I had left my friends behind, was struggling to make new friends in a new town. School had just started and I was feeling like an outsider. At the time, my mom was around eight months pregnant with my younger brother. We were living in Jack's basement. My dad was working late nights at the Pentagon. Most of the talk was about the new baby, my dad's new job, or the house we were building across town. My sister was my only friend. And then there was Jack.

I knew Jack really liked me. In fact, he liked me more than anyone else. He showered me with attention. He made me feel special. I enjoyed that feeling. I needed to feel special, like every other child. Jack provided that at a time when I really needed it. The tragic part, the unfair part, is that Jack took advantage of my innocent need for attention. He attacked it by acting out his sexual fantasies, while at the same time providing me the dire attention that I needed.

And just like that, it clicked. I understood what "x" was. I understood why I volunteered to sit on Jack's lap, acting as though everything was alright. I was trying desperately to pretend that everything was normal, that I had a normal, loving relationship with my grandpa. I tried to make it work. I looked for his attention and he gave it to me. It made me happy, and not because I liked the abuse, but because I needed the love that every child looks for. I was in a lonely place and I was innocent. I was doing what every child would have done in that situation.

When I left her office and drove home I couldn't stop thinking about this new perspective. It was something I hadn't allowed myself to feel before—empathy for that kid's actions. I started to feel more normal, more innocent.

Since Thursday, the disgust for my actions at the age of nine has faded. I have taken a turn for the better. While it will take time to fully understand, I know that I'm going to end up fixing how I feel about myself. Like my enjoyment for math after finally grasping that one concept, I'm eventually going to give that kid the break he deserves. And nobody will be able to take that from me.

Therapy Session 22: August 17, 2010

This session sucked. I went in feeling like everything was going well. Finally, I was thinking about that kid like he was—an innocent child who wanted nothing more than to make everything right for his family and for him. He was resourceful. When I walked out of yesterday's session, I still believed those things about that kid, but what I thought about in that hour was enough to rip me from my progress.

I don't understand the way my mind works. I don't quite get why in one session I can be rational about the abuse, and in another I can be deep in the details, without any defense. I can find myself being manipulated by Jack in ways that I never knew.

As the session started, my therapist asked me what was on my mind. She wanted to know if there was anything specific that was bothering me. I paused, and then told her that I was still uncomfortable with how far I went to show that I loved Jack. I had continued thinking about that after my last session, and the extent to which I pretended that Jack was the greatest grandfather was bothering me. He wasn't that to me. He was my greatest fear.

I talked to my therapist about how my family operated. Whenever I didn't want to engage Jack or participate with Jack in some activity, I was met with two forms of resistance. First, my dad would challenge me for being defiant towards an adult. Second, my mom would challenge me because I wasn't keeping things perfect. There was no chance for me to challenge this resistance. I was a kid. What power did I have?

My therapist set up the lights. I started thinking about my time in the house. I found myself lying on the cement floor of the carport, working with Jack on one of his cars. He always drove shitty cars. Even at that age, I knew that there was something wrong with him for not only driving cars that sucked, but for never knowing how to fix them and pretending like he did. Maybe it was just a ploy to get me alone with him. That one day, when asked if I wanted to work on a car with Jack, my objections were met with strong resistance. I found myself underneath the car, wishing I wasn't.

Within an hour I was inside the car on his lap, my hand on his privates in broad daylight. I started to feel nauseous. I had never thought about that day. I opened my eyes and watched the lights. My mind drifted away from the driveway and towards a shed that was in the backyard. I couldn't quite understand what happened in that shed, but all I thought about was his open-toe sandals and his hairless legs. I don't know why. I don't remember any more details, but the shed is uncomfortable for me to think about for some reason, I guess because I felt vulnerable there. My mind drifted all over the backyard. To the tree that I hid under when I didn't want to talk to anyone, to the basement window that gave me a chance to alert someone if I absolutely had to.

What I realized was that even when I was alone while living in that house, I was experiencing fear. Gut-wrenching fear that a child should never feel. I always knew whose footsteps I was hearing. I always knew when I was in danger, when I was cornered. I became very good at surviving. I managed it the best I could.

That fear has now evolved into a fear of what I can't remember about my past. Every time I remember something new, I feel a strong sense of fear that I'm about to remember something awful, something disgusting. My mind feels like my worst enemy.

Since that session yesterday, I've been a mess. I was forced to experience a more vivid picture of those six months than ever. For twenty-four hours I have felt like I was that kid, dealing with the challenges and awkwardness, and I'm having a hard time removing the feeling.

I called my therapist today and told her I needed a week off. Two EMDR sessions per week were definitely ambitious. I'm exhausted and I realize it's probably too much. I'm having a hard time processing the things rattling around in my head—too much, too often. I hit the liquor store after my session. I felt a great sense of failure for doing that. I wish I didn't.

Therapy Session 23: August 19, 2010

Everyone has a different sense of humor, but there's one thing that I can guarantee makes all of us laugh. It's the classic home video. Dad is standing there with a beer in his hand. In front of him is his son, who is holding a Whiffle-ball bat. Dad is beaming that his son is finally learning the sport of baseball. The pitch is thrown, the Whiffle-ball bat is swung, the ball is missed, and the Whiffle-ball bat proceeds directly to Dad's McNuggets. Guaranteed laughs. How this moment is recorded over and over, yet men still feel the need to proudly hover their privates behind home plate, is beyond me.

If there's one thing I can predict right now, it's that this process of recovery will continue to be unpredictable. As soon as I start to understand the ebb and flow of my mood and emotions, I am unexpectedly derailed. Half way into a sip from my cold can of Coors Light, my McNuggets are introduced to forty miles-per-hour's worth of Whiffle plastic. And just like that, I've lost the perspective and control that I was clinging to so desperately.

After Tuesday's session, I decided that I needed to take a break. There were too many things going on in my head. I wasn't processing everything and gaining the perspective I needed. I was overwhelmed. I woke up Wednesday, called my therapist, and left a message with her assistant telling her that I'd be taking a week off. I'd see her in nine days.

On Thursday, my therapist called me back; she was concerned. I told her why I needed some time off. I explained that I was overwhelmed, that I had been moving too fast and simply needed to gather perspective. She understood my reasons, but still suggested that I come in for my scheduled session. I told her that wasn't necessary. This went back and forth for about fifteen minutes. I was trying to establish control. By the end, we had compromised. I would go to that day's session if she promised not to talk about any of the abuse. In return, we would cancel my following Tuesday session. Fine.

When I arrived at her office, I was still a little annoyed that I didn't get exactly what I wanted. I felt like I had caved. I hated that I always caved. I sat down and crossed my arms, my body language as inviting as a fart-filled sauna.

We started talking. This was the first time I had been visibly mad in a session. But, calmly and coolly, my therapist moved forward. As soon as she realized I was frustrated for not getting my way, she apologized. She didn't realize that it was a control thing. She said that she was so focused on wanting to help me and talk to me, that she may have missed that cue. That calmed me down a little. Still, I retorted by asking if she needed the billable hour that desperately. As soon as it came out of my mouth, I realized how rude it was. I was like a caged pit-bull, ready to hurt anyone who came near. I'm never like that. Now I was assaulting the person who was there to help me. I apologized. To her credit, it really didn't faze her, which was great.

At that point I felt like I had removed some stress. We began talking about why I was feeling what I was feeling.

This went on and around and back again for about twenty minutes. She kept bringing me back to the same conclusion. I was pushing too hard. I was being too tough on myself. It was my idea to have two sessions per week. It was too much at this time.

I agreed. I acknowledged that I thought the two sessions were a bit ambitious. But, she didn't let me off the hook there. She wanted to go back to the conclusion she had made weeks before—the reason why I'm not being kind to myself. It goes back a long way, to the conditioning I received growing up. I have underlying unreasonable expectations for myself and my recovery, and when I don't improve fast enough or realize something new about what I did, I destroy myself. The judgmental and never-satisfied voice inside my head was talking too loudly. She was right again. I knew she was right.

We talked for a while longer about that voice. It was a voice that was never quite satisfied. It was a voice that, even though success was achieved, was wondering why it wasn't better. It was a voice that intended to motivate but was condemning me my entire life.

At the end of the session, I felt really good about everything. She had brought me back to an underlying problem in my life. The same problem that is hampering my recovery and making it impossible to fully love myself or be content with the person I am. She asked if I was still upset. I told her that, no, I was glad that she talked me into coming to talk. We agreed to go back to only Thursday sessions, and we also agreed to dial back the EMDR and sexual abuse work when necessary. Lessons learned. Surprisingly, it was the best session that I have had yet. And, my McNuggets, while still stinging a bit, were going to be okay.

I Am (Persistence): August 24, 2010

I am giving the presentation regardless of the size of this pit in my stomach. I am jumping up on his lap hoping everything will be normal now. I am not dropping the class again. I am letting her lean on my shoulder one more time, waiting for her to realize that she likes me instead. I am the space shuttle mission following the Challenger mishap. I am crying in the dark and then getting back out there. I am going to beat Bobby Riggs to illustrate my point. I am solving this equation, but I need a few more hours. I am Rudy. I am making a deal with myself to not drink until Friday. I am the third ring of the doorbell. I am lying on my back, my nose broken, knowing that I have nine more seconds before I need to get up to knock him out. I am persistence.

Learning to Learn: August 28, 2010

About six years ago I decided to go back to school and get an MBA. The decision to saddle myself with debt and learn the ways of the business world was made from as much disorientation as it was from conviction. It seemed like a good idea, a logical move, I thought. But looking back, I was just biding time before dealing with my past.

So, for two years I pushed through an intense, full-time, top-tier business program. Operating under the Socratic method of teaching, we were to educate one another via discussion and debate. After reading hundreds of pages of material the night before, the following morning in class we were graded on everything we said in a discussion. One stupid comment in class and a scribe in the back of the room docked you a point. One smart comment that furthered the discussion and you gained a point. The points were tallied at the end of the semester, and they represented a large percentage of your final grade. No pressure.

The adjustment to the program was not easy for me. In fact, I could tell it was difficult for quite a few students. We were being forced to abandon our previous ways of operating in the business world, or whatever world we had come from, and learn to operate together as students under extreme conditions—debating and learning together. Two hundred Type A smart-asses, jammed into one building, asked to stop knowing it all and get used to knowing next to nothing. This was like giving a teenage girl a new cell phone and asking her not to send any text messages. It was a drama-fest.

But, within a few months, adjustments had been made and we started to get used to the learning environment. People who I saw as arrogant and overbearing in week one became interesting and thought-provoking. We all started to learn how to learn again.

Recovery is no different. After operating my entire life in survival mode and doing whatever it took to keep myself on top and in control, I was now forcing myself to let go in my recovery. I'm required to open myself up and learn how to learn. Once again, it's not fun. It sucks. But, as in business school, I feel like I'm starting to adjust. I'm starting to understand how to recover. I can better predict when I will have a bad day and why. I can remind myself that it will get better. I can be okay with unhappiness because I know it will fade soon.

I still have a ways to go, and a lot to figure out about myself and my past, but I'm figuring out how to learn, and this time, I don't have to fork out my life savings for the drama-fest.

Therapy Session 24: August 26, 2010

I walked into my therapist's office knowing that I still wasn't ready to think about the abuse. For the last several weeks, I've listened to what my body had to say. The vomit alarm sounded one too many times, so I dialed it back a bit. I learned that moving too fast can be destructive and I had to respect my recovery. So, I'm doing the best I can to be alright with that. I try to convince myself that taking a break doesn't mean that I'm weak.

I sat down in the chair and we traded small talk. I was calm, although anticipating her question about EMDR, aware that she would want to know if I was ready to go back in time again. Seconds later, she suggested that we start up some EMDR if I was up for it. I stopped her there, knowing that it just wasn't in the cards for me at that point. She immediately understood and suggested we just talk through other things that were on my mind.

I focused on one thing. I hadn't been able to shake the feeling that my life is doomed. It sounds ridiculous as I read what I just wrote, but sadly, there is an underlying feeling of condemnation that I have carried with me for years. Before, I just thought it was normal, but lately I've been paying more attention, noticing that every time I start to feel happy, I am subconsciously waiting for the other shoe to drop. It's disturbing.

We talked through this for a while. She linked it to the abuse. I was internalizing everything that was happening and pushing it down deep into my subconscious, slowly developing a feeling that I was damaged goods, that my life wasn't meant to be positive. She also linked it to my upbringing—my always waiting for the one critical comment at the end of a string of compliments. When I heard criticism, I internalized it for a long, long time. In fact, I still hold on to much of the criticism that I heard growing up, while the compliments have disappeared. She said that the fact that I am very sensitive has contributed significantly to both sets of conditioning. It was something that we could fix. My ears perked up. That's what I'm talkin' 'bout.

She followed by commenting that I was still showing signs of being depressed but that this was normal given the circumstances. I hate that word: depressed. It makes it sound like being depressed is a conscious choice. It also makes me feel like I'm miserable, which I'm not. In fact, I'm significantly better than I was six months ago. I'd prefer if people started using the term "temporarily underwhelmed." Yeah, that'll do. Much better.

We wrapped up the conversation and I headed for the door. As I exited, I pushed my head back inside her office and thanked her for not making me look at the lights. She laughed and understood. I felt a little more normal.

Therapy Session 25: September 2, 2010

Until today, all therapy sessions that were directly focused on the abuse were painful to say the least. There seemed to be no immediate return. My therapist would attempt to lift some of the weight of the abuse from the innocent kid, but the weight would remain for a few days at least. After each session, I would quickly spiral into a state of self-hate and unhappiness. And, if we had uncovered something that I hadn't thought about since the abuse, the following days would be also filled with intense fear of the unknown. I was terrified that I would remember something awful, something I couldn't handle. But, after these sessions and the inevitable spiral, I would start putting the pieces back together, processing what I had uncovered until the weight from the memories we had visited slowly began to decrease. This has been the trend. Today was the first time that I uncovered a memory that immediately removed some weight.

I sat down in her office and we caught up. It felt like forever since my last session. I was feeling positive and it was the first time that I answered her question without a tinge of uncertainty. I really meant it when I said I felt good.

We began by talking through what memories we wanted to visit. I told her that I felt like we had covered everything we needed to for the period when we lived at Jack's house. She wanted to make sure I wasn't just avoiding re-visiting my memories of the house, so we talked a little more to make sure that wasn't the case. It was true—I was feeling like we had covered every memory from that time period.

So, we decided to focus on the few years after we moved out of Jack's house. We talked about what I went through when I was ten, eleven, and twelve years old. Encounters with Jack were swift. They were usually a one-day visit and he didn't have a chance to mess with me much. There was less physical contact, mostly just perverted conversations and mind games.

We decided to keep going chronologically. We moved to southern Maryland when I was almost eleven. It was difficult adjusting to another school, trying to find a new set of friends. I was really small for my age.

Visits with Jack were different now. We didn't see them much, but when we did, it was usually for a day or two, with a night or two of sleeping over. At this point I was a little more distant. I knew that I needed to find separation. I needed to make sure he didn't get me alone. For the most part, I was successful, but there were a few times when he got me back into the car alone. I did my best to prevent it, but sometimes it happened.

I started thinking about one time when he was telling me how much I acted like a girl. He was telling me I wasn't masculine enough. I was twelve at the time, and a lot of my friends had started going through puberty which, at this point in my life, was still years away. I remembered feeling so useless and weak, like I was letting men around the world down. I wasn't strong, I wasn't tough, and I wasn't able to defend myself like a real man should. Jack always talked about me being weak, a real momma's boy. Real men didn't depend on their mother's for anything. I was letting him down.

We discussed this and she corrected some of my incorrect thoughts, and afterwards, I drifted back chronologically—back to when we lived with Jack when I was nine. I'm not sure what made me go back in time. I had this memory of him talking to me about his rifles. He was talking about how real men should go hunting. I didn't really have an interest in his guns and he knew that, which is probably why he always talked about them. He was in the car with me sitting there talking. The car was parked. It was just another time when he cornered me in the car, ready to manipulate me into making him feel like a man. I was uncomfortable. On this day, he started talking about guns. He reached under the seat and pulled out a pistol. It was in a small, leather holster. He made me sit on his lap. I was petrified. He put the pistol in my hand and made me hold it. I felt the cold metal. The gun was heavy—too heavy for me to control. I acted like I liked it to make him happy. I wanted to run. I asked him why he had a gun under his seat. He said that he always did. I made a mental note.

I drifted to another scene. This time it was in his study. I was on his lap again. On the far side of the desk was a closet, filled mostly with clothes and paperwork. In the back corner were his rifles. Suddenly, he pulled out a pistol. I didn't see where he had retrieved the pistol, but I knew he had it hidden carefully. I'm not sure if this was the same gun as the one under his car seat. It looked different to me; there wasn't a holster this time. Again, he placed the pistol in my hand. I felt scared, threatened.

I took a deep breath and looked up at my therapist. It was clear that hearing this was sending off alarms. I thought about these memories for a while. I had broken out of the trance I was in. No longer living in the past, I was beginning to process the memories in the present.

We talked about the incidents with the weapons. It became incredibly clear that Jack was sending me a message. There were never any verbal threats or any sort of violence implied, but what he was doing was controlling me with very subtle, passive threats. It became very clear to me as we talked that holding the pistols, knowing that he had one in the car and in the house, was another reason why I didn't tell. It was another reason why I pretended the abuse wasn't happening.

While remembering the guns is a little frightening, I felt anything but scared as we wrapped up the session. I felt relief—much more than I have felt in a while. I had connected a few dots that needed to be connected. I realized that I had been indirectly threatened and that was a contributing factor in my silence. I wasn't hiding the abuse because I secretly liked it, or because I was weak. I hid the abuse because I was afraid and threatened. It was logical, and for whatever reason, learning that really helped me.

I left her office feeling the best I have felt after a session. Another weight had been lifted from the back of the innocent kid.

Labor Day Endeavor: September 6, 2010

Labor Day is one of those holidays that I always enjoy, but I have never fully understood. Who are we celebrating again? Oh, right…us. What did we do again? Oh, right. We went to work and built an enterprising country. How are we supposed to celebrate this achievement again? Shut up, Chris, just enjoy the day off and appreciate the long-awaited bookend to a painfully hot summer. No prob.

I got to thinking this afternoon about what I've achieved this year. I've come a long way in my recovery and I'm proud of that. But, I haven't worked too hard at one of the things I set out to achieve. When I started down this road of capturing my recovery and sharing much of it with the world, one of my goals was to help other people. I think I've given some people a new perspective, but I really haven't done much to share my story and what I've learned along the way.

So, today, in honor of Labor Day, I'm putting myself to work, and as you read this, whenever you read this, please join me. My goal will be to get my story in front of more people who may be able to benefit from my journey. Some people may have never been abused sexually, but they may have children who could be in harm's way one day. Or, some people might know someone who was abused but weren't sure how to broach the subject and help the person feel less alone. There's a chance that I can reach people who were abused and have been in search of someone's story. Regardless, the only way this epidemic is cured is by talking and sharing. It takes hard labor—somewhat uncomfortable labor.

So, please do me a favor and send this story to someone you know, anyone you think could benefit. Send it to several people you care about. Send it to someone you've been thinking about, maybe wishing they are doing well and hoping that if they're struggling in some way, this site may help them feel less alone or less strange or isolated. It doesn't matter if it's Labor Day or not. If you're reading this, please feel comfortable sharing it, for me and millions of other men who had their innocence stolen from them.

The more we share and learn and talk, the less the sexual abuse of children will continue. Happy Labor Day, or whatever day it is now, and thanks for the hard work.

Therapy Session 26: September 9, 2010

I drove home from this session feeling an overpowering sadness. I wasn't feeling sad for me now, or for how far I still had to go in my recovery. I was feeling sad about something else. I was feeling sad for someone else. I was feeling sad for a sluggish adolescent, a defenseless and naïve version of who I am now. However young and simple, he didn't deserve the confusion. It wasn't his fault. The sadness, for that brittle collection of confusion I stopped communicating with a long time ago, was overwhelming.

As I drove, I looked forward to seeing my wife, enjoying a dinner together. But, no matter how hard I tried to celebrate another therapy session in the books, I couldn't shake what was suffocating me. Twenty years of procrastinated sadness all at once. I guess that means the EMDR is working.

When I entered her office I felt really good about everything. I was trending upwards. I knew that. I had the support of everyone I cared about. I knew I wasn't heading in the wrong direction, which was everything to me in order to keep smiling.

We started talking about where we left off last time. I told her I felt good. We talked about the fact that Jack always wanted to talk about guns. He always wanted to make sure I was masculine enough to be his grandson. I started thinking about how hard I tried to be masculine around him. I was in ninth grade. It was December. I lived in Maryland and he still lived in McLean, Virginia at that point, but they would join us for Christmas that year.

My therapist stopped me there. She asked if we could set up the EMDR light box. I said sure—almost reluctantly. She offered up using the hand paddles instead. The hand paddles basically did the same thing as the lights; they stimulated both sides of the brain as the memories were uncovered. The difference was that they would allow me to continue talking without the visual distraction of the lights, while the silver dollar sized paddles vibrated one at a time in the palms of my hands.

We continued. A few weeks before that December, when Jack asked me what I wanted for Christmas, I told him I wanted a Buck knife. I didn't want a Buck knife, but I thought that's what I should say in order to keep the masculine grandson, happy family thing going.

Looking back now, I may have been acquiring my own defense. Knowing about the pistol he had hidden under the front seat of his car and behind the desk of his study, maybe I wanted something that we both knew I had, to provide an equally subtle counter-threat. I'd like to think that, but maybe I'm giving the kid too much credit.

Come Christmas, I unwrapped a Buck knife, held in a plastic camouflage sheath (even though I asked him to buy me the leather sheath instead of the camouflage one). He didn't give a shit. Nobody gave a shit and this little detail didn't matter in order to keep his mission moving—sucking up to his grandson while planning his next sexual encounter.

So, on Christmas of 1987, at 5 p.m., I accepted my Buck knife, in its camouflage lameness, with a huge smile. Everyone loved it. I probably ran over and hugged Jack after I opened it, my family beaming. But, aside from the act, I enjoyed having the knife. It was a little piece of control.

Next, I moved forward in time to my ninth grade Algebra class. It was 1988. I was sitting there, as clueless as the next freshman student, when the door opened and two men in suits whispered to my teacher. I could tell she was startled. She turned and pointed towards me. Embarrassed out of my mind, I stood up and left the classroom with the men in suits. I was going to either be a hero or be totally destroyed socially. The whispering started.

I followed the men. Our Catholic school principal (and rumored pedophile) met me in a golf cart with the two men in suits. Five minutes later we were in the principal's office. The door closed. I sat in front of his large desk in a single chair. Behind me, out of view, were the two men in suits.

They told me about what another family member of mine had claimed. My mind spun. This was the first I had heard of it. They went on saying that Jack was being investigated for the unthinkable. My mind drifted to my principal—only a few feet away—wondering if he was enjoying this conversation. The men in suits explained that they were there to ask about what I knew about my step-grandfather, Jack. I dissolved. I was a crying amoeba. But, for fear of the unknown, I decided to hold true to the story that I have held on to for all of these years. I wasn't molested. Jack had just propositioned me. The interrogation was over. Case closed. I returned to my class. Eyes puffy and red. I made up a story to explain what had happened. But nobody really asked; there were just whispers.

I went home that night after lacrosse practice. My family was aware of what happened to me at school. Either the men in suits had disclosed our conversation to my parents, or I divulged what I had told the Agents—I don't remember. But it doesn't matter, it wasn't the truth. We all sat together in the living room and talked, most likely to make sure that what I told the Agents was, in fact, correct. My parents inquired more, asked a few specific questions. My dad was so mad about the other family member of ours having been molested by Jack. He was furious. I couldn't tell my story. If I did, it would only add to the problems. By my talking, the anger would only turn to rage. Then, someone, I can't remember who, mentioned that there would most likely be a court case. What? Fuck. I couldn't say a thing. There were too many things flying around right now and I definitely couldn't talk. I dialed back and pretended nothing happened. So, I didn't say anything, and everyone seemed okay with that.

My therapist and I talked about this for a while. She could tell that I felt, deep down, that nobody ever really wanted to know the truth about what happened to me over the years. She was right. She brought up something that I hadn't thought about. She said that there could be a chance that my parents were subconsciously accepting my lie in order to keep me out of court, which would have been a trauma in itself. I told her I wasn't sure.

My mind drifted to the few days following that family conversation. Jack had been calling the house over and over. He knew he was being investigated and that the walls were closing in on him. I was his most recent victim, so I knew he was feeling exposed.

He contacted our family the following few evenings. One night he caught me on the phone. He was acting crazy. He said awful things about my mom and dad. There were implied threats that I understood. I was truly scared for my life for the first time.

For the next few nights, I slept with the Buck knife I had received a few years earlier under my pillow. I knew Jack was unstable and my greatest fear was that he would make an unexpected visit. I remembered sitting up in bed, my back to the corner of the room, crying. I didn't sleep well those nights.

One evening that week, our family got a phone call. Jack was dead. He had died of a heart attack while stepping out of the shower. As I think back now, how fitting it was for a pervert like Jack to die, naked, on a bathroom floor, alone. My dad told our family the news. My dad was relieved. It was almost a celebration. My dad then called my uncle. They celebrated, as if God had done us all a huge favor. I pretended to be happy like my dad. I went to my room and cried. It was all too much.

The funeral was at Arlington National Cemetery, with full military honors. The rifles, the pomp and circumstance, the solemnity.

Following the funeral, we all went to Jack's house, the house where I lost my innocence for good, for a post-funeral brunch. Jack's children were there. We all talked and attempted to feel normal. We all wore our best face but the awkwardness was thick.

On the drive home to Maryland that night, my family talked in the car. My mom told us about the conversation she had with Jack's children at the brunch. She told us that they had each said that Jack molested them as well. What was worse, none of them knew the others had been molested. It must have been a long flight back to California for his children.

My therapist asked me how I was feeling. It was clear that I was at a low point. I told her that hearing about the conversation my mom had with Jack's children made me feel worse. It made me feel like everyone had let me down. His children didn't talk when they should have. Maybe if they had, I wouldn't have been molested. And what about my parents? This news about Jack's children should have made them hyper-aware that I probably lied to them about my encounters with Jack. But, sure enough, that night when we got home to Maryland, we agreed as a family to never talk about Jack again. The timer on my twenty-year ticking time bomb began.

The hour was up, so it was time to end the conversation. There's something so awkward about the abrupt end to such a personal conversation, but I guess that's the therapy business. I had covered some traumatic memories. I was feeling alright, but the sadness I was feeling was unlike anything I have felt. As I drove home, I felt twenty years of sadness all at once. All of the feelings I should have felt, the ones I mortgaged, were in the car with me.

This weekend hasn't been one of my better weekends. I didn't go to work on Friday; I needed a break. So, I've been working outside a lot to keep my body moving closer to the speed of my thoughts. And, after a few days of work, the gap between the two is slowly diminishing, which is how this game goes.

The Question From Hell: September 16, 2010

In 1998, when our squadron returned from a six-month deployment to the Middle East, I still had about a year with the squadron before my tour was up. Between training and deployment, I had spent eleven months on a big, gray, floating city—the USS Abraham Lincoln, a nuclear-powered aircraft carrier. It was exciting, but it wasn't exactly the ideal hangout for a restless twenty-three-year-old. So, when our squadron returned from deployment, to put it mildly, the only thing we cared about was making up for eleven months of lost time.

The Hot Tuna was our new ship. The dimly-lit bar was at a busy intersection just off the sandy beaches of Virginia Beach. It was far away from the boardwalk, in a more locally-favored section of the beach. It was where most of the officers hung out back then since most of us lived a few blocks away along the water.

The Hot Tuna lived up to its name. It reeked of sweat, booze, and singles. It was where one, if interested, could easily start up a conversation with a middle school teacher or librarian, and dance away the night in front of a live band playing the perfect spit-swapping music.

That summer was filled with a lot of laughs. We played pranks on the other squadrons. We stole one squadron's bus and gallivanted around town taking rude pictures before returning it with pictures highlighting the trip. We snuck up on the roof of the hangar and painted ridiculous things that only aircrew could see as they entered the break and came in for a landing. It was one of those perfect summers.

What made it more fun, was that we had a recent ROTC graduate join our squadron as he waited to start flight school. The Navy "stashes" people with units in order to fill their time until their spot opens up in flight school. Ensign Swanner was our stash. The meek, nervous, Ensign Swanner was well in over his head hanging out with all of us salty lieutenants who spent half a year in the Arabian Gulf. So, we had a good time trying to loosen him up and help him relax. Unfortunately for Swanner, it was usually at his expense.

One night, we came to the conclusion that the only thing that would help Swanner relax was a dose of The Hot Tuna. Swanner, who had recently broken up with his long-time girlfriend, wasn't at the top of his game. He needed a night out to get his mind off of his college sweetheart.

A group of us walked into "The Tuna" and headed to the bar for a drink. Swanner looked shorter all of the sudden. He whispered to me that he wasn't very good with women, an unnecessary piece of info as I watched him stare at his shoes. I told him it was alright. I said that he shouldn't expect to just get back into the dating game, and that it takes a little time to figure out how to be single again. He relaxed a bit. Then he asked me if I would help him out. Being the most junior, and one of the single officers in the squadron, it was only logical that I be Swanner's wingman.

Feeling pretty comfortable after having logged ten thousand hours at The Hot Tuna that summer, I told him to follow me. I said that I would find two girls that we could talk to, and he might feel more comfortable with me there instead of going it alone. The main piece of advice I had for Swanner as we trolled around the bar, was that he should ask open-ended questions about the women we talked to. Don't talk about yourself—they don't care right now—just focus on them and let them do the talking. He understood.

Within a few minutes we found two single women that met his approval. We walked up together and I said something that started the conversation. Within about five minutes, we were rolling, all enjoying a conversation and letting the women do the talking. Swanner seemed nervous, but since he wasn't talking much, it was going fine.

One of the women said that they needed to use the restroom and that they'd be right back. They left, and Swanner immediately showed his excitement. He was very proud of his social interaction. I was proud of him as well.

But I made sure that he grounded himself. I told him that there was a pretty good chance that the women weren't coming back. It was a common egress technique that I had seen before. If they don't really like you, they'll find away to excuse themselves and then five minutes later you'll find them talking to someone else in a dark corner. No big deal. The single game takes a thick skin. He immediately looked down at the floor. I could tell he felt betrayed and was sliding back to square one.

Just as we started to look elsewhere, the two ladies returned, bubbly and refreshed after their conversation in the restroom. We were both caught off-guard. There was an awkward silence, the first of its kind for our foursome. I could see panic setting in behind Swanner's eyes. And with panic often comes poor judgment. He began to talk. I almost interrupted him, but figured I'd let him continue. What came out of his mouth was as horrific as any question that the singles community has ever heard: "Did you go number one or number two?"

My eyes widened. There was a pregnant pause. Swanner looked at me like the cat that just ate the canary. The women looked disgusted. Within four seconds it was all over. They were gone.

I don't think I've laughed that hard in my life. The cruel single life has its moments that make it all worth it.

The last few weeks have been heavy to say the least. It's been the hardest part of my recovery so far. So, this week, I've been forcing myself to think about the funny moments I've had in my life. There have been so many. I've always liked being around fun, funny people; humor makes me relax. As a result, my awkward life has actually been a blast at times. I forget about that. I've had so many experiences and hung out with so many good people and laughed so hard so many times, that I have to consider myself extremely lucky. Ensign Swanner's question from hell was just one of so many things that I've been thinking about and laughing about this week. It's important to do that right now.

Therapy Session 27: September 16, 2010

On Wednesday, the day before my session, I had a long phone conversation with my sister. For the first time, we broached the subject of whether or not what I was writing and sharing on my blog was too private, whether or not it was a family issue that should be handled within the family. It was an important conversation, sort of the elephant in the room when I talk with my family, and it made me realize how angry I was making some of my family members as I dredged up the past. Some felt misrepresented. Some felt like my perspective may not necessarily be fair. When I defended what I was doing and why, one thing became clear. My anger and my actions are closely tied to the one day that we decided to not talk about Jack ever again. That was the day that I truly realized I was alone, abandoned.

I realized that as I go through this recovery process, my family is supporting me, but not in the way that I was hoping they would. They are very caring people, to say the least, but that doesn't help me much. What I was hoping they would do is join me in my recovery. Rather than cheering from the sidelines, I was hoping they would get down in the trenches with me and figure out why the past was the way it was and why our family is the way it is. As great as every person in my family is individually, as a collective group we operate in an unhealthy way. I want us to figure that out since it is so linked to my abuse. I could have been more clear about what I needed from them but maybe in the back of my head I was hoping they could do it without me having to ask. My idealist side was driving that. My sister suggested that I communicate this better to my parents, that maybe I tell them exactly what I needed. Until that point, I guess I didn't know exactly what I needed. But now it was clear as day. As I hung up the phone with my sister, I was angry and feeling guilty. I was a bad son.

Twenty minutes later, I hit send on an email to my parents, asking them to join me in my recovery by finding a therapist in town to talk about what they're going through and our family past and present. I knew I was asking a lot. Our family isn't exactly therapy-friendly. And I was asking my parents to step far out of their comfort zone to push away their frustrations with me and take a closer look at themselves.

As I exchanged pleasantries with my therapist, I knew what this session would be centered around. One of the things I really like and respect about my therapist is that she lets me lead the process. Not every therapist does that, and it takes someone with confidence and humility to let a patient dictate the pace of their recovery. So, I launched into the conversation that I had with my sister and the email that I sent to my parents. I hadn't received a response, which added to my frustrations.

We talked for a while about what I was feeling and we again drifted to the core of my anger. It was that day that I became truly alone. I told her how my family doesn't like to use Jack's name. He's referred to as "the evil one" or "J." While I understand why they've erased his name from their vocabulary, it sends me right back to that day—the day we removed his name for good. I was deserted, with no way to talk about what I was going through. We had buried Jack and his name, and any chance of my getting help was erased, just like that.

I talked about my guilt for writing publicly about my story. She stopped me there. She wanted to focus on that. After twisting through the topic, we came to the conclusion that I was publicizing my recovery to right a previous wrong. I was finding so much relief in telling the entire world, it was making up for our family burying Jack. It was essential to my recovery. Just as important, was my need to use his name. I want to write his name as much as possible, to prove that this did happen. I was molested and my perpetrator was real, and his name was Jack.

At some point in this conversation, as I talked through my anger, with the vibrating EMDR paddles in the palms of my hands, I must have squeezed the left paddle too hard and I broke it. It made a strange noise and then stopped vibrating altogether. My therapist and I had a good laugh. I guess I was pissed.

We ended the session by talking about the likelihood that my parents may not respond to my email. I knew it was possible and she wanted to make sure I understood why they wouldn't want to do what I asked. She made a very good case for some people simply not being able to go that far into their own issues. She explained that it was a self-preservation thing—an ego-state issue—and that I shouldn't see their inability to do what I asked as a reflection of my parents' love for me. I told her I understood. I left her office and headed home, feeling better and less guilty.

That night, I opened my email and found a response from my parents. They said that they would be willing to drive to Richmond once a week and see a family therapist. They even attached a list of potential therapists. I started crying. This wasn't the manly version of crying, the slow stream of a few tears that slide down the cheek. It was the nine-year-old kid, emotional meltdown type of crying, a shuddering of my core. My wife stood there, her arms around me, in front of my computer and cried with me. It took me about fifteen minutes to pull myself together. I guess it was important to me.

Since Thursday, my optimism has skyrocketed. I feel like I am going to get through this and my family is willing to do whatever it takes to right the previous wrong. Like compounding interest, my optimism allows me to feel good about my hopes of recovery, which then makes me feel good about everything else. It's the opposite of the downward spiral and it's a much more enjoyable ride.

Cranium Conundrum: September 22, 2010

Ah, alas. Fall is finally…falling. This summer felt like the time I rented the movie "Ishtar." Hot, slow, and not funny. But finally, the new television season is beginning, my jeans are back in my dresser, and football season is upon us.

One thing that's front-and-center in the world of football this season is the subject of concussions. For years, players have been knocking their brains from one side of their skulls to the other. I was one of them. When I was a senior in high school, I played on the kickoff return team. I was the guy in the front of the "wedge," the orchestrated chevron of players whose job it was to protect the kickoff returner once he caught the kickoff. My helmet met the helmet of a very large man from T.C. Williams High School one night. He remembers much more than I do. For the rest of the game, I followed my friend Ryan around asking him what sport we were playing. But after shaking off the cobwebs, I was back out there the following Monday. Not a single trainer checked me out.

This is how it used to work. Rather than worry about the long-term impacts, we all dismissed concussions and used our immediate comeback to show how tough we were. Our teammates respected our grit. Our brains did not.

But this season, the NFL is under some serious pressure now that there is medical evidence showing how destructive repeated concussions can be. Some studies have linked concussions to ALS, or Lou Gehrig's disease. The media is all over it. Rules are starting to change and players are being watched more closely.

Today I was cruising along in my pimped out Ford E-150 cargo van (with optional overdrive), listening to my favorite sports radio show, "The Dan Patrick Show." It was a good show, as usual, and it included an interview with former NFL linebacker Chad Brown. He called the show to explain to Dan what it was like having received repeated concussions. It was clear how important it was for him to tell his story. His story was shocking. The emotional roller coaster that he's been on, most likely due to over a dozen concussions throughout his football career, was difficult to hear. He and his wife are moving along, but they're scared by his recent emotional instability and are worried it will lead to something worse.

As I listened to the interview, I couldn't help but make an interesting connection. Everything he was saying about concussions and the lack of medical statistics and research on its affects was staggering. How can we be this far along in neuroscience without knowing more about concussions? It dawned on me that this is the exact frustration that I have with mental health. Everyone sweeps it under the rug and there is very little societal support for those who have mental health problems. Not only that, but both of these issues, mental health and sports concussion research, involve our most prized organ—our brain. How can this information, with so many children, our children, competing in these contact sports, and with so many adolescents and adults suffering from severe mental health challenges, be so discounted?

I think it trickles down to the same core issue: talking about mental health is not fun. It makes us feel vulnerable. For those with sexually abusive pasts, it also causes painful memories to surface, and dealing with those memories feels unbearable. Nobody likes doing it. But if we do, and we include those who are trained to help us, we can improve the lives of so many incredible, but temporarily off-track people.

Similarly, football is what makes me happy in the fall. So many of us get goose bumps at the first kickoff, yet so few of us are willing to dial back this excitement for the safety of the players entertaining us. It's as though we're using them for our gain. No salary is worth that.

I don't have an answer to any of this, but I do see the parallel here and it's likely tied to the human condition. The good news is that we're just starting to move forward. And if the NFL can evolve in regards to mental health and concussions, I think it's time for the rest of us to change.

An Uncertain Goodbye: September 24, 2010

I pulled my van up to Eva's house this morning, right on time. I was eager to see my close friend. For the last six months, I haven't been able to get to Wednesday without thinking about Eva, hoping she was doing alright and looking forward to seeing her on the upcoming Friday. I always enjoyed our conversations. I told her everything, and she didn't blink an eye—always returning serve as quickly as it came at her, with compassion and humor all at once. At ninety-one, she's as sharp as anyone I talk to throughout my day. She reminds me of my grandma, and my wife's grandparents—still as witty and clever as ever.

But, today was different. Today, from the second I saw Eva in her doorway, I could tell something had changed. I didn't know what. I grabbed her hand and walked her towards the van as I always do. When I asked how she was doing, she replied "Not so good, Chris," her voice unsound. Her hair looked different, her posture had changed. It wasn't the same Eva I have been so close to.

We drove to the senior center and I tried to keep the conversation going, but it was clear that she was out of energy. She slumped in her chair. Her hands shook. I got the chills as I drove.

I dropped Eva off and told the site manager that she wasn't feeling well. She didn't really want to talk about it with the site manager, and I watched her slowly walk towards her favorite chair.

I drove back to work to prepare the food for Monday. When I picked her up about four hours later, it looked as though she had aged even more. She told me she felt awful. I asked what was wrong and she said she didn't know, just that she had very little energy and just felt bad. Fearing the worst, I told her again how much she has helped me in my recovery. She always reminded me how little time we have here on earth and how we should live and love and forgive as much as we can. I told her that she reminded me how important it was for me to reconnect with my parents and heal our past. I hated not seeing them. We're all getting older and I hated not being close to them. She liked hearing that. She said, "Well it's good to know I've been kept alive for something good." I kept talking, trying to cram every little thing I could think to tell her into our ten minute drive back to her house. Her head seemed like it was slumped towards the window, her lips quivered.

We got to her house and I parked the van. I helped her out and got the mail out of the mailbox like she always wanted me to do. I held her hand and walked her into the house, slower than we had walked in the morning. I put her things down, and took her sunglasses off. She didn't have the strength to remove them.

I gave her a big hug. I told her I loved her. Without hesitation, she told me she loved me too. She turned and walked towards her son-in-law. I had a golf ball in my throat. I watched her walk for a second and then left the house, got in my van, and drove back to work.

I don't know if I'll see my friend Eva again, but I know that in her six months with me, she has helped me as much as anyone I've ever known. I think she only knows a fraction of that, but that's fine with her.

Radio Silence: September 30, 2010

I read somewhere once that when a childhood sexual abuse survivor goes through the recovery process, their anger transitions as they recover. The anger transitions from being directed towards themselves, to then being directed towards the people who should have protected them from the abuse, and finally, if applicable, it is directed towards the perpetrator.

I'm still in the second phase. My anger is still focused towards my parents. The good news is that I'm no longer mad at myself; the bad news is that I have yet to transition the anger towards the truly guilty party, Jack.

I suspect that this phase is especially difficult on my parents and our entire family. In an effort to respect our family's privacy as we go through this difficult time, sorting out our anger and dealing with the pain that will surface, I am going to stop journaling about my therapy sessions.

This isn't because my parents have censored me. They, to their immense credit, have encouraged me to continue writing as long as it serves my recovery and the recovery of others. I'm doing this because I feel like it's the right thing to do for my recovery right now. I have felt it was right to limit the details of what was happening in recent posts, and that serves nobody. I need to write the ugly things that I am feeling and I don't think I should do that publicly. I need to focus on me right now.

I feel bad for this blanket thank you, because it doesn't even begin to capture my appreciation and respect for the individuals who have supported me throughout this process, but thank you all for being there with me through this. I am forever indebted.

Small World After All?: November 18, 2010

"Every time we turn our heads the other way when we see the law flouted, when we tolerate what we know to be wrong, when we close our eyes and ears to the corrupt because we are too busy or too frightened, when we fail to speak up and speak out, we strike a blow against freedom and decency and justice."

- Robert F. Kennedy

The other day I heard a story on the radio that caught my attention. Apparently, Disneyworld has been embroiled in controversy regarding their famous ride "It's a Small World." For the past several years, there have been all sorts of maintenance problems with the joyful ride. The boats that carry passengers throughout the ride were jamming more and more often on the track, delaying the ride and causing public uproar. After months of inspection, the staff concluded that the track wasn't designed for the increasing weight of the passengers and the maintenance crew was forced to reconfigure the track to better support the cargo. Eventually, once the problem was fixed, the public outcry diminished. But the ordeal has led some to one conclusion: It's not such a small world after all.

All irony aside, it amazed me that fingers were pointed towards Disneyworld for not correctly building and maintaining the ride, when in fact, it was the passengers who were not maintaining a reasonable collective weight. But the track was fixed, Disneyworld apologized for the inconvenience, and all things are back to normal at America's wonderland.

The sad truth is that Americans are overweight, a fact that a large percentage of society is not willing to accept or remedy. It's much more comfortable to conclude that Disneyworld failed to run a properly engineered, safe operation.

"The Oprah Winfrey Show" recently aired a two-part series highlighting male survivors of sexual abuse. Two hundred male survivors of sexual abuse were in attendance, announcing their traumatic pasts on national television for the first time. It was an incredibly powerful series that Oprah herself said may be the show that she is most proud of in her twenty-five years of television.

On the show, Oprah discussed the wide range of destructive behavior that survivors and their loved ones are left with and she brought to light the little societal acceptance for these victims and their families.

One of the survivors made a point that struck me as ironic. He said that so many male survivors of sexual abuse keep their secret to themselves for fear that society will label them a potential pedophile. I thought about this for a while, wondering if I ever felt this fear. It dawned on me that I did. I was always somewhat uncomfortable around children, being so careful not to play with them too much or get too close. I remember being so scared to tell my sister about my abuse because I couldn't bear the thought that she would judge me around her children. It made me sick to think about it and it made me hesitate for years before telling her about my haunted past.

Here I was holding this painful secret to myself, watching it slowly eat me up inside year after year, partly because I was afraid of being judged, or suspected, or considered a threat, when the people that should be watched closely are the ones who weren't talking about their abuse—the ones who surrounded themselves with children, grooming them, while earning the trust of parents. Luckily for me, my sister knew me well, and never suspected that I was a threat to her children, but that doesn't mean that my fear was unfounded.

For thirty years, I have picked up on our society's subtle clues and suggestions that boys who were sexually abused often grow up to be pedophiles. Statistically, this couldn't be further from the truth. Yes, a large percentage of pedophiles were abused as children, but that doesn't mean that the inverse is true. In fact, a very small percentage of boys who were abused grow up to be pedophiles, with so many abuse survivors growing up to be very empathetic, nurturing, wonderful parents and role models for children.

Even now, after I have told my story publicly, I find myself watching a parent to see if they clench their child's hand a little tighter when I'm around. I pray that I don't have people watching me a little closer than others and it affects my actions. I feel myself withdraw around children out of respect for a parent's fears.

Just as overweight passengers find it easier to point their finger towards Disneyworld than face the ugly truth, society finds it easier to suspect someone with a shattered past, than keep a closer eye on the perfect soccer coach, the charismatic priest, or the dedicated Boy Scout leader.

Finding the real truth requires learning about a very uncomfortable subject and talking about it openly and honestly. Sometimes the answer is something we don't want to hear, but we need to set aside our busy lives, set aside our fears, and be strong enough to open our eyes and ears. It may help provide some freedom to those who deserve it.

Life's Dismounts: November 30, 2010

I'm the guy who falls when nobody is looking. I can trip on anything. I can even trip on nothing, usually pulling a small muscle I never knew I had, and then walking it off pretending like nothing happened. I'm also the guy who falls when everyone is looking. I can dismount an escalator as if I'm wearing ice skates, grabbing a perfect stranger for support before apologizing for the accidental grope. Man, what's wrong with this escalator? Sorry. Thanks.

A few weeks ago, I found myself in a conversation with a friend who had just parted ways with her boyfriend of several years. Her sadness was difficult for me to witness. I could feel her unnecessary self-doubt, her loss. As we talked, and as the tears slowly welled up in her eyes when she described the hurt and disappointment, I drifted back to my years wading through the euphoria and madness of single life. I felt awful for her. She was stripped of her usual confidence and optimism.

Since I'm a veteran of botched relationships, commitment challenges, and the post-break-up sadness swamp, I knew I could provide some perspective and maybe even a little wisdom. I started to offer support and guidance, but then I caught myself. She didn't ask for that.

I realized that what I had learned in my single days would offer nothing. My reminders of her value and my hints toward the positive road ahead would change nothing. She needed to sort her way through this stage, and she just needed to let it out and have someone listen and nod. She had slipped, as we all do, and she simply needed an arm to reach for.

For me, the process of recovery from childhood sexual abuse reminds me of the single life and the impending break-ups—the deep feelings of loss and loneliness, self-doubt, shame, and disappointment. Granted, the circumstances and degree of these feelings are far different, but the cycle of recovery is similar.

At first, we are completely lost. We grasp for anything we can hold onto, any little positive feeling of support or reunion we can find. We are disoriented, walking in the dark, bumping into everything. Somewhere along the way though, we improve, but we usually don't notice. Others may notice, but we still feel lost and alone. We continue on, gathering support from those around us, slowly finding our footing. Then, one week, we feel something start to change. A few months later, we feel better. Then, for no obvious reason, we're fine. We're confident, striding through life again.

I don't know where I am in that cycle of recovery, but I feel different. I feel more positive. I feel like I understand people better. I look at situations differently. When I see a homeless person, I don't immediately think of a reason why I don't have spare change. Instead, I wonder when they slipped, how they slipped, and why there wasn't someone there to lean on. I find myself leaning on people, sometimes when they don't even know I'm leaning. I don't need people, specifically those who don't know exactly what I'm going through, to shine optimism in my direction. To me that feels as natural as an NPR sports update. Just as my friend wasn't asking for my solutions in her period of grief, I merely look to grab a little support here and there—and a nod or a smile can be enough.

The Lunchroom Force Field: December 9, 2010

Every child who grows up in a military family knows what it feels like to be on the outside looking in. You spend two years at a school, just long enough to gather some close friends and make a name for yourself, before you are sent back to the starting line at a new school, in a new state, with an entirely new set of social challenges. It's frustrating to say the least—especially when you're shy like I was; slow to open up and show people what I was all about.

As I became more and more aware of the cycle of friendships, I became more and more hesitant to make great friends and then desert them twenty-four months later. It was exhausting and hollowing. But it was a necessary evil, and I always wanted to be liked, so I pressed on in every new environment and worked towards a new group of friends.

One pattern that I noticed in every new setting was that I would always start slow, observing who was cool and who wasn't, and I would adjust accordingly. I often ate by myself at lunch—close enough to the cool kids so that I could hear what they were saying, but not too close as to creep anybody out. Then I would befriend a few people from the cool lunch table who sat next to me in class. I would then prove myself on the soccer field, or in the gymnasium, and get a few more people talking to me. And then, just like that, I would find myself on the inside, with more friends than I had time for. This pattern was eerily similar wherever we moved; it was my socialization pattern. Observe. Listen. Adjust. Test the water. Prove myself when the time was right. And then, voila, one day I would catch myself sitting in the lunchroom, at the cool table, surrounded by friends and I would acknowledge that I had finally breached the lunchroom force field.

I was driving my van today, steering the long stretch from one side of town to the other, when I caught myself thinking. My mind was racing again. But this time it was different. Instead of catching myself pondering my past, the abuse, or my anger, I caught myself pondering an important question: Why did water polo not have horses? Why doesn't it have a single thing to do with polo? Skiing has skis, as does water skiing. Aerobics has music, as does water aerobics. But what's the deal with water polo? I guess I understand why they don't ride horses in the water—that would be awkward television—but where were the mallets? The sweet hats? I guess there is a ball in each sport (of much different sizes), but water polo is far more like soccer than polo. Why don't they call it water soccer?

Instead of being perplexed why my mind was wasting its scant power to ponder the ironic world of water sports, I was excited. I was elated to catch myself thinking about something that had nothing to do with my recovery. Minutes later, I caught myself again, wondering why everyone's cell phone voicemail is the same. First, an explanation about why they didn't answer. Since they didn't answer, they were unable to answer the phone. Second, a list of explicit instructions on how to leave a voicemail, as if callers would be confused when they heard the beep.

This may seem unimportant, but to me it is groundbreaking. It was my moment at lunch when I realized that I was surrounded by more friends than I knew what to do with. I have really progressed. Today I realized that I have breached some sort of recovery force field. I caught a tangible glimpse, and it is something I hope I will never forget.

Ellen: December 13, 2010

One challenge resting in the pile of challenges I face is to improve my ability to deliver compliments, whether to myself or to others. I'm very hard on myself and it carries over to my expectations of others, especially those closest to me. This doesn't mean that I don't think great things of other people. In fact, I admire so many people for a wide range of reasons. But it's the expression of my admiration or respect or love that I struggle with. Consequently, this journal entry is long overdue.

At barely one hundred ten pounds, my wife Ellen is the strongest person I know. No matter how many times we veer off course, she grabs me and keeps me next to her as we find our way again, usually with a smile on her face. Subconsciously, I must have known that she could do this years ago when I bucked my trend of running from relationships and followed my gut, trip after trip, to Chicago to see her.

For the first year and a half of our marriage, Ellen has been asked to accept a different version of a honeymoon phase. She has grown accustomed to returning home from ten-plus hours at a high-stress job, walking in the living room, and finding me in bad shape—either in need of support, or in need of detachment. This was difficult to say the least. Sometimes I would be drunk, trying to numb the pain. Other times I would be silent, avoiding reality altogether.

Many mistakes have been made by both of us. We had to do our best and rely on our love and respect for one another. It was Ellen who always found a way to get us back on course as a team.

This aspect continually goes unnoticed or unmentioned when we hear about the impacts of sexual abuse. There is an incredible strain on the people who love a survivor, especially on a spouse. They are pulled deep into the abyss, whether they are ready or not, and they are asked to navigate their way with very little guidance.

This isn't easy. And, in our case, it required Ellen to seek counseling to, learn more about my recovery process and about how it was severely impacting her. This was one way I saw her strength. She pushed aside her fears and walked into therapy because our relationship was more important. Seeing her do that made me feel stronger and it has kept me moving in the right direction.

Recovery from childhood sexual abuse is an emotional roller coaster for a family, and it takes a unique person like Ellen to navigate the ride so gracefully. Luckily for me, she is my wife. She is amazing. I love you, Ellen.

We Are The Cure: January 11, 2011

When you are done reading this entry, please share this with as many people as you can. I can already sense your hesitation, trust me. Will people think I was abused if I share this? Will I offend someone? Will I stir up something unnecessarily? Will I invade someone's privacy? The answer is no. Progress demands boldness. Unlike currently incurable diseases like Cancer, Autism, Parkinson's, ALS, and Multiple Sclerosis, the sexual abuse of children already has a cure: us. The more we talk, share, and communicate, the more we as a society take a stand against childhood sexual abuse, the faster we will eradicate this disease. So, please, don't hesitate, embrace boldness and share this story.

I've been documenting my recovery from sexual abuse as a child for almost a year now. It hasn't been easy, but I am slowly making well my body and mind—a challenge that so many of you reading this are familiar with. The statistics are horrifying. For men, one out of every six faced some sort of unwanted sexual contact before the age of eighteen, and many of them are challenged to manage the resulting emotions as adults.

Last week, one of these men, Bill Zeller, a brilliant, successful computer science graduate student at Princeton University, put an abrupt end to his challenge. He wrote a four thousand-word letter sharing his darkness of a sexually abusive childhood for the first time. He posted it on Facebook, and then minutes later, he hung himself. Rather than summarize his story, I have included his letter in Appendix 3 of this book. He requested that the letter be disseminated in its entirety, so that others can learn from his story in his succinct and powerful voice.

If you read the letter, it will change you forever. You will understand his darkness and feel some of his pain, if only for a brief minute. You will better understand how hollow life can be for a victim of childhood sexual abuse.

If only Bill would have found a way out of his darkness, he would still be with us. If only there was a way for him to feel less alone, he would still be with us. If only our society freely talked about sexual abuse, not in taboo whispers, but in bold, compassionate, charged proclamations, Bill would still be with us. But we don't feel comfortable doing that. We hesitate, and then we play it safe.

I played it safe for over twenty years. It was all I could do at the time. I didn't have the tools or the surroundings I needed. I didn't have enough people letting me know that it was alright to have been abused, that it wasn't my fault.

So, my darkness grew and grew as I flaunted a successful personal and professional life. I was maneuvering my way forward, tethered to a disease that nobody wanted to recognize, especially me.

Strangely, I was incredibly lucky. I had a family who loved me. I had positive role models. I had great friends who loved to laugh with me. I was gifted and I succeeded at everything I put my mind to. But the disease would grab me tight at times. When it did, I would take it out on myself for not being stronger. I had no idea it wasn't my inadequacy. Then, without warning, I would go into remission. I would feel better. This cycle continued, with every period of sickness being worse than the last. My insides were shutting down.

In my late twenties, after fifteen years of punishing myself for my past, I started thinking about how to make the pain stop. The use of chemicals was only a temporary escape. I had more and more thoughts of how to pull it off, mostly fleeting, but my most common thought was staging a car accident. This way, I wouldn't let anyone down. It would simply be a terrible accident. I would finally be able to take a deep breath and relax.

I haven't written much about the suicidal thoughts I had before I started my recovery. I think because I was afraid I would scare people, or unnecessarily have them worried about my current mental state. But, after reading Bill Zeller's letter, I realized that I was hiding an important piece of my story—the part that reveals the depth of pain that sexual abuse can instill. Maybe it was more than that. Maybe it was because I don't like to think that I was in such a shallow state. It's hard to go back there and feel what I felt. It feels like so long ago.

In the past twelve months I have learned so much about myself, my innocence, and how I deserve to be happy. I have started to feel like "the old Chris" again. It's awkward, frightening and extraordinary at the same time. If only everyone who is suffering from the effects of childhood sexual abuse could feel what I am feeling. If only those who gave up could have found someone to share with.

Bill Zeller was one of millions of men in the U.S. who are currently fighting the effects of childhood sexual abuse. His story, while tragic and terribly sad, is a portal to the cure. We are the cure. Please share.

I Am (Recovery): January 13, 2011

I am the moment he forgot his ex-girlfriend's name. I am the first step out of a wheelchair. I am a deep breath. I am pushing the stick forward and applying full right rudder. I am twelve steps. I am staring in the mirror, watching the corner of my mouth curl. I am his first tears about what he saw in Kandahar. I am control-alt-delete. I am the blood pumping through the veins of a man standing in his kitchen, telling his family he finally received an offer. I am eight hours of uninterrupted sleep. I am Representative Gabrielle Giffords. I am driving an 0-2 slider with a runner on third and two outs. I am the decision to be honest with myself. I am shifting my weight to my back foot to keep the tip out of the water. I am no longer playing catch and release with my meals. I am feeling the things I thought were forever lost. I am recovery.

Nice To Meet Me: June 15, 2011

Life is like a good suspense film. As soon as you think you have things figured out, just as you unravel the mystery and whisper your theory to the person next to you, you find out that you had things wrong. This is most often the case when evaluating the people we meet in life. We categorize people instantly, rather than pushing through their exterior and getting to know them on a personal level. I'm guilty. I've always conveniently bucketed personalities, if for no other reason than because it made things easier for me. But just as I would start feeling brilliant for having everyone figured out, every few months throughout my life, someone would surprise me and turn my bucket upside down. The bully who pushed me around in gym class, the annoying girl who only cared about criticizing others, the quiet guy dressed in black with the nose ring. One of them would somehow, usually by accident, show me that there was a lot more to their uninviting exterior. It was always a pleasant surprise and a lesson learned. But what I didn't expect to learn at the age of thirty-seven, is that one of the people I had wrong…was me.

At this point I've lost count of my months in recovery, not because I don't care about how I'm doing, but because the timeline doesn't matter anymore. I've stopped over-analyzing every therapy session, every bad day, every setback, and I've learned to be very comfortable with where I am. It's where I am and nothing will change that. I've learned to relax and smile again.

Consequently, Jack isn't much more than a name to me now. Jack is four letters that are assigned to a part of my past, and that's all. About three months ago, after returning from work, I made a snap decision to grab my car keys and drive the ninety minutes up Interstate 95 to Arlington

National Cemetery. I'm not sure why, but suddenly I was ready to re-visit the pile of dirt that pushed me into this self-discovery. I had no big speech planned. I had no expectations.

I parked my car in the visitor's lot, strolled to the information desk, and told the clerk which grave I was visiting. Within ten minutes I was walking up to a quiet section of the military graveyard, underneath an oak tree. Jack's gravesite. It was a beautiful day. I stood there and just stared at the ivory-colored tombstone. Part of his headstone was broken from what looked like a lawn mower incident. I smiled. I didn't say much. I didn't feel much. I just stood there and looked down on his plot. I was surprised at how little it mattered, how little this section of grass meant to me. After about ten minutes, I left. It was uneventful. I walked confidently back to my car, started it up, and drove home.

I had this incredible sense of relief as I drove. I don't know what I was expecting, but the fact that I was uninspired, or unaffected, was empowering. It was a non-event, which was the biggest event of all. We buried Jack in Arlington Cemetery when I was fourteen years old. Soon after, my family and I buried the memories of Jack, and now, twenty-three years later, I had buried Jack once and for all.

Since that day in Arlington, I have taken incredible strides in my recovery. I haven't been burdened by the raw anger towards my past, my family, my loss of innocence. I have resumed my relationship with my parents and in doing so, I have been reminded how important it is to have them in my life. I have found hobbies that I didn't know mattered to me. Don't get me wrong, I still have a lot of work to do, but I understand where I've been and I like where I'm headed. My self-constructed exterior has been unraveled and my own bucket overturned. I like who I see underneath. It's nice to meet me.

My Life: As A Survivor

I always pictured this day differently. I imagined I would be sitting here, giddy, writing the final section of my book, feeling completely recovered and free from my past. I'd be "recovered."

For some reason, I expected this day to be more like a romantic comedy, when all things are perfect, and birds are chirping and people are skipping around with shit-eating grins. I don't know why. Maybe because that's the way we visualize "happiness."

What I have learned is that recovery is not that simple. It's not a "voila" moment, or a valiant crossing of a finish line. It's not perfect, like most things in life. Instead, recovery is a life-long journey that takes daily maintenance to navigate normal ups and downs.

Don't get me wrong. The benefits of recovery are too long to list. I'm experiencing life as I always dreamed. I feel emotion again. I feel love for myself. I feel compassion. I have genuine friends and relationships that I truly cherish. I have so much hope and excitement for my future, I feel like a child at times.

I've learned that my past is exactly what it was before I started therapy. It hasn't changed. I still have the same twisted story of abuse, but how I think about my past and myself is different. It still makes me mad when I watch television and learn about another boy who was molested by some coach, while the staff or university knew about the coach's tendencies for years, and decided to look the other way to protect the institution. I still have bad days when I get down on myself when I shouldn't, or when I drink too much to temporarily escape something that is bothering me. I'm still taking an anti-depressant. I still have challenges to face. But that's okay. I can manage all of this because of what I have learned in therapy. I understand myself and my coping mechanisms, my weaknesses and my strengths. Because of therapy, I will continue to take strides.

I wouldn't trade my life with anyone.

Appendix 1: Resources

For men and women overcoming sexual abuse:

Websites

www.1in6.org This site is focused on helping men who were abused as boys and for the family and friends who are also looking to support him. This site is very professional, incredibly safe and informative, and has been the most help for me overall. My wife and family also used this site regularly to better understand what I was going through.

www.malesurvivor.org This is a helpful anonymous message board for men with a sexually abusive past. It has facilitators for anyone who needs someone to speak with. It hosts a range of men, from those who have just thought about their past for the first time and need to tell someone, to men who have been in therapy and well into their recovery for decades. I used this site at the very beginning, until I started therapy, and it was a great way to feel less alone.

www.RAINN.org Excellent support and resources for men and women. This site includes an online hotline to report any sort of abuse.

www.darkness2light.org This site is focused on the prevention of childhood sexual abuse. It shows you steps you can take to educate your children, their teachers, or you as parents. You can also become a national facilitator for this program – something my family members and I have considered doing one day.

www.imavictim.com Heath Evans, survivor and former NFL fullback, started a foundation to raise awareness of childhood sexual abuse and to find ways to prevent abuse. This site provides a place for survivors to anonymously post their story. It is a wonderful site to find out how many of us there are – we are definitely not alone.

Books

Victims No Longer To this point, I haven't found a better book for my situation. It focuses on the male incest survivor, and is written by a psychologist who specializes in the topic. It's accurate, well written, and empowering. It played a key part in my recovery.

Abused Boys This book has been incredibly helpful for me and my family. Since it is focused on boys, it covers the specific issues that men face as adults – somewhat different from what women will face. It also includes many stories that help validate what you are feeling.

I Never Told Anyone This has a pretty good collection of stories, mostly from women. It is an older book but my first therapist swore by it and suggests it for most of her patients at the beginning of therapy.

Playing with Fire This book saved my butt. Written by pro hockey player Theo Fleury, it's actually more hockey than abuse stories, but it does a good job of connecting with people who are in the early stages of facing what happened.

Killing Willis I haven't read this but it was recently released by Todd Bridges, from Diff'rent Strokes. It details his painful journey.

Searching for Angela Shelton This is a documentary, and I have only watched the trailer, but it follows a woman, Angela Shelton, on a journey across America to confront her past.

For partners, family and friends looking to support someone overcoming sexual abuse:

Websites

<u>www.1in6.org</u> (Male survivor specific) This site is a great resource for family and friends. It is well written and to the point. It also has a great resources section.
<u>www.darkness2light.org</u> Maybe a good way for a friend or family member to support the abused person in their life is by becoming a national facilitator for prevention of childhood sexual abuse.

Books

<u>**Allies in Healing**</u> This book has helped my wife tremendously. It covers all of the emotions that a survivor goes through, and it also covers what a spouse of a survivor is feeling. It can be helpful to family members as well, but it is more focused on the spouse.

Therapy Related Resources:

<u>**EMDR**</u> (Eye Movement Desensitization and Reprocessing). This is the technique that I used in therapy. It is commonly accepted and is known to be one of the best techniques to help men overcome sexual abuse trauma.
<u>www.1in6.org/get-help/finding-and-evaluating-therapists</u>
This is the best resource that I have found for shopping for the right therapist. This guide will help make sure you get in the right hands for you.

Appendix 2: Creative Writing

Before you read this Appendix, I want to provide some context since this is a departure from the style of the rest of the book. This is the first of five "creative writing" exercises that I used to express my anger towards Jack during my recovery. Since he died when I was fourteen, I was never able to confront him, and for some, confronting a perpetrator is an important part of recovery. Instead of unloading my anger directly, I decided to come up with fictitious scenarios where Jack, who I believe went to hell, is forced to feel some of the same things his victims felt due to his abuse. In the five posts, I make him feel five emotions: anger, disgust, insecurity, helplessness, and shame. Looking back now, I realize that these posts may seem odd to some, but that is alright. It served my recovery, and for that reason, I wanted to include these entries in the book. In several of these creative writing exercises, I punish Jack, emotionally and physically. In no way do I condone any sort of physical or emotional abuse to anyone, including a perpetrator. That would go against everything that I stand for. Since it is make-believe and occurring in my creative version of Jack's hell, I hope that readers will understand what I was trying to achieve.

[belieber14]: May 19, 2010

Jack: Hello?

belieber14: Hiya! There you are! I wuz starting to get worried about u! I wuz afraid u didn't know how to type! LOL!!!!

Jack: Who is this?

belieber14: Who do u think, Jack?! I'll give u 1 guess.

Jack: I have no idea. Where am I?

belieber14: Booooooooring! Hahaaha. Well, it's not like we don't have 4ever to kill, but I'll come clean just because I am xcited and it takes you foooorever to type. I am ur first dose of ur eternity spent in hell. Since u clearly s...u...c...k at typing, our evil creative team thought ur eternity should b spent IMing—and the boss thought it was soooo important for u to start with me—I think cuz I keep it so reeeelz!

Jack: I don't know what you're talking about. Who is your boss?

belieber14: sheesh. Duh! Do I really have 2 spell it out? He's Beelzebub........ya'know.............Mephistopheles. Beueller...Beuller...the Devil, u turd!!! LOL! Oh, and can u type faster—it isn't that hard.

Jack: What? What is happening here? Why am I sitting at this machine?

belieber14: ok, ur dim, so i will start from the beginning. U definitely missed the last 20-some yearz! Haha! So here's the deal, and pay attention, fucko, cuz I am already annoyed with u. Haa! LMFAO!! For the last 20 years since u died, u have been in a hell holding tank, designed especially for u until we were ready to start the fun stuff. Did they play the Justin Bieber music that I requested??!!!! I luv JB—I am suuuuuch a Belieber!!!! Ha!

Jack: I sat in the dark and listened to stupid music for so long. I can't handle any more. When the music stopped, this little computer turned on. I'm in an empty room and my hands are secured to the keyboard. Please, don't turn the music back on, and get me out of here you bitch.

belieber14: WTF??? eeeeeasy, tuff guy!! Ha! By "stupid" you better not be referring to the biggest pop star since MJ!!!!!! RIP, KofP!!! Getting 2 the point. OMG, u r soooooo distracting…where wuz i…oh…so yeah, u were in the holding tank becuz there r so many of u molester-types 4 the boss 2 take care of and u each get a special version of your own eternity that takes like sooo long for the evil creative team 2 come up with. Yours only took 20 years, so consider yourself lucky. Ok, so…this "little computer" (duh, forgot you died before laptopz!) is what u will be looking at 4…ev…er!!!

Jack: My eternity?

belieber14: yup. Ur dead. U know that, right? u got lucky and died stepping out of the shower just as those molestation allegations surfaced from ur family member, dummy!!!

Jack: I do remember that, but those allegations were false. I didn't do anything.

belieber14: aha…u should so b on the cover of US weekly!!!! U forget who my boss is. He saw it all (and helped you along, I might add). u molested more than just 1 family member. U soooo overdid it. and it didn't take much convincing on his part—it wuz lyke u went all Jason Bourne, u over-achiever!!!

Jack: Ok. Fine. I did it. But I was molested as a boy by my grandfather so it wasn't my fault.

belieber14: what, r u typing with ur fucking nose? Faster, you bird!!! Haha! LOL!!!!! JK. I don't give a shit, excuse the language, about what your fucking grandpa was up 2, even tho I know he rolled thru here a little while back (and I must say, we all like the work he did!!!! LOL!). Anyway, this is ur hell for what u did, Jack!!! Deal wid it. plus, u get 2 hang with us on IM instead of experiencing eternal happiness with that other guy…ahem…the "G" word. Don't say it…it makes my ears burn. Sike!!!! Duh, we r on IM!!! I can't hear shit!!!! Hahah!

Jack: Why are you writing like that? It's annoying. What is an IM?

belieber14: snap! You hear that boss?! That's the best compliment he could have given me!!!! Hah! I deserve my own star in Hollywood. It's like I have my masters in evil!!! Ahaha! So, basically, you get 2 spend ur first part of eternity instant messaging (IM'ing, duh!!) with me…a rude, annoying 4teen year old!!! My orders r 2 make you feel uncontrollable anger. Apparently, it's only 1 of sooooo many things you'll get to feel in hell 2 make up 4 what your victims went thru, but my boss sayz, angering peeps is what I do bezt, so i got first dibs on u, Jack!!!! He totally meant that as a compliment. But, O…M…G, thatz just the beginning. I'm female, and I'm smarter than u. Since u always thought boys were superior (and sexy), and u think ur so smart—guess what?!!…drum roll…I'm what angers u most! Hahaha!!!!!!! I even got to play my fav muzic, just cuz i knew u would h8 it!!!!!! OMG!!!

Jack: This is absolutely ridiculous. Stop talking like that. This is a waste of my time.

belieber14: How many words wuz that? 11? 11 words takes u 25 minutes?!!!! Talk about waste of time. Did you eat lead popsicles growing up? Duh!!!!! By my records, u do deserve this, Jack. My evil self is almost humbled to be in ur presence. but I'm not!!!! Hahahahaha. But seriously, I can't waste ur time. All u have is time. And all I have is soooooo much stuff 2 chat about until da boss says it's time 4 someone else 2 chat with u...in like....4ever!!!!! So. Where do we start, Mr. liar pants??!!

Jack: I refuse to engage with you, you idiot.

belieber14: OMG!! Like...how...rude. Here's the probs. U have no choice. But, since u just called me the "i" word, u just bought some more time listening to...u guessed it...Justin Bieber!!!! Hit it boss.....ttyl!!!

[TrucknBranMan]: May 26, 2010

TrucknBranMan: Breaker 1-9 for a radio check?

TrucknBranMan: I said, breaker 1-9 for a radio check?

TrucknBranMan: Key up, sandbagger. I know yur there.

Jack: hello?

TrucknBranMan: There y'ar. Was 'fraid yude dun ripp'd yur own face off, good buddy.

Jack: Who is this?

TrucknBranMan: Thought yude nev'r ask, ole timer. I've only been waitin' furever. Ma'names Ukobach, but mose people jus' call me Squirt.

Jack: Get me out of here you son of a bitch. I can't take it anymore.

TrucknBranMan: I see you been hav'n a good 'ole tahm with ma good buddy, Amduscias? 'Ole Amduscias is a tuff one. He'll grind yuh down allraaht. He sure does laaak his music. And, yur what we truckers cawl, a terlet mouth. Let's clean'er up a bit, eh?

Jack: Are you talking about the evil girl who made me listen to terrible music forever? She introduced herself as the devil's assistant and went by belieber14. I just spent millions of years crying in anger. Fucking get me out of here. You are all evil.

TrucknBranMan: Takes wun to know wun, terlet mouth. Yeah, the boss sayd he wonted you to work with 'ole Amduscias first….er..whatever he told you his nayme wuz. He'll git ya angry, heh?!!!! LOL!!!

Jack: I tried to kill myself over and over, but I couldn't move. I had to listen to this stupid music. Help me.

TrucknBranMan: Well, yur shoppin' at the raaht strip mawl, Jack. I'm here to help ya.

Jack: Thank god.

TrucknBranMan: Wull, not so fast, partner. Lemme tayke a step back fur a sec. I ain't no…"G" word, but I ayom here to help. I gawt that terrble music shut off for ya, so liss'n up. Laaak I said, they cawl me Squirt. I'm a truck drivin' fool. In fact, I drive so much, I ain't gawt time to show'r. I'm whut us truck'r folk cawl a "Dirty Dan"…er, someone who eats and drives real good, but don't got no tayme to show'r. That's 'cuz I'm trayin to sayve up moolah for a little venture me and me O.L. are startin'.

Jack: I don't know what you're talking about. What's O.L.?

TrucknBranMan: Well….SHE….is ma Ole Lady…yu gawt yur ears on raaht? We'z gawna start us up a new venture…all entrepreneur-laaak…well, wuntz we raize 'nuff moolah. Yep, yur typin' with one of the future proprietors of the first ev'r Brancake House.

Jack: What? You are insane. You dumb jackass.

TrucknBranMan: Terlet Mouth. You got laaak one more chance to clean'r up. Truck'r folk don't cuss online. Ain't classy. Wur wuz I? Raaht, the Brancake House. So me an the O.L. have corner'd the market on frah'd bran products. Bran muffins? Frah'd. Bran Pancakes? Frah'd. We won't surve nuth'n if it ain't 1) bran and 2) frah'd. Only problem's the smell of the place at the end of the day, but we're workin' on some air fresh'ner systems to keeper' smellin' fresh as a Wawa. We also been tossin' round sellin' underwear fur customers who may…yuh know….squirt on ax'dent. We wuz gonna make'um brown in color – fer cammo, ya know cause of the intestinal reaction…but I don't want to git in the micro-details. Plus, thass a lil' too much terlet talk. As stated, we truckers lyke to keep er classy online, of course.

Jack: That is the stupidest fucking idea I have ever heard. You are creating a business that caters to people who accidently shit their pants after eating food that you create…food that sounds like the most disgusting, bowl-wrenching food ever.

TrucknBranMan: Looks laaak 'ole Squirt is gonna be takin' the gloves off, terlet man. I wuz gonna make yur next eternity quick, but now we got biz'ness, you'n me.

Jack: Your business should be spent sending me back to Earth, asshole. I am a good man and I treated people well on Earth.

TrucknBranMan: Man, you dun almost made me choke on my Brancake (by the way that's copyraaahted). You know you dun molested so many innocent people. Remember those …uh…lyrics to that one Justin Bieber song that you dun memorized for sure… "It's funny how things change 'cause now I see." Damn, good buddy—you don't see much. I thawt you wudda realized you done mess'd up so many people's lives. Well, I guess all Amduscias did was to make ya feel anger laaak yur victims felt and not teach ya much of anything. Guess that's where I'm comin' in, Terlet Jack. I'm here to teach u what feeling disgusted feels laaak. U know, that's what ur victims all felt like when you molested 'em? They all felt so disgusted…and many of them still do. When u feel disgusted, it's laaak ur nothin' but a squirt o' turd. Wait a sec. I done got me a brain'storm happn'n.

Jack: What are you talking about?

TrucknBranMan: Who ever said a redneck, ratchetjaw, dirty dan, can't be brill'yant. You, good buddy, are com'n fur a raaaayde.

Jack: What?

TrucknBranMan: Yur next eternity will be spent...well...nice n' disgusted...ridin' with me in my rig. Yur gonna be my new, brown pair of Brancake House underwear. With all the brancake eat'n I been doin, and with all the lacka shower'n....there ain't no good thing to say 'bout my Brancake underwear....well....'sept that their camouflage'd brown...the idea of yur's truly, mark'ting genius. Let's just say...it ain't gonna be dry and it ain't gonna be fresh. Perfect fur you molest'r-types that need to lurn a little 'bout the word disgusted.

Jack: No. Please. Don't. I can't.

TrucknBranMan: Yep, good buddy. I can. And I did...jus now...an I think a little squirt came out. Taaym to join me, Terlet Jack. Yeeeehaw, over n' out.

[AlexCupcheck]: June 19, 2010

AlexCupcheck: Hello everyone, and thank you for joining us on Confidence In Jeopardy! I'm your host, Alex

Cupcheck! Tonight we have three new contestants. First, from a small town in…

Jack: Help, what's going on?

AlexCupcheck: Excuse me everyone for the interruption, but one of our contestants is clearly in need of attention. Can I help you, Jack?

Jack: What is happening? I'm back at my little computer. Am I no longer in the awful truck with the bran man?

AlexCupcheck: Jack, please type faster, and stop interrupting. You have no idea what you're doing to my ratings right now. But, since you've already derailed the show, we might as well quench your thirst for knowledge. After all, our show is all about knowledge. Now, what do you need?

Jack: Where am I? What's happening? Who are you?

AlexCupcheck: Obviously, my fantastic intro was lost on you. Once again, my name is Alex Cupcheck, and I'm the brilliant host of Confidence In Jeopardy!, one of hell's most successful game shows. Full disclosure, we borrowed a few things from the earthly game, "Jeopardy!," but we all think our version has so much more to offer. And, Jack, if you must know, Alex is my stage name. My real name is Belphegor, but nobody calls me that. You, my digested-bran-smelling friend, are one of three lucky contestants. The good news is the top two scorers in Confidence In Jeopardy! will be returned to earth to live wonderful lives of bliss and riches. The third, the one with the least amount of points at the end of three questions, will be forced to play Eternal Jeopardy! with me. Which, I must say, will suck. You got what you need? You understand?

Jack: Uh, ok. I'm pretty good at "Jeopardy!." I just want to go back to my normal life on earth…and being rich will be nice.

AlexCupcheck: I completely understand your excitement, but remember you have two worthy opponents. That said, yes, you technically have a sixty-six percent chance of advancing to earth.

Jack: Ok, that's great, let's go, Alex. Time for these two other guys to learn a few things.

AlexCupcheck: Duly noted, Jack. Okay, sorry everyone for the rude interruption. As I was saying, tonight we have three new contestants. First, hailing from Southwest Israel, a professional banker for a large corporation and bookie in his free time…wow, that's quite a combination…please welcome, Melchom! Second, a PhD of Human Interaction and Aggression, who I hear plays a mean game of bocce ball, please say hello to, Sonneillon! And finally, fresh off a bran-tastic second eternity, a very subpar lawyer who loves watching "The McLaughlin Group" and molesting young boys and girls in his free time, please welcome, Jack!

Jack: Hey…why'd you have to say that…?

Sonneillon: Jack, I wouldn't put up with that from Alex if I were you.

AlexCupcheck: Shut it, Jack. And, don't antagonize him, Sonneillon. Everyone, please give a round of applause for our three contestants. Now, let's begin…Confidence…In…Jeopardy! Melchom, since you seem to know the most about money, you can begin.

Melchom: I'll take "Chinese Literature" for one thousand, Alex.

AlexCupcheck: Good choice. Here we go:
他寫了战争艺术

AlexCupcheck: Yes, Sonneillon. You buzzed first.

Sonneillon: Who is, Sun Tzu?

AlexCupcheck: That is correct! Sun Tzu is the author of the famous Chinese military treatise, "The Art of War."

Jack: Hey, wait a second. That first part was in Chinese. I'm American. That's not fair.

AlexCupcheck: Jack, you better start thinking and stop interrupting. That's already one question out of three. You need to get at least one of the next two to stay out of Eternal Jeopardy! And trust me; you'll want to stay out of Eternal Jeopardy!

Jack: This is ridiculous.

AlexCupcheck: No, it's not. It's a quality program with fantastic ratings and a loyal following…well, until today's show. Okay, where were we. Ah yes, Sonneillon. Nicely done. Your turn.

Sonneillon: I'll take "Mathletes" for five hundred, Alex.

AlexCupcheck: Ok. For five hundred dollars: 12,345,678,987,654,321

AlexCupcheck: Melchom, you buzzed just before Sonneillon.

Melchom: What is 111,111,111 multiplied by 111,111,111?

AlexCupcheck: Absolutely right!! Well done, Melchom.

Jack: Hey, this is fucking ridiculous. These questions are too hard.

Sonneillon: I totally agree with you, Jack. I think Alex is trying to make you lose.

AlexCupcheck: Sonneillon, stop it. Jack, you're going to need to stop complaining and find a way to get this last question because time is running out and Eternal Jeopardy! is not something you should be flirting with right now. Okay, so…Melchom…it's back to you. Pick the final question and Jack's last chance to return to earth for lots of good times and money.

Melchom: I'll take "Justin Bieber Lyrics" for two thousand, Alex.

AlexCupcheck: Wow, great choice. If Jack gets this answer correct, you realize, Melchom, that you will lose Confidence In Jeopardy! because this answer is worth two thousand dollars?

Jack: I'm ready. I can do this. I know this. I spent an eternity listening to Justin Bieber music.

AlexCupcheck: Okay. Here it is, the final question: "One love. My one heart. My one life for sure."

AlexCupcheck: Jack, you buzzed first. Wow, your chance for a return to earth.

Jack: The first line in the chorus for "One Time"!!!!! Yes!! Yes!! Yes!!! I knew it!!! I'm outta here, hell…good riddance!!!

AlexCupcheck: I have good news and bad news, Jack. First, the good news. Yes, you had the answer correct. Now, the bad news. You didn't put your answer in the form of a question. So, unfortunately, you're wrong and, you've just earned the spot in Eternal Jeopardy!

Jack: What? What? This isn't happening.

AlexCupcheck: Unfortunately for you, it is happening. And you're starting Eternal Jeopardy! right now.

Jack: Wait, wait. It's not fair. I answered it right. It's not fair. Wait…why is there a large sandbag being lifted above my lap?

AlexCupcheck: It is fair. Any idiot knows you need to answer in the form of a question. And that sandbag isn't the bag you should be worried about. You wore your protective cup, right? I hope you did, because in Eternal

252

Jeopardy!, every time you get a question wrong, the sandbag is released.

Jack: Wait. No. Don't. I'm not wearing a cup. I won't get any questions right. The questions are too difficult. Don't do this to me. No!

AlexCupcheck: You seem to be losing your confidence fast. Well, that is only fair. That is what you did to your innocent victims, Jack. Don't you realize that? You caused them to lose confidence in themselves by taking away their innocence at a very young age. No child can retain their confidence when that happens. So, you'll be able to feel that now. Well...in addition to some other feelings due to the fact that you didn't wear your cup. Ok, here we go...first answer of Eternal Jeopardy!...: вечный ад

Jack: Whoa...no...I don't speak Russian.

AlexCupcheck: I don't think that was right...nor was it in the form of a question, Jack. Might want to brace yourself...

Jack: Noooooooooo!

[AussieYobbo]: July 19, 2010

AussieYobbo: Oi!

AussieYobbo: Oi! Oi! Oi!

Jack: Alright, alright. Who is this? I need help. Please. I can't move. My legs are numb, I must be paralyzed.

AussieYobbo: G'day Mate!! 'Bout toyme you snapped to. Ya Yanks continue to surproyze me with yer drama. "Moy legs are numb"…"I must be paraloyzed". Stop yer wankin' an let's have us a chinwag.

Jack: A what?

AussieYobbo: Forget it….let's chat, ya nong.

Jack: What did you call me?

AussieYobbo: Crikey, you're as cunning as a shithouse rat. Jus' listen, bloke. Man…several pailings short of a fence, are ya? Ok, royht, where wuz I? Uh…Paraloyzed, royht. So yer clod hoppers ain't paraloyzed, boofhead. They're…uh…stuck.

Jack: Stuck? Is it because of all this wet sand around me? What's all this sand here for? Is this from the bag of sand that landed on my lap over and over when I was forced to play Eternal Jeopardy!? Please. No more bags of sand. I'm losing my mind. I can't take the pain. I'm not smart enough.

AussieYobbo: Come off it, Jack, I think that's the smartest thing I ever heard you say. And, yeh, I heard 'bout yer cruids gettin' smashed by the 'ole sandbagger. Heard they took quite-a poundin' from me mate, Alex Cupcheck. How's that bugger?

Jack: Just shut up and get me out of here. Who are you?

AussieYobbo: Don't come the raw prawn with me, mate. I'm here to help ya. M'names Choronzon, but most blokes 'round here jus' call me Yobbo. Like I said, I'm here to help ya, mate.

Jack: Help me? Well what are you waiting for? Every time I move I feel myself sink a little in this sand. Just get me out. Now.

AussieYobbo: Well, don't chuck a wobbly on me, Jack. First off, it ain't that simple. Mate, yer so dim you wouldn't know the tram were up you 'til the bell rang. I'm here to help, not here to perform magic. Second, I'll start by telling ya what's in yer royht pocket.

Jack: Uh…yeah. There's a piece of plywood in my pocket.
AussieYobbo: Wait a sec, mate, that ain't plywood. That's a boom'rang. You don't hear me makin' fun of you Yanks and yer slingshots. So, you'll need that there boom'rang to help you get out of the quicksand.

Jack: Quicksand? What? This is quicksand? Why am I in quicksand?

AussieYobbo: Bloody hell, do I look like the boss? All's I know is I'm s'posed to turn yer ears into arseholes and make 'em shit on yer shoulders, figuratively speaking. Jus' doin me job, Jack.

Jack: Fuck you. Just stop talking and tell me how to move.

AussieYobbo: Royht...this'll be more fun than me thought. So, liss'n good there, Jacko. The Boom'rang is yer ticket out of that sandy mess.   Just chuck that boom'rang into that tree in front of you and knock yerself off a voyne so you can climb out, and then yer safe, no drama.

Jack: This is ridiculous. I don't have my glasses on. I lost them when I tried to punch the BranMan. I don't deserve this. You said, throw it at that vine? Whatever, here it goes.........AAAh! My nose! I broke my nose. I missed the vine; the boom'rang came back and hit me in the face. And I sank a little further down in the quicksand when I threw it.

AussieYobbo: Royht. Boom'rangs come back, Jack. Guess ya never learn'd to throw a boom'rang right—you was too busy touchin' young boys and girls, eh Jack? Have another go, ya mug.

Jack: Fuck off. I didn't do anything wrong. They were as guilty as I was.   One more throw and I'm out of here...AAAH! My teeth! I just hit myself again. That really comes back fast. I wish I had my glasses.

AussieYobbo: Bloke, yer gettin' close, but I should warn ya that yer droppin' a little further in the 'ole quicksand, mate.

Jack: This is so fucked up. Every time I try, I end up hurting myself more. I'm never going to get out of here.

AussieYobbo: May your chooks turn into emus and kick your dunny door down. You jus' hit the 'ole nail on the head, Jacko. You know those people you molested, mate? Those people have been conditioned, by you, to defeat themselves. Since ya took their childhoods away, they've become victims, and they've unknowingly sabotaged themselves throughout loyfe, jus to fit in as victims, the only thing they know how to be, since they never had a choice, mate. Some moyht say that their loyves felt a bit helpless and self-defeating. You know the feeling, Jacko? Ain't no easy way out, mate.

Jack: Oh, fuck you. Not another way for me to feel what those children felt. I didn't do anything. Get me out of here. Someone, help me.

AussieYobbo: No worries, mate. Since you don't appreciate me help, how 'bout some help from me mate, KB?

Jack: KB?

AussieYobbo: Yep, KB's a King Brown snake, one of Australia's most dangerous snakes. And one of very few species that can handle the 'ole quicksand. Maybe he'll help ya? KB will be there in a jiffy.

Jack: Oh no…I hate snakes. I think I've just figured out this boom'rang…AHHH!

[HipsterChick]: December 28, 2010

HipsterChick: Dude, your face is messed up.

HipsterChick: Did you hear me, or am I wasting my time with you? Your face took a total beating from that boomerang. It's going to make my job more difficult.

Jack: Hello? Please help me. I'm done. Just put an end to this.

HipsterChick: That was such a lame thing to say. Just hold still, man.

Jack: Hold still? Where am I? Who are you? Oww!!

HipsterChick: I said hold still. Whole Foods is closed so if you knock over my organic coffee and tofu salad, I'll walk.

Jack: Oww. What was that? Who are you?

HipsterChick: That was me finishing the "E," and if you don't hold still, the next letter will look even worse. My peeps call me MC Ink, but my real name is Uphir. Stop moving.

Jack: I just spent forever getting out of quicksand. I was bit by a snake. My nose was broken. I don't feel well. Owww! Hey. What the hell was that?

HipsterChick: That was the "L." It's like so funny that you said "hell." It gets me every time one of you says that. "What the hell." Do you have any idea how dumb you sound? The next thing you'll say is that you like Coldplay.

Jack: What is a Coldplay?

HipsterChick: Forget it. Now, I need to dot the "I," so if you move, it'll look like another "L," and that won't make sense.

Jack: What won't make sense? What are the letters? Why is my forehead stinging? I just want to be left alone. I'm so sorry for what I've done. I've done terrible things.

HipsterChick: Don't apologize to me, I love what you did. You're keeping me in business, pal , and after this I should be able to get a sweet new pair of skinny jeans and some new cans for my DJ show tonight. Now hold tight while I get the "H" done. No squirming.

Jack: Are you giving me a tattoo?

HipsterChick: No, I'm standing here, dipping this device in ink, and then I'm baking cookies on your forehead. Yes, I'm giving you a tattoo.

Jack: Why?

HipsterChick: You'll see. Just hold tight. It's your final eternity, Jack, so it's important that we get this right. The "P" is going to hurt a bit. Here it goes.

Jack: Oww. Shit. Are you serious? This is my final eternity? What does that mean?

HipsterChick: It means that you are going to have some freedom, Jack. The Boss worked out a deal with that fancy guy in the sky. These things happen every now and then. But these deals come with a price and that's what I'm working on.

Jack: What? You mean I'm going back to earth? Really?

HipsterChick: Jack, you're a few prongs shy of a trident, aren't you? No, you're not going to earth. Hold tight, here's the "O"

Jack: Ahh.

HipsterChick: You've being given a Get Out of Hell card. I guess The Boss thought you were too annoying for us and you have the option of going to heaven with all of the other losers if you want. But we're giving you a going away present—something that will show everyone what you've been up to. The rest is up to you.

Jack: That's great. I can't believe it. I'm finally getting out of here.

HipsterChick: Yeah, I can't believe it either. I thought you were down here for good, but stranger things have happened, like the time I hosted a totally sweet dance party in my basement and everyone ended up wearing the same pair of skinny jeans and the same t-shirt. We're all so original, so what are the odds of that?!

Jack: I don't know what you're saying, but I'll take it. I'm ready. Oww!

HipsterChick: You're not ready. That was the "D." Two letters left.

Jack: So what are you spelling? So far, it spells "ELIHPOD." Is that some sort of hell word?

HipsterChick: Yeah, it's a hell word. We have words from hell. No, you idiot. But you surprised me, Jack; I didn't think you could keep track of the letters. It's not the best work I've ever done, but it's sweet. It reminds me of the sixteenth tattoo I got on my ankle. And, here's another "E." One more letter, the "P," and we're done. Hold still…and…there we go.

Jack: ELIHPODEP? What the hell is that?

HipsterChick: It's you, Jack. Don't you know? Oh…wait. I forgot, you need a mirror. Let me swing your chair around, buddy.

Jack: It says "PEDOPHILE." What? Oh, no. You didn't. I'm going to have to wear this on my head forever?

HipsterChick: That's the deal. But what you get in return is your freedom. If you ask me, it's an easy price to pay. But I guess I'm not factoring in your time with Belieber14, TrucknBranMan, AlexCupcheck, and AussieYobbo. Apparently you learned some things about what you've done to so many innocent children. Apparently you learned enough to get The Boss to broker a deal. He never keeps peeps around once they've learned something. We only like empty souls here. Well, that and skinny jeans, bumper stickers, tattoos, turntables, and indie rock!

Jack: Ok. I understand. I will continue my eternity with my past tattooed to my forehead for everyone to see. I can manage that as long as it's not down here.

HipsterChick: That settles it, dude. Now I can enjoy my organic tofu-soy salad. My work is done. You're out of my hands. The Boss has spoken, and you're a free man. But, if you even slip, don't forget that The Boss can broker another deal, and I hope he does. If you come back I can teach you so much about music and ink you up some more.

Jack: Thank you, Uphir. You have no idea how…

HipsterChick: Shut up. Get out.

Appendix 3: Bill Zeller's Letter (unedited)

I have the urge to declare my sanity and justify my actions, but I assume I'll never be able to convince anyone that this was the right decision. Maybe it's true that anyone who does this is insane by definition, but I can at least explain my reasoning. I considered not writing any of this because of how personal it is, but I like tying up loose ends and don't want people to wonder why I did this. Since I've never spoken to anyone about what happened to me, people would likely draw the wrong conclusions.

My first memories as a child are of being raped, repeatedly. This has affected every aspect of my life. This darkness, which is the only way I can describe it, has followed me like a fog, but at times intensified and overwhelmed me, usually triggered by a distinct situation. In kindergarten I couldn't use the bathroom and would stand petrified whenever I needed to, which started a trend of awkward and unexplained social behavior. The damage that was done to my body still prevents me from using the bathroom normally, but now it's less of a physical impediment than a daily reminder of what was done to me.

This darkness followed me as I grew up. I remember spending hours playing with legos, having my world consist of me and a box of cold, plastic blocks. Just waiting for everything to end. It's the same thing I do now, but instead of legos it's surfing the web or reading or listening to a baseball game. Most of my life has been spent feeling dead inside, waiting for my body to catch up.

At times growing up I would feel inconsolable rage, but I never connected this to what happened until puberty. I was able to keep the darkness at bay for a few hours at a time by doing things that required intense concentration, but it would always come back. Programming appealed to me for this reason. I was never particularly fond of computers or mathematically inclined, but the temporary peace it would provide was like a drug. But the darkness always returned and built up something like a tolerance, because programming has become less and less of a refuge. The darkness is with me nearly every time I wake up. I feel like a grime is covering me. I feel like I'm trapped in a contimated body that no amount of washing will clean. Whenever I think about what happened I feel manic and itchy and can't concentrate on anything else. It manifests itself in hours of eating or staying up for days at a time or sleeping for sixteen hours straight or week long programming binges or constantly going to the gym. I'm exhausted from feeling like this every hour of every day.

Three to four nights a week I have nightmares about what happened. It makes me avoid sleep and constantly tired, because sleeping with what feels like hours of nightmares is not restful. I wake up sweaty and furious. I'm reminded every morning of what was done to me and the control it has over my life.

I've never been able to stop thinking about what happened to me and this hampered my social interactions. I would be angry and lost in thought and then be interrupted by someone saying "Hi" or making small talk, unable to understand why I seemed cold and distant. I walked around, viewing the outside world from a distant portal behind my eyes, unable to perform normal human niceties. I wondered what it would be like to take to other people without what happened constantly on my mind, and I wondered if other people had similar experiences that they were better able to mask.

Alcohol was also something that let me escape the darkness. It would always find me later, though, and it was always angry that I managed to escape and it made me pay.

Many of the irresponsible things I did were the result of the darkness. Obviously I'm responsible for every decision and action, including this one, but there are reasons why things happen the way they do.

Alcohol and other drugs provided a way to ignore the realities of my situation. It was easy to spend the night drinking and forget that I had no future to look forward to. I never liked what alcohol did to me, but it was better than facing my existence honestly. I haven't touched alcohol or any other drug in over seven months (and no drugs or alcohol will be involved when I do this) and this has forced me to evaluate my life in an honest and clear way. There's no future here. The darkness will always be with me.

I used to think if I solved some problem or achieved some goal, maybe he would leave. It was comforting to identify tangible issues as the source of my problems instead of something that I'll never be able to change. I thought that if I got into to a good college, or a good grad school, or lost weight, or went to the gym nearly every day for a year, or created programs that millions of people used, or spent a summer or California or New York or published papers that I was proud of, then maybe I would feel some peace and not be constantly haunted and unhappy. But nothing I did made a dent in how depressed I was on a daily basis and nothing was in any way fulfilling. I'm not sure why I ever thought that would change anything.

I didn't realize how deep a hold he had on me and my life until my first relationship. I stupidly assumed that no matter how the darkness affected me personally, my romantic relationships would somehow be separated and protected. Growing up I viewed my future relationships as a possible escape from this thing that haunts me every day, but I began to realize how entangled it was with every aspect of my life and how it is never going to release me.

Instead of being an escape, relationships and romantic contact with other people only intensified everything about him that I couldn't stand. I will never be able to have a relationship in which he is not the focus, affecting every aspect of my romantic interactions.

Relationships always started out fine and I'd be able to ignore him for a few weeks. But as we got closer emotionally the darkness would return and every night it'd be me, her and the darkness in a black and gruesome threesome. He would surround me and penetrate me and the more we did the more intense it became. It made me hate being touched, because as long as we were separated I could view her like an outsider viewing something good and kind and untainted. Once we touched, the darkness would envelope her too and take her over and the evil inside me would surround her. I always felt like I was infecting anyone I was with.

Relationships didn't work. No one I dated was the right match, and I thought that maybe if I found the right person it would overwhelm him. Part of me knew that finding the right person wouldn't help, so I became interested in girls who obviously had no interest in me. For a while I thought I was gay. I convinced myself that it wasn't the darkness at all, but rather my orientation, because this would give me control over why things didn't feel "right". The fact that the darkness affected sexual matters most intensely made this idea make some sense and I convinced myself of this for a number of years, starting in college after my first relationship ended. I told people I was gay (at Trinity, not at Princeton), even though I wasn't attracted to men and kept finding myself interested in girls. Because if being gay wasn't the answer, then what was? People thought I was avoiding my orientation, but I was actually avoiding the truth, which is that while I'm straight, I will never be content with anyone. I know now that the darkness will never leave.

Last spring I met someone who was unlike anyone else I'd ever met. Someone who showed me just how well two people could get along and how much I could care about another human being. Someone I know I could be with and love for the rest of my life, if I weren't so fucked up. Amazingly, she liked me. She liked the shell of the man the darkness had left behind. But it didn't matter because I couldn't be alone with her. It was never just the two of us, it was always the three of us: her, me and the darkness. The closer we got, the more intensely I'd feel the darkness, like some evil mirror of my emotions. All the closeness we had and I loved was complemented by agony that I couldn't stand, from him. I realized that I would never be able to give her, or anyone, all of me or only me. She could never have me without the darkness and evil inside me. I could never have just her, without the darkness being a part of all of our interactions. I will never be able to be at peace or content or in a healthy relationship. I realized the futility of the romantic part of my life. If I had never met her, I would have realized this as soon as I met someone else who I meshed similarly well with. It's likely that things wouldn't have worked out with her and we would have broken up (with our relationship ending, like the majority of relationships do) even if I didn't have this problem, since we only dated for a short time. But I will face exactly the same problems with the darkness with anyone else. Despite my hopes, love and compatability is not enough. Nothing is enough. There's no way I can fix this or even push the darkness down far enough to make a relationship or any type of intimacy feasible.

So I watched as things fell apart between us. I had put an explicit time limit on our relationship, since I knew it couldn't last because of the darkness and didn't want to hold her back, and this caused a variety of problems. She was put in an unnatural situation that she never should have been a part of. It must have been very hard for her, not knowing what was actually going on with me, but this is not something I've ever been able to talk about with anyone. Losing her was very hard for me as well. Not because of her (I got over our relationship relatively quickly), but because of the realization that I would never have another relationship and because it signified the last true, exclusive personal connection I could ever have. This wasn't apparent to other people, because I could never talk about the real reasons for my sadness. I was very sad in the summer and fall, but it was not because of her, it was because I will never escape the darkness with anyone. She was so loving and kind to me and gave me everything I could have asked for under the circumstances. I'll never forget how much happiness she brought me in those briefs moments when I could ignore the darkness. I had originally planned to kill myself last winter but never got around to it. (Parts of this letter were written over a year ago, other parts days before doing this.) It was wrong of me to involve myself in her life if this were a possibility and I should have just left her alone, even though we only dated for a few months and things ended a long time ago. She's just one more person in a long list of people I've hurt.

I could spend pages talking about the other relationships I've had that were ruined because of my problems and my confusion related to the darkness. I've hurt so many great people because of who I am and my inability to experience what needs to be experienced. All I can say is that I tried to be honest with people about what I thought was true.

I've spent my life hurting people. Today will be the last time.

I've told different people a lot of things, but I've never told anyone about what happened to me, ever, for obvious reasons. It took me a while to realize that no matter how close you are to someone or how much they claim to love you, people simply cannot keep secrets. I learned this a few years ago when I thought I was gay and told people. The more harmful the secret, the juicier the gossip and the more likely you are to be betrayed. People don't care about their word or what they've promised, they just do whatever the fuck they want and justify it later. It feels incredibly lonely to realize you can never share something with someone and have it be between just the two of you. I don't blame anyone in particular, I guess it's just how people are. Even if I felt like this is something I could have shared, I have no interest in being part of a friendship or relationship where the other person views me as the damaged and contaminated person that I am. So even if I were able to trust someone, I probably would not have told them about what happened to me. At this point I simply don't care who knows.

I feel an evil inside me. An evil that makes me want to end life. I need to stop this. I need to make sure I don't kill someone, which is not something that can be easily undone. I don't know if this is related to what happened to me or something different. I recognize the irony of killing myself to prevent myself from killing someone else, but this decision should indicate what I'm capable of.

So I've realized I will never escape the darkness or misery associated with it and I have a responsibility to stop myself from physically harming others.

I'm just a broken, miserable shell of a human being. Being molested has defined me as a person and shaped me as a human being and it has made me the monster I am and there's nothing I can do to escape it. I don't know any other existence. I don't know what life feels like where I'm apart from any of this. I actively despise the person I am. I just feel fundamentally broken, almost non-human. I feel like an animal that woke up one day in a human body, trying to make sense of a foreign world, living among creatures it doesn't understand and can't connect with.

I have accepted that the darkness will never allow me to be in a relationship. I will never go to sleep with someone in my arms, feeling the comfort of their hands around me. I will never know what uncontimated intimacy is like. I will never have an exclusive bond with someone, someone who can be the recipient of all the love I have to give. I will never have children, and I wanted to be a father so badly. I think I would have made a good dad. And even if I had fought through the darkness and married and had children all while being unable to feel intimacy, I could have never done that if suicide were a possibility. I did try to minimize pain, although I know that this decision will hurt many of you. If this hurts you, I hope that you can at least forget about me quickly.

There's no point in identifying who molested me, so I'm just going to leave it at that. I doubt the word of a dead guy with no evidence about something that happened over twenty years ago would have much sway.

You may wonder why I didn't just talk to a professional about this. I've seen a number of doctors since I was a teenager to talk about other issues and I'm positive that another doctor would not have helped. I was never given one piece of actionable advice, ever. More than a few spent a large part of the session reading their notes to remember who I was. And I have no interest in talking about being raped as a child, both because I know it wouldn't help and because I have no confidence it would remain secret. I know the legal and practical limits of doctor/patient confidentiality, growing up in a house where we'd hear stories about the various mental illnesses of famous people, stories that were passed down through generations. All it takes is one doctor who thinks my story is interesting enough to share or a doctor who thinks it's her right or responsibility to contact the authorities and have me identify the molestor (justifying her decision by telling herself that someone else might be in danger). All it takes is a single doctor who violates my trust, just like the "friends" who I told I was gay did, and everything would be made public and I'd be forced to live in a world where people would know how fucked up I am. And yes, I realize this indicates that I have severe trust issues, but they're based on a large number of experiences with people who have shown a profound disrepect for their word and the privacy of others.

People say suicide is selfish. I think it's selfish to ask people to continue living painful and miserable lives, just so you possibly won't feel sad for a week or two. Suicide may be a permanent solution to a temporary problem, but it's also a permanent solution to a ~23 year-old problem that grows more intense and overwhelming every day.

Some people are just dealt bad hands in this life. I know many people have it worse than I do, and maybe I'm just not a strong person, but I really did try to deal with this. I've tried to deal with this every day for the last 23 years and I just can't fucking take it anymore.

I often wonder what life must be like for other people. People who can feel the love from others and give it back unadulterated, people who can experience sex as an intimate and joyous experience, people who can experience the colors and happenings of this world without constant misery. I wonder who I'd be if things had been different or if I were a stronger person. It sounds pretty great.

I'm prepared for death. I'm prepared for the pain and I am ready to no longer exist. Thanks to the strictness of New Jersey gun laws this will probably be much more painful than it needs to be, but what can you do. My only fear at this point is messing something up and surviving.

I'd also like to address my family, if you can call them that. I despise everything they stand for and I truly hate them, in a non-emotional, dispassionate and what I believe is a healthy way. The world will be a better place when they're dead--one with less hatred and intolerance.

If you're unfamiliar with the situation, my parents are fundamentalist Christians who kicked me out of their house and cut me off financially when I was 19 because I refused to attend seven hours of church a week.

They live in a black and white reality they've constructed for themselves. They partition the world into good and evil and survive by hating everything they fear or misunderstand and calling it love. They don't understand that good and decent people exist all around us, "saved" or not, and that evil and cruel people occupy a large percentage of their church. They take advantage of people looking for hope by teaching them to practice the same hatred they practice.

A random example:
"I am personally convinced that if a Muslim truly believes and obeys the Koran, he will be a terrorist." - George Zeller, August 24, 2010.

If you choose to follow a religion where, for example, devout Catholics who are trying to be good people are all going to Hell but child molestors go to Heaven (as long as they were "saved" at some point), that's your choice, but it's fucked up. Maybe a God who operates by those rules does exist. If so, fuck Him.

Their church was always more important than the members of their family and they happily sacrificed whatever necessary in order to satisfy their contrived beliefs about who they should be.

I grew up in a house where love was proxied through a God I could never believe in. A house where the love of music with any sort of a beat was literally beaten out of me. A house full of hatred and intolerance, run by two people who were experts at appearing kind and warm when others were around. Parents who tell an eight year old that his grandmother is going to Hell because she's Catholic. Parents who claim not to be racist but then talk about the horrors of miscegenation. I could list hundreds of other examples, but it's tiring.

Since being kicked out, I've interacted with them in relatively normal ways. I talk to them on the phone like nothing happened. I'm not sure why. Maybe because I like pretending I have a family. Maybe I like having people I can talk to about what's been going on in my life. Whatever the reason, it's not real and it feels like a sham. I should have never allowed this reconnection to happen.

I wrote the above a while ago, and I do feel like that much of the time. At other times, though, I feel less hateful. I know my parents honestly believe the crap they believe in. I know that my mom, at least, loved me very much and tried her best. One reason I put this off for so long is because I know how much pain it will cause her. She has been sad since she found out I wasn't "saved", since she believes I'm going to Hell, which is not a sadness for which I am responsible. That was never going to change, and presumably she believes the state of my physical body is much less important than the state of my soul. Still, I cannot intellectually justify this decision, knowing how much it will hurt her. Maybe my ability to take my own life, knowing how much pain it will cause, shows that I am a monster who doesn't deserve to live. All I know is that I can't deal with this pain any longer and I'm am truly sorry I couldn't wait until my family and everyone I knew died so this could be done without hurting anyone. For years I've wished that I'd be hit by a bus or die while saving a baby from drowning so my death might be more acceptable, but I was never so lucky.

To those of you who have shown me love, thank you for putting up with all my shittiness and moodiness and arbitrariness. I was never the person I wanted to be. Maybe without the darkness I would have been a better person, maybe not. I did try to be a good person, but I realize I never got very far.

I'm sorry for the pain this causes. I really do wish I had another option. I hope this letter explains why I needed to do this. If you can't understand this decision, I hope you can at least forgive me.

Bill Zeller

Please save this letter and repost it if gets deleted. I don't want people to wonder why I did this. I disseminated it more widely than I might have otherwise because I'm worried that my family might try to restrict access to it. I don't mind if this letter is made public. In fact, I'd prefer it be made public to people being unable to read it and drawing their own conclusions.

Feel free to republish this letter, but only if it is reproduced in its entirety.